Second Arrivals

Second Arrivals

Landscape and Belonging in Contemporary Writing of the Americas

Sarah Phillips Casteel

New World Studies

A. James Arnold, Editor

University of Virginia Press

Charlottesville and London

University of Virginia Press

© 2007 by the Rector and Visitors of the University of Virginia

All rights reserved

Printed in the United States of America on acid-free paper

First published 2007

9 8 7 6 5 4 3 2 1

Library of Congress Cataloging-in-Publication Data

Casteel, Sarah Phillips, 1974–
  Second arrivals : landscape and belonging in contemporary writing of the
Americas / Sarah Phillips Casteel.
     p.   cm. — (New World studies)
  Includes bibliographical references and index.
  ISBN 978-0-8139-2638-4 (acid-free paper) — ISBN 978-0-8139-2639-1 (pbk. :
acid-free paper)
  1. English literature—North America—History and criticism. 2. English
literature—Minority authors—History and criticism. 3. Caribbean literature,
English—History and criticism. 4. English literature—20th century—History and
criticism. 5. Landscape in literature. 6. Minorities in literature. 7. Emigration and
immigration in literature. 8. Place (Philosophy) in literature. 9. Garden writing.
10. Installations (Art) I. Title.
PR9175.C37 2007
820.9′920693—dc22

                                                                    2007004160

For my family and their many arrivals

Contents

Acknowledgments

THIS BOOK has been greatly enriched by the insights and perspectives of a series of exceptional teachers, colleagues, and friends with whom I have had the good fortune to be in contact over the past decade. I am indebted to Michael Dash and Rob Nixon for first posing the questions about identity and displacement that laid the foundations for my thinking about the relationship between landscape and belonging. In addition, during my graduate studies at Columbia, Gauri Viswanathan, Rachel Adams, Winston James, Jim Shapiro, Sandhya Shukla, and Joey Slaughter offered invaluable intellectual guidance, and I am particularly grateful to Rachel for her ongoing encouragement.

Since coming to teach at Carleton, I have found myself surrounded by generous and compassionate colleagues, and I would like to give special thanks to Christine Duff, Jack Healy, Brian Johnson, Jan Schroeder, and Ming Tiampo for reading and offering helpful comments on individual chapters of the manuscript. I am also grateful to Carleton University for awarding me a GR-6 grant that enabled me to carry out further research. In addition, I have benefited from the thoughtful advice of Sukeshi Kamra, Barbara Leckie, and Winfried Siemerling, as well as the friendship and intellectual companionship of Jan, Ming, and Catherine.

Finally, my deepest thanks go to my husband, James; my parents, Mark and Ruth; and my sister, Emma, for their wisdom, patience, and unflagging support; and to my son, Harry, for taking just enough naps during his first year of life to enable me to finish my work on the manuscript. The experiences of immigration and arrival that have shaped my own family's history over many generations and across several continents provided much of the inspiration for this book.

I WOULD like to express my gratitude to the artists Jin-me Yoon and Isaac Julien for generously allowing me to reproduce their work here. The excerpt from "Islands Vanish" from *Land to Light On* by Dionne Brand is used by permission of McClelland & Stewart Ltd. The excerpts from "Indian Reservation: Caughnawaga" and "Pastoral of the City Streets" from A. M. Klein's *Complete Poems. Part 2: Original Poems, 1937–1953* are used by permission of the University of Toronto Press.

In addition, I thank the journal *Interventions* (http://www.tandf.co.uk) for permitting me to reproduce in revised form my article "New World Pastoral: The Caribbean Garden and Emplacement in Gisèle Pineau and Shani Mootoo," *Interventions* 5.1 (2003): 12–28. Rebecca Walsh and the editors of *Interventions* aided me significantly in refining the argument and conceptualization of this article, which eventually became the basis for chapter 5. Portions of chapter 3 originally appeared as the Horst Frenz Prize essay "Joy Kogawa's Native Envy: New World Discourse in *Obasan* and *Itsuka*," *Yearbook of Comparative and General Literature* 51 (2003–4): 159–66, for which I thank the American Comparative Literature Association. Portions of chapter 6 originally appeared as "Dynamics of Inclusion and Exclusion in the Landscape Aesthetics of Jin-me Yoon," *Exclusion/Inclusion: Economic and Symbolic Displacements in the Americas*, ed. Patrick Imbert, Amy D. Colin, and Daniel Castillo Durante (New York: LEGAS, 2005), 159–66, and I am grateful to Patrick Imbert for including me in a very stimulating colloquium at the University of Ottawa in the spring of 2004 that resulted in this publication. As well, I would like to extend my thanks to A. James Arnold, Cathie Brettschneider, Ellen Satrom, and the two anonymous readers at the University of Virginia Press for supporting the publication of this book.

Introduction

Landscaping in the Diaspora

> For me, for the writer's gift and freedom, the labor and disappointments of the writing life, and the being away from my home; for that loss, for having no place of my own, this gift of the second life in Wiltshire, the second, happier childhood as it were, the second arrival (but with an adult's perception) at a knowledge of natural things, together with the fulfillment of the child's dream of the safe house in the wood.
>
> —V. S. Naipaul, *The Enigma of Arrival*

THIS BOOK identifies contemporary diasporic writers across the Americas who articulate alternative forms of emplacement. They do so by engaging rural and wilderness settings and the modes of landscape representation with which these settings are associated. Their writing is distinguished by an attention to landscape that is uniquely informed by experiences of cultural and geographical displacement. At the same time, these writers' sensitivity to the politics of landscape representation reflects their New World location.

In Jewish American author Philip Roth's dystopian novel *The Plot against America* (2004), for example, the rural's relationship to exclusionary national ideologies is revealed when urban Jewish boys are exported to the American heartland by the "Office of American Absorption" to be de-ethnicized. The narrator's brother returns from a summer-long stint on a Kentucky tobacco farm with his hair tinted blond, a taste for bacon, and a twang in his voice. In a visual analogue to Roth's novel, Korean Canadian photographer Jin-me Yoon inserts herself into the Prince Edward Island countryside, raising vital questions about how "natives" are differentiated from "tourists." Yoon's jarring photographs remind us that rural areas are traditionally the site and source of authentic national identity; it is for this reason that the introduction of minority presences into these areas can have such an unsettling effect. By appropriating rural and wilderness landscapes, especially iconic ones, diasporic writers of the Americas such as Roth as well as visual artists such as Yoon position themselves to contest exclusionary narratives of the nation.

Current theorizations of diaspora do not favor the reading of landscape from the vantage point of the displaced that is advanced by the writers and artists considered in this book. Diaspora studies tends instead to polarize mobility and sedentarism, often celebrating the former while neglecting, or even disparaging, the latter. In a critique of the American academy's model of diaspora studies, a founding editor of the journal *Diaspora* observes that "there is no doubt that in American diasporic discourse today, routedness is more interesting than rootedness" (Tölölyan 67). This orientation may be attributed in part to a longstanding affirmation in the United States of mobility, which is associated with the values of individuality and freedom in the national imagination (Tölölyan 69–70). But the privileging of mobility—while perhaps more pronounced in literary studies than in the disciplines of anthropology or geography—extends beyond U.S. articulations of diaspora studies.

Paradoxically, place is both ubiquitous in conversations about diaspora across the disciplines and at the same time undertheorized.[1] In part, the resistance to a deeper engagement with place reflects anxieties about the politics that adhere to it. In keeping with their suspicion of territorializing metaphors, and informed by contemporary anthropology's reinterpretation of culture as unbounded by geography, cultural theorists have attempted to distance themselves from the original meaning of diaspora as a dispersion from a fixed homeland. In an influential essay, Stuart Hall distinguishes between an "imperializing" conception of diaspora that is premised on a necessary return to a fixed geographical location and an alternative conception of diaspora that does not sustain a stable idea of a homeland, instead recognizing the impossibility of return. The original model of a diaspora is, of course, that of the Jews, and it is no accident that Hall's example of the former, "backward-looking" version of diaspora politics is Zionism.[2] Other critics have suggested, however, that even the Jewish diaspora does not support such a territorializing model and have questioned whether the Jewish diaspora is itself centered around a stable point of origin.[3]

An attempt to shift the terms of diasporic discourse away from the language of territorialization is evident, then, both in taxonomies that construct an opposition between the Jewish model of diaspora and more "progressive" models and in revisionary accounts of the Jewish diaspora itself. While critics such as Hall acknowledge the depth and importance of geographical origins and their imaginative recovery, they nonetheless seek to de-emphasize the role of territory in their theorizations of diaspora. Several of the governing metaphors of contemporary cultural criticism—Paul Gilroy's slave-ship chronotope, Gilles Deleuze and Félix Guattari's nomadism, Arjun Appadurai's five "landscapes" of globalization—register the extent to which place has fallen out of favor, these spatial metaphors serving to emphasize movement rather than location. The spatial turn in critical theory has enabled important new insights into the production of (post)colonial, diasporic, and globalized environments. Yet one less fortunate—and indeed rather paradoxical—consequence of the spatial turn and the more dynamic concept of space that has attended it has been a tendency to put an exaggerated stress on displacement, dislocation, and movement at the expense of place.[4] Spatial designators such as "terrain," "landscape," and "borders" are more often than not metaphorized in contemporary criticism.

Diaspora studies' critique of territorializing discourses has played an important role in dispelling myths of origin. Yet it also has had less salutary consequences where this critique has been extended indiscriminately to *all* forms of emplacement. The hyperemphasis on movement in diaspora studies makes it difficult to register the extent to which the intensification of a population's mobility renders the need for viable forms of emplacement more, rather than less, urgent (see Gupta and Ferguson 10–11). Thus, although it may seem commonsense, it bears underlining that, as James Clifford reminds us, "the term *diaspora* is a signifier, not simply of transnationality and movement, but of political struggles to define the local, as distinctive community, in historical contexts of displacement" ("Diasporas" 308).

The Country and the City

One of the means by which diasporic writers of the Americas are reinventing place is by engaging rural and wilderness landscapes. This engagement signals an insistence upon geographical place as both meaningful and compelling, a move that should not be dismissed too hastily as merely nostalgic. Instead, their works warrant careful consideration for the ways in which they revisit traditional sites of identity construction, often in order to challenge the myths of identity that such sites previously were made to support. In so doing, these writers demonstrate the flexibility of landscape and botanical imagery, which is revealed in their work to serve a great variety of ideological and cultural programs. At the same time, however, in recuperating sites laden with a long history of associations, they risk reproducing the very conceptual structures whose exclusionary power they aim to contest. Both the possibilities and the risks of an attachment to landscape will be explored in the readings of novels, poetry, garden writing, and visual art that follow.

The two poles of contemporary diasporic discourse—movement and sedentarism, or the global and the local—find their spatial counterparts in the customary opposition between the city and the country. Conventionally, the city has been widely perceived as the space of diversity and movement, while the country is negatively associated with homogeneity and containment. Rural spaces connote conservative models of identity and belonging associated with repressive nationalisms and fascist movements, as well as racisms such as that of the U.S. rural South. In particular, the pastoral has been stigmatized either as outmoded or, following Raymond Williams, as complicitous in the exploitation of the working class.

In order to distance itself from such ideologically compromised modes of thinking, diaspora studies has placed an exaggerated stress on the virtues of mobility. Consequently, the city becomes the focus of intense scrutiny, while landscape and depictions of nature seldom figure in such discussions.[5] Theorists of diaspora devote considerable attention to the phenomenon of "the global city," privileging the city as offering "advantages" to diasporic populations (Cohen 168) and as exposing the limits of national narratives (Chambers, ch. 6). The city is assumed to be the site that poses the deepest challenge to the logic of a designated space for every race. In such accounts, the city comes to stand in for modern (diasporic) life itself.[6]

The urban orientation of diaspora studies is reinforced by globalization theorists' identification of "global" or "world" cities as the nodes of transnational flows. Since the 1980s, numerous studies have recognized cities as the hubs of global and transnational networks.[7] Such studies point to cities as spaces that become detached from their national contexts, thereby illustrating globalization's disarticulation of the nation-state. The global city, unbounded by the nation-state, is typically inhabited by international professionals at one end of the class spectrum and by immigrant workers at the other (Sassen 226). The extranational affiliations of both groups exemplify the "denationalization" of the city. Thus, if urbanism has for some time been allied with modernism and modernity, it has now come to be closely associated with postmodernity and globalization as well.

The denationalization of the city, which these theorists celebrate, may also be understood as limiting the possibilities for emplacement among diasporic and minority populations. The modern metropolis as we have conventionally imagined it is the theater in which new forms of belonging are worked out. For many, however, the city would appear to disallow an extensive experience of belonging insofar as it remains deeply bound up with modernist tropes of alienation and exile. While the city may be more accommodating of marginalized populations, then, it also significantly curtails these populations' claims to belonging.

Rural and wilderness spaces, by contrast, are frequently imagined in national narratives as the essence or heart of the nation, and for this reason they remain off-limits to minority presences even when—or perhaps especially when—the city is at its most accessible. Accordingly, in a Canadian context the artist Richard Fung complains that, contrary to the official discourse of multiculturalism, "in a country whose identity is tied to a romantic image of the land, people of color are discursively tied to the urban landscape—and the inner city, at that" (168). Fung's charge is borne out by the opposition that Trinidadian Canadian author Shani Mootoo encountered to the Canadian wilderness scenes that she had planned to include in her novel *He Drown She in the Sea* (2005): "The editors apparently wanted Mootoo to focus more on the Caribbean part of the book. . . . In other words, Trinidadian immigrants aren't supposed to be parsing the sights and sounds of B.C. mountains and seashores. They are allowed, Mootoo says, to write about Canadian cities. . . . Immigrant writers are, apparently, not permitted to appropriate Group of Seven landscapes" (Gessell B8).

As Fung's and Mootoo's comments suggest, the nation is conventionally (and prejudicially) defined in both temporal and spatial terms: its citizens, who are ostensibly united by a shared descent or historical identity, are imagined as occupying a common and defined territory.[8] National identity is typically located in characteristic landscapes (the Swiss Alps, the American West, the Canadian North). In such cases, landscapes become what Anthony D. Smith terms "ethnoscapes," in which "the terrain invested with collective significance is felt to be integral to a particular historical culture community or *ethnie,* and the ethnic community is seen as an intrinsic part of that poetic landscape" (150).

National identification with rural and wilderness landscapes may be couched not only in terms of character traits (for example, individualism and freedom in the case of the American West) but also in genealogical and racial terms (landscape as ancestral homeland). Myths of origin are often linked to remote natural spaces that lie far from the contaminating influence of the city; hence, the long trek deep into the Amazonian jungle that Alejo Carpentier's protagonist makes in *The Lost Steps* (1953) in search of the primordial origins of human music and culture. The relationship between rural landscapes and national representation is indeed a profound one, as is evidenced by the close historical ties between landscape painting and nationalist programs (Andrews 158–59).

For the very reasons that diaspora criticism has tended to avoid rural spaces—their ostensible racial homogeneity, conservatism, and xenophobia, as well as their associations with myths of origin—the writers and artists discussed in this book make such spaces the focus of their critique. By introducing minority presences into iconic landscapes, they contest a spatial vocabulary of the nation that would contain minorities within the city and bar them from the exurban spaces that represent an uncontaminated national essence. At the same time, they undermine a spatial logic that reads the rural as populated by spatially bounded, sedentary "natives."

Refusing to observe the carefully policed boundaries of iconic rural and wilderness landscapes and the exclusionary definitions of national belonging that they naturalize, these writers and artists intrude upon such landscapes and transform them into more inclusive and heterogeneous spaces. We might describe this gesture as a "second arrival," a phrase that I have borrowed from V. S. Naipaul's *The Enigma of Arrival*. The motif of the second arrival indicates a move to the countryside that succeeds the diasporic subject's initial arrival in the metropolis, but it also suggests taking a second look and coming to a new way of seeing as a result. Moreover, it usefully breaks down the binary opposition of home and away, native and tourist, revealing arrival to be an ongoing process of becoming.

The Anxiety of New World Origins

My aim in identifying the urban bias of diaspora studies is not to dispute the social fact of greater concentrations of immigrant populations in cities.[9] Rather, I seek to draw attention to the symbolic value and appeal of the rural for diasporic writers and artists. To call attention to this dimension of diasporic consciousness is not, however, to diminish the importance of mobility and urban experience, nor of the wide and complex range of localizations that may be found in between the two poles of city and country. Instead, what interests me are the insights that might be generated were we to return the two poles of mobility and stasis, or city and country, to a more dialectical relationship. How might diaspora studies imagine a more tensive and processual relationship between place and displacement?[10] Upon what kinds of metaphors would such a model rely, and what new readings of place might it enable? Furthermore, what might be gained by situating such a model of diaspora studies within a New World context? What does a hemispheric American framework contribute to discussions about contemporary identity that extend beyond the borders of the Americas? While a fuller answer to these questions will come in the individual readings developed in the chapters that follow, I would begin here by pointing to the specific pressures that the New World situation brings to bear on origins, belonging, and ancestral homeland.

The question of place has a special resonance in the Americas, where traditional modes of emplacement currently are being reimagined. The Caribbean in particular has emerged as a key site from and through which to theorize the relationship between identity and place. Because of the decimation of its autochthonous populations, the radical ruptures of the Middle Passage, slavery and indentureship, and the patterns of internal and external migrations that characterize its societies, the Caribbean has produced some of the most innovative thinking about origins and place. At the same time, Canada and the United States, both in their settler colonial past and in their multicultural present, also have struggled to develop viable metaphors for belonging. The inaccessibility of narratives of autochthony for the majority of their populations, combined with their imperfectly pluralist national ideologies, have encouraged the interrogation of received notions of citizenship and belonging, particularly on the part of minorities. With their acute awareness of the discontinuous character of origins, both Caribbean and North American writers and artists have advanced incisive critiques of myths of origin and national belonging.

Thus, if ideologies of fixed origins are by now widely discredited, in the Americas myths of origin have always been especially tenuous, as the Martinican writer Edouard Glissant indicates when he identifies New World societies as "composite" rather than "atavistic." Glissant, surely one of the most perceptive observers of such phenomena, suggests that while atavistic cultures rely heavily on genesis and creation myths, composite cultures are too acutely conscious of their creolized condition to authorize themselves via genealogical narratives. Instead, they emphasize contact and entanglement (*Traité* 194–95). Accordingly, Glissant defines the Caribbean as a "multiple series of relationships" or "field of relationships" (*Caribbean Discourse* 139, 253).

Glissant observes that composite New World societies such as those of the Caribbean develop strategies of diversion: rather than reverting to the desire for a single origin or "identity-root," the practice of diversion enables a "return to the point of entanglement" (*Caribbean Discourse* 26). "The idea of creolization demonstrates that henceforth it is no longer valid to glorify 'unique' origins that the race safeguards and prolongs," he maintains (140). And rather than laying an exclusive claim to *territoire,* composite cultures instead approach land as *terre:* a land to which they are deeply connected, but not in an absolute sense that would call for the violent suppression of competing claims (*Traité* 177; see also 193). The contrast that Glissant draws (following Deleuze and Guattari) between *l'identité racine-unique* and *l'identité-rhizome* similarly functions to eschew absolute territorial claims in favor of provisional and nonexclusive ones (*Traité* 21). Notably, however, Glissant's distinction between *terre* and *territoire* does not deny the meaningfulness of place. He rejects such a view—"La mondialisation, conçue comme non-lieu"—in favor of an emphasis on the particularity of individual places (*Traité* 192).

As Glissant suggests, while the New World has historically figured in the European imagination as an Edenic site of origins, nativist identity formations remain largely unavailable to most of its inhabitants, who can lay no claim to autochthonous ties to the land, and whose histories are characterized (to a greater or lesser degree) by a sense of rupture rather than continuity with the past. Trinidadian Canadian writer Dionne Brand's expressive phrase "the Door of No Return" signals the extent to which narratives of origin and return are confounded by New World circumstances and by the Middle Passage in particular:

> That fissure [between the past and the present] is represented in the Door of No Return: that place where our ancestors departed one world for another; the Old World for the New. The place where all names were forgotten and all beginnings recast. In some desolate sense it was the creation place of Blacks in the New World Diaspora at the same time that it signified the end of traceable beginnings. Beginnings that can be noted through a name or a set of family stories that extend farther into the past than five hundred or so years, or the kinds of beginnings that can be expressed in a name which in turn marked out territory or occupation.
>
> (*A Map to the Door* 5–6)

Brand's Door of No Return symbolizes the failure of narratives of origin for the African diaspora in the New World. Yet not only members of the African diaspora but also settler populations in the Americas exhibit an uncomfortable awareness of their nonindigeneity and discontinuous past. At its most acute, this awareness produces what Lois Parkinson Zamora identifies as the Americas' underlying common condition: the "anxiety of origins." Zamora observes in *The Usable Past* that the obscured and disrupted character of origins in the Americas has resulted in the creation of innovative narrative strategies capable of "encompassing multiple origins or imagining absent ones" (8). Moreover, contrary to the customary reading of America as free of the burden of history, New World writers' problematic relationship to origins does not convince them to abandon a sense of connection with the past. As a consequence of the Americas' composite character and their resultant anxiety of origins, the creation of viable modes of belonging and of "Americanness" becomes one of the central projects of New World cultural production. Landscape has played a key role in this project, both historically and in the contemporary moment.

Colonial Pastoral and Its New World Legacies

Studies of New World discourse, preeminently Edmundo O'Gorman's *The Invention of America,* stress that rather than recording direct impressions of the new landscape and its inhabitants, European chroniclers "invented" the New World by imposing preexisting assumptions onto it, which in turn came to inform New World experience. Building on this insight, Lois Parkinson Zamora, J. Michael Dash, and other scholars of New World studies have suggested that writers of the Americas are distinguished by their heightened awareness of the discursive character of the New World and of the capacity of writing and other forms of representation to shape New World perspectives. In this context, landscape representation takes on a special function, contributing significantly to the construction of New World identities. While differences among the literatures and arts of the Caribbean and North America must not be underestimated—differences reflected, for instance, in the distinctive modes of landscape representation that they tend to favor—they share a common colonial inheritance of the centrality of nature to definitions of New World identities, as well as a self-consciousness with regard to their discontinuous genealogies and problematic relationship to indigeneity.

Since the fifteenth century, European pictorial and textual representations of the New World have introduced a series of what geographer Denis Cosgrove calls "landscape ideas."[11] The landscape ideas that circulated in the literature of the early explorers drew on a range of Golden Age, Arcadian, and wilderness imagery in an effort to assimilate new and often disturbing experiences. While both "soft" and "hard" primitivism informed the literature of exploration and settlement, the pastoral or "soft" pole lent itself more readily to the domestication of the new environment. In Columbus's diary, for example, conventional pastoral features such as the cultivated landscape, the myrtle tree, and the nightingale serve to familiarize the landscape. Columbus's repeated comparisons of the landscapes he encounters to the greenness of Andalusia in the months of April and May function to domesticate foreign surroundings. Other Renaissance explorers, including Ralegh, Barlowe, and Cartier, also drew heavily on pastoral imagery of a pleasant and abundant landscape. Their accounts likely influenced the pastoralism of *The Tempest,* as well as that of seventeenth-century poems such as Michael Drayton's "To the Virginian Voyage" (1606) and Andrew Marvell's "Bermudas" (1681), which promote a vision of the New World as Arcadia (see Marx, ch. 2; Hamlin 119–21). Painting of the early colonial period similarly pursued a pastoral vision of the New World, as for instance in sixteenth-century Dutch painter Jan Mostaert's "A West Indian Scene" (ca. 1540–50), which represents the Caribbean terrain as a pastoral landscape drawn from classical antiquity (see Honour 22–24).

In the eighteenth century, colonial pastoral was reinvigorated by Bernardin de Saint-Pierre's popular novel *Paul et Virginie* (1788). The novel, which Bernardin calls in his preface "mon humble pastorale" (29), transplants two French women to the Île de France (Mauritius) and presents an idealized portrait of the natural and simple way of life that the women and their children enjoy on the island.[12] Similarly, Chateaubriand's *Atala* (1801) situates Arcadia in a specific New World location among the Natchez Indians in the "New Eden" of the southern United States. Nineteenth-century colonial discourse, although increasingly drawn to the sublime, continued to rely on pastoral motifs to characterize colonial landscapes. In what Mary Louise Pratt dubs the "monarch of all I survey scene," the surveillance of the colonial landscape inscribes the desire for mastery over colonial space. When the nineteenth-century travel writer John Stewart exports metropolitan conventions to describe a Jamaican plantation as though it were an English village, he at the same time asserts the priority of England as the authentic and superior pastoral landscape: "The negroes houses are grouped together, and stand isolated from all the other buildings, forming a sort of rustic village, inclosed [*sic*] by a stone wall, and displaying an intermixture of gardens and various fruit-trees, which has a pleasing sylvan appearance" (qtd. in Renk 33). In such descriptions, the gentleness of the pastoral imagery masks a colonizing drive to appropriate territory (see Renk 33–34).

Pastoral representations of New World landscapes not only inscribed colonial control but also facilitated settler cultures' creation of a sense of place. A revealing example of the settler colonial pastoral is the Canadian Oliver Goldsmith's long poem *The Rising Village* (1825, revised 1834), a reply to his great-uncle's poem *The Deserted Village* (1770).[13] In *The Deserted Village,* the emigration of a group of dispossessed British (or, likely, Irish) peasants is depicted as their expulsion from a pastoral world: "These far departing seek a kinder shore, / And rural mirth and manners are no more" (lines 73–74). The younger Goldsmith's *The Rising Village* inverts the pattern of its English predecessor by arguing that the pastoral landscape can be recreated in the New World, specifically in Acadia (Nova Scotia). The Acadian wilderness that confronts Goldsmith's settlers initially compares unfavorably to Britannia's "charming prospects" (line 29). Yet, eventually, the "savage tribes" and wild beasts that threaten the settlers are displaced by "the peaceful arts of culture":

> Here crops of grain in rich luxuriance rise,
> And wave their golden riches to the skies;
> There smiling orchards interrupt the scene,
> Or gardens bounded by some fence of green;
> The farmer's cottage, bosomed 'mong the trees,
> Whose spreading branches shelter from the breeze;
> The winding stream that turns the busy mill,
> Whose clacking echos o'er the distant hill;
> The neat white church, beside whose walls are spread
> The grass-clod hillocks of the sacred dead.
>
> (1834 ed., lines 455–64)

In *The Rising Village,* the departure of the land's native inhabitants—human and animal—transforms "bleak and desert lands" into a pastoral village. The evacuation of the land's indigenous inhabitants converts nature from a hostile wilderness into a benevolent force, thereby naturalizing the settlers' presence in that landscape. Nature rewards Goldsmith's settlers for their labors with a pastoral abundance and a newly anglicized landscape.

While lacking the domesticating capacity of the pastoral, the sublime also played an important role in establishing a sense of distinct American identity, sites such as Niagara Falls becoming emblems of an American wilderness experience unavailable in Europe (see Kornhauser; McKinsey). Among New World settler societies, landscape was frequently called upon to distinguish the Old World from the New. In such narratives, landscape compensates for the perceived absence of history by offering up grandeur in the form of spectacular scenery, while particularized botanical imagery lends a sense of American specificity. Accordingly, the nineteenth-century painter Thomas Cole and his Hudson River School colleagues privileged the unparalleled sublimity of the U.S. wilderness in their landscape paintings. Well into the twentieth century, the wilderness experience continued to be cited as generative of a North American identity. Lawren Harris, one of the Group of Seven painters who in the early twentieth century contributed to the shaping of Canadian nationalism, wrote in 1926 that "the top of the continent is a source of spiritual flow that will ever shed clarity into the growing race of America, and we Canadians being closest to this source seem destined to produce an art somewhere different from our southern fellows—an art more spacious, of a greater living quiet, perhaps of a more certain conviction of eternal values" (qtd. in Andrews 158).

Recently, revisionary scholarship on the Group of Seven has exposed the masculinist and racialist ideology that is inscribed in its wilderness aesthetic and construction of Canadian nationhood.[14] Such scholarship emphasizes how settler colonial landscape aesthetics emptied the land of indigenous presences and substituted a white male presence. Like the American West, then, the Canadian wilderness as a privileged site of national identity formation is now being challenged, not only in the critical literature but also by creative writers and artists both through their insertion of diasporic presences into the landscape and through their acknowledgement of prior indigenous claims on the land.

Critical Pastoralism, the Marvelous, and the Gothic

Postcolonial writing of the Americas has continued to rely heavily on landscape to generate a distinctively American poetics. One strain of such landscape imagery takes the form of critical pastoralism, which, like settler colonial pastoralism, capitalizes on pastoral's capacity for emplacement. Yet this version of pastoral runs contrary to perceptions of the mode as simplistic and ideologically conservative, a view popularized by Raymond Williams. In his influential *The Country and the City,* Williams attacked the pastoral for mystifying class relations and masking the exploitation of rural people. Williams's powerful critique has shaped subsequent discussions of the mode. British critics in particular have called for a "post-pastoral" poetry, viewing pastoral as "a challenge to be transcended" by contemporary writers, who must break out of the "closed circuit" of pastoral and antipastoral (Gifford 55, 57).[15]

A contrasting view, however, has been advanced by U.S. critics, who have favored a more dialectical model that allows for a greater range of both formal and ideological positions. Most famously, Leo Marx in

The Machine in the Garden posits a multifaceted and versatile pastoral when he distinguishes between "complex" and "simple" pastoral. In Marx's account, complex pastorals contain within them a "counter-force" that juxtaposes the ideal with a more realist vision: "Most literary works called pastorals—at least those substantial enough to retain our interest—do not finally permit us to come away with anything like the simple, affirmative attitude we adopt toward pleasing rural scenery," he writes. "In one way or another, . . . these works manage to qualify, or call into question, or bring irony to bear against the illusion of peace and harmony in a green pasture" (25).

The distinction that Marx develops between complex and simple pastoral opens up the possibility of a critical mode of pastoral that nonetheless may be understood as operating within a pastoral framework, one that encompasses both a utopian and a historicizing dimension. Following Leo Marx, Lawrence Buell's study *The Environmental Imagination* emphasizes pastoral's "ideological mobility," its capacity to be simultaneously conservative and oppositional. Buell points to pastoral's "multiple frames" and "ideological multivalence" to illustrate the difficulty of reducing pastoral to a single ideological or class position. Such a reading understands the mode as potentially having both conservative and innovative functions. In its contemporary, complex form, then, pastoral is defined not so much by a strict adherence to classical convention as by the manner in which it brings into tension idealizing and historicizing visions of landscape.[16] Diasporic writers exploit this double-edged quality of pastoral so that they may assert the need for place while simultaneously registering the historical realities of displacement.

Pastoral is not, however, the only mode of which diasporic writers of the Americas have availed themselves in their efforts to rethink place. Caribbean writers are noted for their emphasis on landscape, but their landscape aesthetic is on the whole less receptive to the pastoral than the North American examples that I discuss. Instead, they tend, as Glissant suggests, to pursue less "European" modes of landscape representation that reach beyond the bounds of realism. Preeminently, the Cuban writer and musicologist Alejo Carpentier draws inspiration from the natural environment in the course of theorizing what he claims as a uniquely American mode of aesthetic expression: the marvelous real. In his classic essay "On the Marvelous Real in America," Carpentier recounts that "when André Masson tried to draw the jungle of Martinique, with its incredible intertwining of plants and its obscene promiscuity of certain fruit, the marvelous truth of the matter devoured the painter, leaving him just short of impotent when faced with blank paper. It had to be an American painter—the Cuban, Wilfredo Lam [*sic*]—who taught us the magic of tropical vegetation, the unbridled creativity of our natural forms with all their metamorphoses and symbioses on monumental canvases in an expressive mode that is unique in contemporary art" (85). For Carpentier, the "baroque" quality of America significantly derives from "the unruly complexities of its nature and its vegetation, the many colors that surround us, the telluric pulse of the phenomena that we still feel" ("Baroque" 105). In his account, American nature, in combination with a distinctive history of discovery and mixture of cultures, is generative of a singularly American artistic imagination and poetics.

More recently, the Guyanese writer and land surveyor Wilson Harris has evoked a landscape animated by ancestral spirits and "nature's chorus" and has argued against a view of landscape as mere background, implicitly rejecting an anthropocentric approach. "It seems to me," Harris explained in a 1996 BBC broadcast, "that, for a long time, landscapes and riverscapes have been perceived as passive, as furniture, as areas to be manipulated; whereas, I sensed, over the years, as a surveyor, that the landscape possessed resonance" (40). In Harris's view, it is the writer's responsibility to attune himself to this landscape and to the consciousness that it embodies by departing from realist aesthetic modes that muffle "the music of living landscapes."

This dynamic conception of landscape is pursued in contemporary Caribbean writing not only with reference to the marvelous but also with the related discourse of the gothic. Like the pastoral and the marvelous, the gothic has long-standing ties to colonial landscapes, including Caribbean settings, which have served as convenient spaces onto which gothic fantasies about the relationship between self and other could be projected. As Joan Dayan and Lizabeth Paravisini-Gebert have shown, writers since the early nineteenth century have drawn inspiration from such historical events as the Haitian Revolution and such cultural forms as obeah and voodoo to generate gothic plots.[17]

Gothic is a mode notable for its ideological elasticity, having produced versions that have served both conservative and radical political and social agendas. Accordingly, in the eighteenth and nineteenth centuries, novelists on either side of the slavery debate deployed gothic conventions to advance their political agendas (Paravisini-Gebert 230–31). And while the "imperial Gothic" mode as characterized by Patrick Brantlinger expressed anxieties about the viability of the civilizing mission of empire at the very height of the British Empire's power, it did not necessarily attack the moral legitimacy of that mission. Other versions of gothic, however, are more insistently contestatory in their elaborations of such gothic motifs as the past that has been suppressed, tortuous familial relationships and bloodlines, and transgressive sexuality and desire. While gothic narratives on the whole tend to be preoccupied with a troubling past and its relationship to the present, postcolonial gothic excavates repressed histories expressly in order to challenge the dominant political and social order.

The dynamic vision of landscape advanced by the marvelous and the gothic coincides with the landscape poetics of Glissant, who maintains that chaos, excess, and instability govern the treatment of nature in the Other America. Glissant identifies the "language of landscape" as integral to this literature, in which landscape "stops being merely decorative or supportive and emerges as a full character" (*Caribbean Discourse* 105).[18] Glissant defines a New World landscape aesthetic in opposition to the symmetry and order that characterize European landscape representation: "There is something violent in this American sense of literary space. In it the prevailing force is not that of the spring and the meadow, but rather that of the wind that blows and casts shadows like a great tree" (*Caribbean Discourse* 145; see also *Soleil* 25). Thus, in keeping with the tradition that I outlined above, Glissant's approach in singling out landscape as central to his poetics has been to distance New World from European treatments of nature.

Glissant also tends in his critical writing to distinguish implicitly between North American literature and the literature of the Other America, so that the landscape aesthetic that he outlines apparently pertains primarily to the Caribbean and Latin America. But at a striking moment in *Caribbean Discourse,* he indicates that a more comprehensively hemispheric discussion of landscape aesthetics may be warranted. In his essay "Quebec," he observes that "it is valid to introduce into our vision of Caribbean landscape—mountains and seas, sand flats, contorted hills—the same swirling movement of the Quebecois landscape." "I am curious," he declares, "about how the imagination functions there" (172–73).[19]

Following Glissant's lead in this passage, I would like to suggest that without neglecting cultural, historical, and aesthetic divergences between North America and the Caribbean, it is illuminating to consider the function and treatment of landscape as a site of diasporic emplacement in a comparative hemispheric context. Overly sharp distinctions among regions of the hemisphere may prevent us from registering the full range of modes of landscape representation that operate in a given region. Thus, even as this study contrasts the pastoralism of a number of North American writers with the versions of the marvelous and the gothic elaborated by some of their Caribbean colleagues, it also problematizes neat oppositions of this kind. It does so by looking back to the landscape ideas introduced in New World discovery and settlement narratives as well as forward to ongoing efforts to interrogate and revise them. My contention is that underlying the diverse visions of American nature that surface in the course of such an exercise, we may locate a common project in which many contemporary writers and artists of the Caribbean and North America are engaged: that of reimagining the New World landscape as infused with history and as subject to competing claims.

THE CHAPTERS that follow examine works by diasporic writers and artists of North America and the Caribbean that explore experiences of dislocation against a rural or wilderness background. In so doing, the chapters identify a series of landscape ideas that cut across a wide range of genres and media. Part I suggests that the pastoral mode proves particularly well suited to the project of New World emplacement. Although considered by many critics to be a "dead" mode, or at least a highly conservative one, pastoral is revived in contemporary writing of the Americas in a manner that reveals its long-standing emphasis on displacement and dispossession. Chapter 1 considers the politics of V. S. Naipaul's controversial attachment to the English pastoral landscape of Wiltshire, as well as Derek Walcott's rejection of the English pastoral in favor of Camille Pissarro's brand of French ruralism. Chapters 2 and 3 then turn to North America and to the critical pastoral mode deployed by Jewish American authors Bernard Malamud and Philip Roth as well as Japanese Canadian author Joy Kogawa. These discussions demonstrate the strong appeal of the pastoral for ostensibly urban-oriented diasporic authors as well as the significant risks that the mode poses, particularly with regard to competing Native North American claims on the land. Roth's and Malamud's protagonists identify uncritically with settlement and pioneer narratives, while Kogawa collapses together the historical experiences of First Nations peoples and Japanese Canadians in her effort to assert a bond between her protagonists and the Canadian landscape.[20]

Part II takes some distance from the pastoral mode to explore generic and expressive possibilities that extend beyond fiction and poetry as well as beyond the literary itself. Chapter 4 turns from fiction and poetry to garden writing, a genre that in the hands of Jamaica Kincaid and Michael Pollan becomes a sharply probing tool of historical and cultural inquiry. Chapter 5 continues to engage the space of the garden, as Shani Mootoo, Gisèle Pineau, and Maryse Condé recast the relationship between territorialized and deterritorialized narratives of identity through intertextual allusions to a variety of discourses about island nature, including those articulated in the literature of exploration, natural science, and anthropology. In their novels, these discourses coexist so that no single reading of the Caribbean landscape can obtain a stable authority. Instead, in Mootoo, Pineau, and Condé, the recourse to the marvelous and the gothic challenges the rationality of colonial and scientific narrative. Their juxtaposition of a variety of landscape ideas within a marvelous framework enables a comprehensive reconsideration of constructions of Caribbean nature.

While the majority of the chapters focus on fiction and poetry, this study acknowledges the inherently visual character of landscape representation both by opening with a discussion of Naipaul's and Walcott's engagements with European painting traditions and by concluding with a chapter on installation art. Exclusionary colonial and postcolonial constructions of national landscapes have often been most forcefully inscribed in visual representations, and as a result some of the most powerful challenges to these representations have come from visual artists. Accordingly, chapter 6 gives special attention to British Caribbean filmmaker Isaac Julien and Korean Canadian photographer Jin-me Yoon in order to examine how artists working with alternative expressive media such as photography, video, and installation art condense the juxtapositions of landscape and dislocation with which this book is concerned and illuminate the new insights that they yield into the desire for place.

PART I

Critical Pastoralism

1   V. S. Naipaul's and Derek Walcott's Postcolonial Pastorals

> No other literature is so botanical as English, so seeded with delight and melancholy in the seasons. . . . Boundless as its empire became, England remained an island, a manageable garden to its poets, every one of whom is a pastoralist.
>
> —Derek Walcott, "The Garden Path"

THIS STUDY is concerned with representations of New World landscapes. Yet it begins in the Old World, more specifically in Wiltshire, England, and Pontoise, France, the respective settings of works by two of the Caribbean's most celebrated writers: V. S. Naipaul and Derek Walcott. Naipaul's *The Enigma of Arrival* (1987) and Walcott's *Tiepolo's Hound* (2000) attest to the influence of European landscape ideas on a generation of anglophone Caribbean writers who came of age in the 1950s. Both works further show how received landscape ideas became subject to interrogation as the Caribbean writer's encounter with the European landscape produced a critique of colonial landscape representation as well as a new sense of place. In Naipaul and Walcott, this interrogation hinges on a tension between an idealizing vision of nature on the one hand, and a historicizing view on the other. This tension is fundamental to the pastoral, a mode that Naipaul celebrates but that Walcott is more apt to disclaim. Yet both authors' treatments of the landscape of empire may be considered as operating within the pastoral mode when it is understood in the critical and complex sense that I will be elaborating over the next three chapters. In *The Enigma of Arrival* and *Tiepolo's Hound*, Naipaul and Walcott begin to rethink the relationship between nature and culture in an attempt to articulate a postcolonial sense of place, producing two key examples of what Rob Nixon has termed the "postcolonial pastoral."[1]

The Enigma of Arrival, Naipaul's heavily autobiographical novel of English rural life, and *Tiepolo's Hound,* Walcott's verse biography of the Impressionist painter Camille Pissarro, are sustained explorations of the relationship of the postcolonial subject to European landscape representation. In *Enigma*, Naipaul's narrator, who closely resembles Naipaul himself, obeys a Thoreauvian impulse to "strip [his] life down" and "to avoid vanity" by withdrawing into a cottage on the grounds of a manor in rural Wiltshire near the ruins of Stonehenge. The novel portrays the narrator embarking on a "second life," in which his initial period of exile in London is followed by the experience of a "second, happier childhood as it were, the second arrival (but with an adult's perception) at a knowledge of natural things" (88). In Wiltshire, Naipaul's narrator finds himself in an unmistakably pastoral landscape that had once housed shepherds and their flocks. The narrator's "second arrival" brings him into close contact with nature, which not only heals and renews him but also brings about significant shifts in his way of seeing. *Enigma* documents the narrator's education in nature and in the seasons and is above all a testament to the narrator's sense of being in harmony with his landscape for the first time.[2]

Continually impinging upon this rural idyll, however, is the classic Naipaulean problem of placelessness. The manor upon whose grounds the narrator is living was built in part with colonial wealth, a revelation that recalls the plantation economy that brought the narrator's Indian ancestors to Trinidad. Naipaul's pastoral idyll is also suspended for a good eighty pages by the story of the narrator's journey from Trinidad to England twenty years prior, as well as of his travels throughout the Caribbean and Central America. Moreover, rather than narrating the life chronologically, so that the idyll would serve as an end point to the journey, Naipaul moves from the idyll to the journey and then back again to the idyll, repeating details and entire episodes along the way. The cyclical structure of the book, which accords with its attention to seasonal time, underscores the narrator's contention that his pastoral episode offers no permanent remedy for his rootless condition. The dissonant and unresolved quality of Naipaul's pastoral coincides with critical assessments of the pastoral as a tensely dialectical mode; at the same time, it also signals the ambivalent character of Naipaul's politics.

In Walcott's book-length poem *Tiepolo's Hound,* the Caribbean-born painter Camille Pissarro serves as a kind of double for the narrator, as well as for the Caribbean artist more generally. Here, as in Naipaul's *Enigma,* the narrator bears a close resemblance to the author himself. Revisiting some of the material from his earlier verse autobiography *Another Life* (1973), Walcott finds points of identification between his own artistic formation and that of Pissarro. Walcott is a painter as well as a poet, and in *Tiepolo's Hound* he for the first time includes reproductions of his paintings.[3] The large author photograph on the dust jacket of *Tiepolo's Hound* shows Walcott at the easel, paintbrush in hand, and the analogy that Walcott draws in the poem between his life and Pissarro's further underscores his own vocation as a painter. Pissarro, born in St. Thomas in the Danish Virgin Islands in 1830 to Sephardic Jewish parents and a founding father of the Impressionist movement in France (where he arrived in 1855), also shares the narrator's Caribbean upbringing. The two lives are intertwined in the poem, as Pissarro journeys to Paris to satisfy his "longing for the center" and the narrator searches for an elusive hound that he had once glimpsed in a painting.

In *Tiepolo's Hound,* Walcott's Pissarro becomes emblematic of the Caribbean artist and his displaced condition, enduring "the same crisis / every island artist, despite the wide benediction / / of light, must face," of whether to leave the Caribbean and go into exile (24). Pissarro suffers the humiliations of any "island boy," feeling both bound to and rejected by the European artistic tradition to which he has apprenticed himself:

> Success at home meant nothing, this was the centre
> of opinion; for a Danish colonial Jew
>
> from a dirty, backward island to enter
> the museum's bronzed doors, that would never do.
>
> (61)

The poem's focus on Pissarro's life serves to underscore its central theme of displacement; as a Jew of Portuguese ancestry and Caribbean birth who settles in the France of the Dreyfus Affair, Pissarro is marginalized several times over. At the same time Pissarro, who exhaustively painted the French countryside around Pontoise, exhibits a profound interest in nature and a preference for rural landscapes that the narrator shares. Not only Pissarro's Pontoise but also a variety of other European and Caribbean rural landscapes feature prominently in the poem and in the paintings that accompany the text. The celebration of nature is one of a number of Walcottian themes—including the rejection of History, the value of apprenticeship, and the devotion to simple things—that become associated with Pissarro in *Tiepolo's Hound.* Thus, as in *Enigma,* in *Tiepolo's Hound* the theme of Caribbean exile is explored against the backdrop of a European rural landscape, and the pastoralism that results is sharply double-edged. While Naipaul attends primarily to the European pastoral landscape, however, Walcott's emphasis is ultimately on the local Caribbean setting.

Enigma and *Tiepolo's Hound* share a number of thematic and formal concerns. Indeed, despite Walcott's attack on *Enigma* in a review in the *New Republic,* these may be the works in which the two Nobel laureates come closest to one another. Both are heavily autobiographical narratives that to a certain extent conceal their autobiographical content—*Enigma* is subtitled "A Novel" and *Tiepolo's Hound*'s ostensible subject is Pissarro. But more significant is the emphasis both works give to visual perception and landscape representation, Naipaul to English aesthetic traditions and Walcott primarily to French and Italian ones. While Walcott has long filled his poetry with allusions to painters and works of art, it is perhaps more surprising to find phrases such as the following in Naipaul: "In winter the trees went bare and brushlike, as in the watercolors of Rowland Hilder" (6). And in *Tiepolo's Hound,* Walcott deepens his long-standing emphasis on the visual by reproducing his own paintings alongside the text of the poem.

Moreover, the title of each work refers to a painting, and at the same time contains a curious displacement. While Naipaul derives his title from the surrealist Giorgio de Chirico painting "The Enigma of Arrival" (1912), a reproduction of which he finds in the Wiltshire cottage, the painting was in fact given its name by Apollinaire, suggesting a disconnect between language and image that will be a central concern of Naipaul's postcolonial pastoral. The displacement in Walcott's title is even more thorough: the identity of the painting to which the title alludes is in question throughout the poem. Perhaps it is not a Tiepolo painting at all that the narrator remembers but rather a considerably earlier painting that also features a hound: Paolo Veronese's "The Feast at the House of Levi" (1573), which was itself retitled to appease the Inquisition, and which is housed in Venice, not in New York as the narrator remembers—but then again perhaps it is not. Thus, Naipaul's and Walcott's titles hint at enigmatic gaps between language, visual representation, and the object of representation that are thematic of the problem of landscape art in a (post)colonial setting.

In keeping with their shared emphasis on the visual and on landscape aesthetics, rural landscapes predominate in both *Enigma* and *Tiepolo's Hound.* What we might identify as their pastoral qualities—their slow-moving pace, quiet, contemplative mood, and their privileging of the rural—has raised doubts about both works. Naipaul's choice of setting has left some of his more sympathetic readers, such as Sara Suleri, puzzled by the book's "oddly bucolic tone" (167), while prompting those more wary of Naipaul's politics to accuse him of shying away from the racial complexities of the urban setting. Related misgivings have been expressed with regard to Walcott's poem. One reviewer complains that *Tiepolo's Hound* is not angry enough: "It would be nice to see more rage and less quiet. Stillness and poise and grace centre the European eye—a more persistent paranoid vision might better reveal the deep obfuscations and abstractions that inform the great wrongs of colonial history" (Kinsella 14). A central question raised by both works, then, is why do they adopt a pastoral setting and sensibility? Given the ideological baggage that the pastoral carries in a postcolonial context, what accounts for Naipaul's and Walcott's recourse to this mode?

Colonial Pastoral and the "Mobile Museum"

To describe *Enigma* or *Tiepolo's Hound* as a "postcolonial pastoral" is to posit the existence of a "colonial pastoral" that provokes the articulation of an alternative vision of landscape. Indeed, both *Enigma* and *Tiepolo's Hound* are concerned with developing a new "art of seeing," to use Walcott's phrase. But what constitutes the colonial pastoral in a New World context? On the one hand, colonial pastoral may refer to the pastoral or Edenic vision that European explorers imposed on the New World when they first encountered it, and to which Europeans often continued to adhere in spite of mounting evidence of the falseness of this vision. As I suggested in the introduction, colonial pastoral also designates the practice common among settler colonial cultures of pastoralizing the new surroundings as a means of domesticating them for the purposes of settlement. To apply a pastoral vocabulary to an unfamiliar landscape, as Oliver Goldsmith does to Nova Scotia in *The Rising Village*, is to imagine that landscape as habitable and to encourage others to do the same.

Colonial pastoral may also indicate, however, the dissemination in the colonies of images of rural European landscapes and the impact of this transmission on the colonial subject. This last version of colonial pastoral is highlighted in a scene in Jamaica Kincaid's *The Autobiography of My Mother* (1996) in which a young Dominican girl accidentally smashes a china plate that is the prized possession of her caretaker. The plate, which had been the object of the girl's "obsessive curiosity," depicts an English rural vista:

> I would look at it and wonder about the picture painted on its surface, a
> picture of a wide-open field filled with grass and flowers in the most tender

shades of yellow, pink, blue, and green. . . . This picture was nothing but a field full of grass and flowers on a sunny day, but it had an atmosphere of secret abundance, happiness, and tranquillity; underneath it was written in gold letters the one word HEAVEN. Of course it was not a picture of heaven at all; it was a picture of the English countryside idealized, but I did not know that, I did not know that such a thing as the English countryside existed. And neither did Eunice; she thought that this picture was a picture of heaven, offering as it did a secret promise of a life without worry or care or want. (8–9)

In this passage, Kincaid calls attention to the prominence in colonial settings of visual representations of rural European landscapes as well as to one of the means by which such images were disseminated. At the same time, Kincaid's heroine violently resists the plate's privileging of the metropolitan landscape by shattering the plate and the English pastoral image it displays. This episode points to both the prevalence of pastoral constructions of England in her colonies and the colonial subject's desire to dislodge this construction.

Yet the dissemination of landscape imagery in the colonies may also instill a desire to visit the metropolitan landscape, to find "confirmation" of what has been seen in reproductions and read about in books. In *The Pleasures of Exile*, the Barbadian writer George Lamming observes that the Caribbean student was consumed by the myth or "idea" of England before he left his homeland, a myth that he inculcated through his colonial education. It is in the context of Lamming's discussion of the "idea of England" that we can understand Naipaul's narrator's statement in *Enigma* that, upon arriving in England for the first time, "I had come to London as to a place I knew very well" (134), or, regarding Wiltshire, that "though I hadn't truly seen those views before or been in their midst, I felt I had always known them" (36).[4] The idea of England that Lamming attributes to the generation of Caribbean immigrants that arrived in England in the immediate postwar period has many facets, but one feature is certainly the visual image of the English pastoral landscape.

If the rural has been central to the English sense of place, particularly since the late nineteenth century, that emphasis on a rural Englishness is both carried over into and stimulated by the colonial setting. Williams notes in *The Country and the City* that industrialization and the new forms of political control that England exerted over her colonies in the late nineteenth century encouraged an increasingly idealized image of rural England to emerge, so that rurality became central to an idea of England as home. This rural image of Englishness was in turn transmitted from white colonists to Britain's colonial subjects.[5] In the colonies, in the words of one critic, "architecture, art, and spectacle all created a sense that England's landscape, aesthetic forms, and rituals were the images of home that every colonial of every social class ought to retain. These images became the interior landscape of the colonized mind" (Renk 31–32).

The precise character of this interior landscape is illuminated by a repeated motif in Derek Walcott's poetry: the "mobile museum."[6] In *Tiepolo's Hound,* we learn that several books of reproductions that the narrator had studied as a child in St. Lucia supply the contents of this museum:

> Fragile little booklets, reproductions in monochrome,
> RENOIR, DÜRER, several Renaissance masters
>
> were our mobile museum, the back yards of home
> were the squares of Italy, its piazzas our thick pastures.
>
> (13–14)

In this broken quatrain, the rhyme "masters/pastures" underlines the prominence of landscape painting in the Western artistic tradition to which Walcott apprenticed himself and suggests a connection between colonial rule and landscape representation, while "monochrome/home" indicates the difficulty of assimilating the local landscape to this imported aesthetic. Both themes also figure prominently in Walcott's earlier verse autobiography *Another Life,* which cites books of reproductions to which Walcott was exposed as a child, including *The English Topographical Draughtsmen* and a "sky-blue book" containing "the shepherdesses of Boucher and Fragonard" (ch. 9; 3.7–8). In addition to these reproductions, Walcott was influenced by his father's practice of copying European paintings and drawings, as he recalls in his early essay "Leaving School" (1965):

> On the drawing room walls of our house there were relics of [my father's] avocation: a copy of Millet's *The Gleaners,* a romantic original of sea-birds and pluming breakers he had called *Riders of the Storm,* a miniature oil portrait of my mother, a self-portrait in water colour and an avenue of pale coconut palms. These objects had established my vocation, and made it as inevitable as that of any craftsman's son, for I felt that my father's work, however minor, was unfinished. Rummaging through stuffed, dark cupboards, I sometimes came across finely copied verses, evidence of a polite gracile talent, and once on a sketchbook of excellent pencil studies. I treasured the books he had used:

two small, blue-covered volumes on *The English Topographical Draughtsmen*
and on *Albrecht Dürer,* and thick-ridged, classical albums of John McCormack,
and I think, Galli Curci. (28)

Notably, a number of Walcott's father's copies were of European agricultural scenes. Among his father's legacy to him are "a fine sketch of a
cow" and an oft-mentioned copy of Millet's "The Gleaners," confirming
that the idea of Europe transmitted by such means was frequently rural.
"Remember 'The Hay Wain' / in your museum, Thomas Craven's book?"
the narrator asks his painter friend Gregorias in *Another Life* (ch. 12;
3.9–10), referring to Constable's well-known 1821 painting. This autobiographical material is reworked in *Tiepolo's Hound,* in which Walcott's
father's copy of *The English Topographical Draughtsmen* resurfaces:

> From my father's cabinet I trace his predecessors
> in a small blue book: *The English Topographical Draughtsmen,*
>
> his pencil studies, delicately firm as theirs,
> the lyrical, light precision of these craftsmen—
>
> Girtin, Sandby, and Cotman, Peter De Wint,
> meadows with needle spires in monochrome,
>
> locks and canals with enormous clouds that went
> rolling over England, postcards from home,
>
> his namesake's county, Warwickshire.
>
> (11)

In passages such as this one, Walcott records the transmission of visual
images of rural Europe—"meadows with needle spires," "locks and canals
with enormous clouds"—through reproductions as well as through his
father's artistic labors. He also alludes to the ambiguous meaning of
"home" that results from this familiarity with European landscapes. His
father's name, Warwick, suggests a connection to an ancestral rural English landscape where there is in fact none—or at least none that Walcott
would want to claim, as he insists later in the poem.

Naipaul, too, vividly describes the circulation of landscape imagery in
the colonial Trinidad of his childhood, imagery that inspired the narrator's move to Wiltshire. In *Enigma,* Naipaul's narrator has a fantasy of
England just as his aristocratic Wiltshire landlord has a fantasy of India
and Africa, and the emblem of this fantasy of England is a pastoral scene
of cows on a grassy hillside that was depicted on the labels of the milk

tins of the narrator's childhood. The narrator returns repeatedly to this milk-label image of England: "I had seen the cows on the hillsides against the sky. . . . And they had seemed like the cows in the drawing on the label of the condensed-milk tins I knew in Trinidad as a child: something to me as a result at the very heart of romance, a child's fantasy of the beautiful other place, something which, when I saw it on the downs, was like something I had always known" (84). In Wiltshire, the narrator attempts to locate the real landscape that corresponds to that of the fantasy of the milk label; indeed, he at times feels as though he is entering the drawing, although this is an impression that he will later come to revise.

In addition to the milk-label image, Naipaul's narrator's "advance information" about rural England is derived from a Constable painting of Salisbury Cathedral, which lies near his new home in Wiltshire: "It was Salisbury. It was almost the first English town I had got to know, the first I had been given some idea of, from the reproduction of the Constable painting of Salibury Cathedral in my third-standard reader. Far away in my tropical island, before I was ten. A four-color reproduction which I had thought the most beautiful picture I had ever seen" (7). Constable is the narrator's primary visual guide to his new landscape, and at the same time a key contributor to his idea of England.[7] As with Walcott's books of reproductions or Kincaid's china plate, in Naipaul mass-produced images of the English landscape are the primary conduits of the colonial pastoral.

Yet because Naipaul is a less visually minded writer than Walcott—even in the case of the de Chirico painting, it is the title of the painting rather than the painting itself that draws his attention—his emphasis is primarily on the transmission of landscape imagery through poetry and novels. His visual reference points are fewer and less rich than those of Walcott, whose poetry is densely laden with allusions to artistic traditions. Walcott's poetry is replete with phrases such as "in the saffron of Tiepolo sunsets" (7) and "the dusty olive / of Cézanne's trees" (19) that seamlessly introduce an allusion to a painter or artwork in order to convey a quality of light or color. Naipaul's visual references, by contrast, are less essential to the fabric of his writing and bespeak the child's visual imagination rather than a mature adult one, as is indicated by his citations of E. H. Shephard's illustrations for *The Wind in the Willows* (187) and a Pre-Raphaelite painting reproduced in his *Nelson's West Indian Reader* (171). More resonant in Naipaul are the allusions to English poetry: the father of the narrator's neighbor Jack is "a Wordsworthian figure: bent, . . . going gravely about his peasant tasks, as if in an immense Lake District solitude" (16).

The Wiltshire cattle are compared to those of Gray and Goldsmith: "No lowing herd winding o'er the lea here, as in Gray's 'Elegy'; no 'sober' herd lowing to meet their young at evening's close, as in 'The Deserted Village'" (84–85). In *Reading and Writing* (2000), Naipaul refers to his "private literature anthology," a version of Walcott's "mobile museum" that comprises the works of literature available to him growing up in Trinidad.[8] In addition to indicating the limited availability of books on the island, Naipaul's notion of the private anthology also suggests the extent to which foreign books were domesticated in the child's mind.

In his early essay "Jasmine" (1964), Naipaul describes his childhood practice of melding English novels onto his own Trinidadian landscape: "The process of adaptation was automatic and continuous. Dickens's rain and drizzle I turned into tropical downpours; the snow and fog I accepted as conventions of books. Anything—like an illustration—which embarrassed me by proving how weird my own recreation was, anything which sought to remove the characters from the make-up world in which I set them, I rejected" (17).[9] Yet the foreignness of the literary material was not always so easily overcome, as Naipaul illustrates through the anecdote of the jasmine flower with which he ends his essay. While on a visit to British Guiana, Naipaul smells a scent familiar to him from his childhood. When he queries his hostess, she identifies its source as jasmine, a flower whose name Naipaul had known from his reading but which he had not associated with the flower that has now been pointed out to him:

> Jasmine! So I had known it all those years! To me it had been a word in a book, a word to play with, something removed from the dull vegetation I knew.
>
> The old lady cut a sprig for me. I stuck it in the top buttonhole of my open shirt. I smelled it as I walked back to the hotel. Jasmine, jasmine. But the word and the flower had been separate in my mind for too long. They did not come together. (22)

Walcott's Pissarro suffers from similar confusion regarding the flowers in France, "whose names he never knew, or that would vary / from their names in the islands" (36). This peculiarly botanical sense of displacement and the devaluation of the local landscape that tends to accompany it—Naipaul's characterization of Trinidadian vegetation as "dull" would surely be disputed by many—is indeed a favorite motif of Caribbean literature. In Jamaica Kincaid's *Lucy* (1990) it is the daffodil, in Merle Hodge's *Crick Crack Monkey* (1970) it is the apple, for Naipaul's

Mr. Biswas it is the English seasons, but the problem is always the same: the gap that opens up between the local landscape and the landscape represented in books and art.

The Caribbean subject's sense of familiarity with the metropolitan landscape often comes at the cost of an ability to fully apprehend the local landscape. Naipaul's narrator recounts that it is only when he flies over Trinidad for the first time as he departs for England that he recognizes that Trinidad *has* a landscape. From the vantage point of the airplane, he sees "a landscape of clear pattern and contours, absorbing all the road-side messiness, a pattern of dark green and dark brown, like camouflage, like a landscape in a book, like the landscape of a real country. So that at the moment of takeoff almost, the moment of departure, the landscape of my childhood was like something which I had missed, something I had never seen" (105). It is striking how often and how powerfully the various forms of cultural, psychological, and economic displacements from which the Caribbean subject suffers are expressed in terms of landscape and botanical imagery. As I will suggest in chapter 4, perhaps the greatest practitioner of this mode of expression is Jamaica Kincaid. In novels such as *Lucy* and particularly in her garden writing, Kincaid highlights the oddly dislocated character of the Caribbean landscape by reminding us of the historical imposition of foreign names on local flora and by noting the absence of local plants in the botanical gardens established throughout the colonies.

In *Another Life*, Walcott's narrator had drawn attention to the problem of the denigration of the local landscape:

> from childhood he'd considered palms
> ignobler than imagined elms,
> the breadfruit's splayed
> leaf coarser than the oak's.
> (ch. 1; 2.24–27)

In a striking passage in *Tiepolo's Hound* that is reminiscent of Kincaid, Walcott again takes up the theme of the disconnect between the local and metropolitan landscapes and the devaluation of the local landscape that results:

> The empire of naming colonised even the trees,
> referred our leaves to their originals;
>
> this was the blight on our minds, a speckled disease.
> In the convulsive olives of Van Gogh's Arles,

lime trees tried to be olives they could not become,
not less real than reproductions in a book,

but certainly less hallowed. Reality was riven
by these reproductions, and that blight spread

through every noun, even the names we were given,
the paintings we studied, the books we loved to read.

The gommier in flower did not mimic the dogwood
or snow at the roots of white cedar, or Queen Anne's lace,

an apple orchard, or April's autumnal firewood;
they were, like the breadfruit, true to their sense of place.

(92)

Here and throughout *Tiepolo's Hound,* Walcott describes the profound
effect—"the blight on our minds"—of the circulation of landscape imagery in the Caribbean islands, which alienates the colonial subject from
his very physical surroundings and which elevates not only metropolitan
culture but also metropolitan *nature* above its colonial counterpart. Walcott suggests in these lines that nature is itself colonized by "the empire
of naming." In referring to the colonization of nature, Walcott brings
about a significant rapprochement of nature and history; nature does
not stand apart from culture in this reading but instead they are thoroughly entangled.[10] At the same time as pursuing an entangled reading
of New World nature, Walcott also locates a certain resistance in Caribbean natural phenomena, which remain "true to their sense of place."
This key passage from *Tiepolo's Hound* suggests that the articulation
of a postcolonial sense of place will depend on a reconceptualization of
nature itself.

Ways of Seeing

Born on islands that were physically transformed in the service of plantation economies, and raised on images of idealized foreign landscapes,
Naipaul and Walcott are deeply preoccupied with the problem of landscape representation. Both writers are acutely aware that landscape is
always a creation of history. Accordingly they are highly self-conscious
in their presentation of landscape; Naipaul's narrator calls attention to his
"way of looking" (15, 19, 59), while Walcott refers to the "art of seeing" (7). As critics have noted, *Enigma* opens with Naipaul's narrator
struggling to see the Wiltshire landscape through the rain, which blurs

his vision. Several days later, when the Wiltshire valley becomes outlined with snow, the landscape slowly comes into focus for him. This opening motif expresses in visual terms a pastoral tension between misrecognition and recognition—or idealization and historicization—that will structure the book. This tension is also central to *Tiepolo's Hound*, in which Walcott problematizes visual perception and visual memory through the figure of the hound that the narrator had once seen in a painting but cannot now relocate. Walcott's focus on Impressionism, a school of painting that shifted attention to the effect of the physical environment on the artist's awareness, reflects his interest in the problem of perception.

One of the primary obstacles to vision for Naipaul and Walcott is the set of images and assumptions that I have described as colonial pastoral. Just as Renaissance travelers to the New World arrived with preconceptions about the landscape that hindered their ability to see, so the colonized subject comes to the European landscape with a set of preabsorbed images that cloud his vision. By adopting a critical attitude toward these preabsorbed images, the Caribbean writer becomes able to see the European landscape less allusively. Thus, Naipaul's narrator writes that after twenty years in England, "The man who went walking past Jack's cottage saw things as if for the first time. Literary allusions came naturally to him, but he had grown to see with his own eyes. He could not have seen like that, so clearly, twenty years before. . . . The simplicity and directness had taken a long time to get to him; it was necessary for him to have gone through a lot" (173). But this question of clear vision not only concerns the perceptual interference of inherited pastoral images; it is also tied to the deeper political and aesthetic assumptions that inform those images. In both *Enigma* and *Tiepolo's Hound*, the narrators vacillate between two models of landscape representation that coexist within their complex pastorals: an idealized, coherent vision of landscape on the one hand and an experiential, fragmentary vision of landscape on the other.

Learning How to Read History in the Landscape in The Enigma of Arrival

In his review of *Enigma* in the *New Republic*, Walcott writes that his response to the excerpts of the book that appeared in advance of its publication was to "cheris[h] them as the tenderest writing Naipaul had ever done" (28). Initially, Walcott celebrated the arrival of a new, gentler Naipaul that these excerpts appeared to announce. Yet upon reading the book in its entirety, Walcott became dismayed at the return of the familiar Naipaulean bitterness: "Then the book began to disfigure itself. The old distemper set in. The elation and gratitude shriveled and puckered and once again left the teeth on edge, the scour on the tongue" (28). *Enigma* ultimately confirmed Walcott's original opinion of Naipaul, whose "direction," Walcott claims, "has always been clear" (27).

Walcott's conflicted response is typical of the book's broader reception; it has been heralded as a breakthrough by some and at the same time condemned by others as "the most intense of all [Naipaul's] fantasies" (Cudjoe 213). While one camp argues that *Enigma* radically challenges essentialist conceptions of place and identity, the other complains that the book, whose attachment to the English landscape only encourages suspicions that Naipaul is overly enamored of Englishness, represents an intensification of Naipaul's colonialist obsession with England as well as his racial anxiety.[11] This contradictory response reflects the ambivalent character of Naipaul's later work. Naipaul is notorious for his location of Caribbean societies outside of history and his insistence on their in-authenticity. Yet counterbalancing Naipaul's Eurocentrism and cultural conservatism is his more recent emphasis on what one critic calls "gestures of return and reconciliation" (Mustafa 7). What, then, are the politics of Naipaul's pastoral?

Upon arriving in Wiltshire, Naipaul's narrator seeks confirmation of his idea of rural England, just as he had sought confirmation of his idea of London upon his arrival there twenty years prior. The narrator's inten-tionally paradoxical characterization of his arrival in London—"I was like a man entering the world of a novel, a book; entering the real world" (129)—holds true of his Wiltshire experience as well. Yet as in London, the narrator's arrival in Wiltshire is marked by a series of misreadings of the new landscape and its inhabitants. Reflecting on his early days in Wiltshire, the narrator revises those initial impressions with the benefit of the perspective that time and the act of narration now afford him. The central gesture of *Enigma,* I would argue, is this recording and revision of false impressions of rural English life.

The correction of misperceptions occurs on a number of levels in *Enigma.* In "The Journey," the section of *Enigma* that suspends the rural idyll, the young narrator in London had struggled to shed his fantasy of what properly constitutes a writer's material. Now, in the Wiltshire scenes that precede and follow "The Journey," the narrator must confront his attraction to an idea of the rural as timeless, ancient, and at "the begin-ning of things." When he was a child in Trinidad, streams had made him think of "the beginning of the world, the world before men, before the settlement" (44), and this child's fantasy thrives in Wiltshire, where

his "vision of the world before men" is encouraged by the proximity of
Stonehenge as well as a nunnery that may have figured in the Arthurian
legend. At certain moments in the narrative, Naipaul's narrator is able to
sustain the myth of the rural as untouched by time: "The view through
which I walked, was of a nature almost unchanged since Constable's day"
(204). Yet more frequently he is confronted by evidence of change: "Here
was an unchanging world—so it would have seemed to the stranger. So
it seemed to me when I first became aware of it: the country life, the slow
movement of time. . . . But that idea of an unchanging life was wrong.
Change was constant" (32). In passage after passage, the narrator contrasts his initial, uninformed impression of Wiltshire with the more edu-
cated one that supplants it, so that the narrative comes to have something
of the demystifying force of Williams's *The Country and the City*.

Naipaul's Wiltshire landscape is a landscape of illusion, populated by
buildings that "pretend" to be older than they are by mimicking earlier
architectural styles or by disguising their true function. The "country-
cottage effect" of a neighbor's house turns out to be contrived rather
than a natural feature of the landscape, and the narrator makes a similar
discovery regarding his own cottage. He mistakes a "rustic" stable on
the grounds of the manor for a forester's hut and clings stubbornly to the
romantic notion even after recognizing his mistake. Similarly, a squash
court is built to look like a farmhouse; a shed is disguised as a cottage.
The Edwardian manor and its grounds are themselves playful creations
of the landlord's family—a "modern fantasy," a "gratuitous expression
of great security and wealth" (195) rather than "natural expressions of
a particular place" (193). Thus, architecture in Naipaul's Wiltshire constructs a sense of continuity with the past rather than expressing a natural
inheritance of the land's inhabitants. Yet not only architecture but nature
itself participates in the illusion. A young growth of trees suggests the
presence of a deep forest of older growth behind, but the forest fails to
materialize. The cows that had at first seemed such perfect incarnations
of those pictured on the condensed-milk tins are, as the narrator discovers, not only not milk-producing but also have genetic defects caused by
overly mechanized breeding techniques. Ultimately, the narrator comes
to see nature itself as constructed: "Nothing was natural here; everything was considered. Grass and trees concealed as much engineering as
a Roman forum. Just one cut with the mower did away with the idea of
wilderness outside the back door of my cottage" (219–20).

With this last insight, Naipaul moves his pastoral out of the realm of
myth and into that of history. In *The Middle Passage* (1962), Naipaul

had begun to understand Caribbean nature as entangled with history: "So many things in these West Indian territories, I now begin to see, speak of slavery. There is slavery in the vegetation. In the sugarcane, brought by Columbus on that second voyage when, to Queen Isabella's fury, he proposed the enslavement of the Amerindians. . . . And just as in the barren British Guiana savannah lands a clump of cashew trees marks the site of an Amerindian village, so in Jamaica a clump of star-apple trees marks the site of a slave provision ground" (182–83).[12] If, as this passage suggests, Trinidadian nature supplies a record of history, *Enigma* reveals that the metropolitan landscape is also entangled with history. In *Enigma*, Naipaul identifies the emergence of a new social order by tracing changes in the configuration of the rural English landscape. Just as the Trinidadian landscape is not static but is transformed as a result of its constant interaction with history, so too the Wiltshire estate's grounds dramatically alter with the decline of the British Empire. Part of the narrator's education in nature in Wiltshire is learning how to read history in the landscape.

In keeping with this demystifying and historicizing bent, Naipaul's narrator highlights connections between the estate on which he now resides and the colonial economies that in the nineteenth century had brought his Indian ancestors to Trinidad as indentured laborers. The narrator describes the Wiltshire estate as the "apotheosis" of those colonial plantations on which his ancestors had labored, and notes that the estate, which was once "enormous," had been created partly out of the wealth of empire. Now considerably shrunken in size, the estate is falling into disrepair, its grounds increasingly untended and its buildings decaying. The decline of empire is written onto the English landscape, and the passing of the estate and the empire that supported it is strongly associated in the narrator's mind with nature's cyclical logic of decay and renewal. Naipaul's Wiltshire pastoral is deeply implicated in a history of dispossession that both predates and includes the modern imperial age; in Naipaul's novel, English pastoral and colonial displacement are coextensive rather than antithetical.

In a later passage in which he advances an entangled reading of nature, Naipaul considers the particular meaning of gardening in a Caribbean setting. Naipaul recalls the unfamiliarity of gardens for him as a child in Trinidad, and observes that gardening primarily signified servitude to colonial subjects in the Caribbean: "That instinct to plant, to see crops grow, might have seemed eternal, something to which the human heart would want to return. But in the plantation colony from which I came—a colony created for agriculture, for the great flat fields of sugarcane, which were the point and explanation of everything . . . —in that colony, created by the power and wealth of industrial England, the instinct had been eradicated" (238).[13] Yet while the narrator identifies the loss of an "instinct to plant" as one consequence of colonization, he also points to a new landscape idea that emerged in the transition from a plantation society to a postslavery and postcolonial one. Note his description of the vegetable gardens grown by former estate workers in postwar Trinidad on land redeemed from swamp: "The straight lines of these vegetable plots, the human scale, the many different shades and textures of green, gave us a new idea of agriculture and almost a new idea of landscape and natural beauty. The vegetable growers were Indian, but these vegetable plots were like nothing in peasant India. . . . English allotments in a tropical and colonial setting! Created by accident, and not by design; created at the end of the period of empire, out of the decay of the old sugar plantations" (225–26). Thus, the creation of a landscape becomes expressive of a postcolonial identity; the Indian vegetable growers use skills gleaned from their colonial education to construct a new relationship with the land. This insight into the way in which landscapes are made rather than inherited by their human inhabitants is central to *Enigma* and establishes it as a complex, rather than merely nostalgic, pastoral.

In *Enigma,* Naipaul's narrator initially seeks remnants in the landscape around Salisbury of an uninterrupted wholeness, of an idealized preindustrial England that represents an ancient way of life. He interprets evidence of the many changes occurring in the landscape—increased mechanization, buildings being torn down, deaths and new arrivals—as signs of "decay" and of the belatedness of his arrival. Even a hedge is for him "a vestige, a memory of another kind of house and garden and street, a token of something more complete, more ideal" (17). But subsequently, in a less tragic mood, the narrator renounces his quest for an idealized past: "I lived with the idea of change, of flux, and learned, profoundly, not to grieve for it. I learned to dismiss this easy cause of so much human grief. Decay implied an ideal, a perfection in the past. But would I have cared to be in my cottage while the sixteen gardeners worked? . . . Wasn't the place now, for me, at its peak? Finding myself where I was, I thought—after the journey that had begun so long before—that I was blessed" (210). This is a critical turning point for Naipaul's narrator, who, if he does achieve a new vision, achieves it here in his shift from a language of tragic belatedness to one of affirmation. Naipaul's use of the word "blessed" in this passage sounds surprisingly like Walcott, who tends to favor a quasi-religious vocabulary of faith, devotion, and bene-diction. Yet Naipaul's narrator arrives at this new vision while on one of his daily walks, indicating that it represents a temporary moment of en-lightenment rather than a wholesale alteration in his outlook, as accords with the cyclical logic of the book.

Indeed, even as Naipaul does much to demystify the colonial pastoral in such passages and to revise his infamous earlier statements regarding the stasis and uncreativity of Caribbean societies, there is more than a hint of nostalgia for an older imperial order in Naipaul's often elegiac book, as we see for instance in the references to the sixteen gardeners who had once tended the estate's grounds. Naipaul's narrator wistfully imagines the "order" that this troop of gardeners would have created on the grounds, one that could never be replicated today: "Sixteen! How could anyone not running a plant nursery find sixteen gardeners nowa-days or pay their wages? How different the hamlets and villages round about must have been then, how many working people in little houses!" (61). The underlying note of nostalgia and the romanticization of labor that this passage contains distances Naipaul from Walcott, who is far less susceptible to the fantasy of the English manor village to which Naipaul's narrator repeatedly succumbs.

The conflicting interpretations of *Enigma*—the debate over whether it announces a shift in Naipaul's politics—reflect the ambivalent vision of the novel. It is in distancing himself from his earlier, highly mythologized view of rural England that Naipaul can be seen as moving toward a new perspective. Yet he has difficulty sustaining this more complex pastoral vision, and wavers between falling back on an old way of seeing and attempting something more radical. Rather than coexisting in a produc-tive tension that yields new insight, these two ways of seeing lead to an impasse—a blockage symbolized by the choking fit that the narrator suffers before his departure from the valley—and as a result Naipaul's demystification of the colonial pastoral remains incomplete. The affirma-tion of change erodes toward the end of the book as the narrator reverts to his earlier habit of bemoaning the decay of the old order. Naipaul's ambivalent politics expose the contradictions of the pastoral mode at their most intense; his Wiltshire idyll is simultaneously the culmination of his fantasy of England and its undoing.

The Real and the Ideal in Tiepolo's Hound

A comparable but ultimately less paralyzing conflict between two ways of seeing emerges in *Tiepolo's Hound*. While in *Another Life* Walcott's visual reference points were drawn primarily from the Old Masters, in *Tiepolo's Hound* he distances himself somewhat from that set of influences by juxtaposing the Old Masters' idealizing vision with the more realist vision of Pissarro and his fellow Impressionists.[14] The seventeenth-century pastoral painter Claude Lorrain and his eighteenth-century successors Boucher and Fragonard had painted "golden cattle in luminous pastures" (39), improving on nature in accordance with the classical ideals of beauty, harmony, and order. This idealizing vision is not available to Walcott's Pissarro, who lives in the age of industrialization and the machine:

> By now the hallowed pastorals were besieged
> by factories, stations, by the charred verticals
>
> of factories' chimneys, palm stumps on a beach
> that made the imperilled poplars precious, the calls
>
> of dove and skylark rarer, till every
> frame held bending smoke and the raw noise
>
> of industry. He painted the ordinary
> for what it was, not eulogies of Pontoise.
>
> (53)

Responding to recent discoveries regarding the nature of color and perception, the Impressionists rejected the belief in the transcendent in favor of a transient reality subject to both the artist's attitude and the passing of time (as Monet's serial paintings of haystacks, cathedrals, and waterlilies demonstrated).[15] Eschewing the balanced and harmonious composition of neoclassical landscape painting, they cropped their compositions to emphasize movement and the partial nature of their experiential perspectives.

While Claude's idealized landscapes engaged the viewer in a complete and transcendent experience, the Impressionists' particularized landscapes attempted to capture the moment of perception:

> Time, petrified in every classic canvas,
> denied the frailty of the painter's hands,
>
> acquired an intimacy with its origin, Claude,
> David, and the Venetian schools presumed
>
> a privilege given by the gods or God,
> while Time's blasphemous fire consumed, consumed.
>
> Now sunlight is splintered and even shade is entered
> as part of the prism.
>
> (43)

For the Impressionists, "vision was not the concentrated gaze / that took in every detail at a glance" (43). In accordance with the Impressionists' understanding of time, Walcott's Pissarro "learnt to look / at the instant with no pretext of stasis" (55). Walcott admires the fragmented, incomplete quality of Pissarro's Impressionist landscapes, which is underscored by the bare patches that Pissarro occasionally left on his canvases. Pissarro's bare patches are in turn echoed by the openness of Walcott's broken quatrains, which enact an analogous fragmentation of space. At the same time, through their transformation of a traditional verse form, Walcott's broken quatrains encourage a new approach to the familiar, in keeping with his poem's broader objective of interrogating conventional ways of seeing.[16]

A pastoral dissonance between the real and the ideal is also generated in *Tiepolo's Hound* by the poem's sustained comparison of the religious painting of the Venetian baroque to the naturalistic conventions of Italian genre painting. The way of seeing suggested by baroque religious painting, which is represented in the poem by the motif of baroque "ceilings huge with paradisal glow" (70), is one that posits a transcendent ideal and an Eternal Time.[17] Genre painting's contrasting orientation toward the everyday is represented by the hound that the narrator remembers having once seen in a painting by Tiepolo or Veronese.[18] The elusive hound points to the transience of everyday life: the hound is "the hunched phantom / at the feast's surfeit, not saints possessed / / by their own radiance" (119). The hound's way of seeing is affiliated in the poem with the Impressionist's emphasis on the fleeting moment. It focuses on the mundane detail and insists on the partial and inconclusive nature of perception. It is unstable, doubting, and subject to inaccuracies such as the "mistake" of the poem's title.

To view Veronese's "Feast at the House of Levi" at the Accademia in Venice—the painting that the narrator at one point realizes may contain the hound he seeks—is to gain insight into the narrator's way of seeing. The painting was retitled "Feast at the House of Levi" because the Inquisition deemed its carnivalesque depiction of the Last Supper to be heretical. Marginal figures including Turks, Moors, a dwarf-jester, a cat, and, of course, the hound crowd Veronese's large canvas, which covers an entire wall of the museum. Because of the vast size of the canvas, these marginal figures are portrayed in enough detail to suggest the plurality of their perspectives on the biblical scene. Particularly striking in this regard is a Moor on the extreme far left of the canvas who is cut off at the shoulders—a framing figure who is cropped from many standard art book reproductions. He peers onto the canvas from its edge, only partially present to the action of the painting, and gives us an alternative point of view on it.[19] Instead of supporting the illusion that the painting provides a complete vision, this figure, together with a fiercely expressive Moor situated to his immediate right, hints at a world that is excluded by the boundaries of the canvas.

Like the Moors on the far left of the "Feast at the House of Levi," Walcott's elusive, remembered hound offers a decentered perspective on Veronese's painting. In the painting the narrator remembers, the hound is at once both marginal and central. The focal point of the painting is ostensibly the feast, but the viewer's eye is drawn to the hound, who (placed slightly off-center in the foreground of the painting below Christ) stands out because of the "bright vermilion" of his thigh. In the poem, the hound thus becomes the figure for marginality and the potential for a revisionary postcolonial rereading. Drawing inspiration from the hound, Walcott's corrective mode of perception calls attention to other neglected and marginalized elements such as the myriad displaced figures with which it is associated in the poem: the members of Pissarro's Sephardic Jewish family, the "turbanned Moors at the edge of a feast" in Old Masters paintings, and the narrator himself.

The revisionary mode of perception represented by the hound is applied to Camille Pissarro as art-historical subject as well. In standard studies of Impressionism, Pissarro's Jewishness and his Caribbean provenance receive only passing mention,[20] but for Walcott these become the critical features of Pissarro's biography. Walcott's emphasis is always on Pissarro's status as outsider, and, in his reading, the Impressionists are likened to marginalized colonials: "they were the Academy's outcasts, its niggers / from barbarous colonies, a contentious people!" (45). Because of his Jewishness, Pissarro remained an outsider even among these outsiders, as the Dreyfus Affair made painfully clear. Yet at the same time, Walcott emphasizes Pissarro's centrality to French art history, for Pissarro is at once an interloper among the Impressionists and their father figure. Walcott's favorite linguistic trick for expressing this interpenetration of the colonial and the metropolitan is to point out that the letters of the word "Paris" are contained in Pissarro's name. Like the hound, then, Pissarro is at once marginal and central.

Walcott expands on this theme of the centrality of the "island boy" Pissarro to European art history by arguing for the influence of a Caribbean aesthetic on the Impressionist movement. As Walcott sees it, Pissarro's artistic vision is crucially shaped by his island upbringing; Caribbean memories and a Caribbean sense of light and color continually intrude into his European life. "The island blazed at the back of his mind" (48), Walcott writes, attributing the originality of Pissarro's vision to his Caribbean sensibility:

> He paints in dialect, like an islander,
> in a fresh France; when his swayed poplars tilt
>
> you can catch an accent in their leaves, or under
> his formal clouds a hill's melodic lilt.
>
> (53)

Walcott depicts Pissarro as encouraging his friend and pupil Cézanne to adopt a more tropical palette,

> to change his dingy palette to colours
> brightened by his tutor's tropical eyes,
>
> a different language for a different light,
> more crystalline, more broken like the sea
>
> on island afternoons, scorchingly bright
> and built in prisms. He should learn to see.
>
> (56)

Thus, Walcott makes a case for the indebtedness of the Impressionists to Pissarro's Caribbean way of seeing, and most profoundly to a Caribbean sense of reality as fragmented, prismatic, and multiple. In so doing, however, Walcott does not dispense with the transcendent vision of the Old Masters, which still holds considerable appeal for him, but instead maintains a productive tension between these two perspectives—one that is analogous to a pastoral juxtaposition of the rural idyll with what Leo Marx describes as "a more complicated order of experience" (25).

In reclaiming Pissarro for the Caribbean, Walcott calls into question our understanding of Impressionism as a French artistic movement and problematizes the very distinction between metropolitan and colonial cultures in much the same way that Naipaul exposes the economic dependency of the English pastoral estate on colonial wealth. Walcott's revisionist history of Impressionism is less a matter of rewriting art history than of presenting Europe and the Americas as thoroughly imbricated. This interdependency is highlighted in *Tiepolo's Hound* through the verbal play on "Paris"/"Pissarro" and the interweaving of the colonial and metropolitan landscapes. Walcott's references to European painters are often so densely woven into his poetry that they cannot be disentangled from his Caribbean vision, and as he has done throughout his career, he insists on the value of apprenticeship to European tradition rather than on the need to shed European influences. Accordingly, in *Tiepolo's Hound* he argues that paint transcends the limitations imposed by empire and history, for "page and canvas know one empire only: light" (58). Pissarro "was Art's subject as much as any empire's" (29), Walcott writes; "the paint is all that counts, no guilt, no pardon, / / no history" (58).

This acceptance of "foreign" influences generates a special kind of reciprocity between European and Caribbean landscapes in *Tiepolo's Hound,* so that, for instance, the St. Lucian town of Canaries is "framed in the cubes of Aix-en-Provence" (19); while for Pissarro, the "white cries" of gulls and nurses in Paris "recalled those Sundays of Charlotte Amalie's / and the bays of his childhood paradise" in St. Thomas (47). Contributing further to this sense of reciprocity is the interaction between the Caribbean settings of Walcott's paintings and the predominantly European orientation of his verse, which appear on facing pages of the book. So, too, in *Enigma* the English landscape continually evokes Trinidad, just as Trinidad had once been the screen onto which the English landscape had been projected. Naipaul's narrator is reminded of his childhood landscape by the English one, even when the resemblance is apparently lacking, as with a snow drift that recalls for him a Trinidad beach (44).[21] Thus, the curious side to the mobile museum is that rather than ensuring the dominance of the metropolitan landscape over the colonial one, it creates an unstable reciprocity between them. This interpenetration of the two landscapes and the interdependency between metropole and colony that it underscores is characteristic of Naipaul's and Walcott's postcolonial pastorals. It serves to unsettle the fixity of place, challenging the myth of a homologous relationship between an individual and his native landscape.

Pastoral and a Postcolonial Sense of Place

In an illuminating discussion of a postcolonial sense of place, George Handley identifies three ways of conceiving the relationship between nature and history. The first possibility is to seek out nature as an escape from history and human responsibility. The second is to regard the natural environment from a purely economic and utilitarian point of view. As Handley notes, the problem with both of these approaches is that they pull nature "up and out of its historical roots, either by means of converting it into a commodity of nostalgia or one of vindication" (2). However, there is also a third option: to understand nature and human history as interlocking. It is this perspective that informs Naipaul's and Walcott's landscape aesthetics. Both authors bring nature and culture into a closer relationship, challenging colonial pastoral's reading of New World nature as outside of history. In addition, they call into question the myth of a "natural" relationship between an individual and a landscape, opening up the possibility of a more flexible and inclusive model of belonging.

Significantly, Naipaul's and Walcott's critiques of the colonial pastoral do not result in a displacement of the rural in favor of the urban as perhaps one might have expected. In *Enigma* and *Tiepolo's Hound*, both of which contain a preponderance of rural and agricultural imagery, the pastoral setting remains the primary one. Instead of a departure from the rural landscape and its pastoral associations, what we find in Naipaul and Walcott is a reconfiguration of the rural that makes possible their articulation of a postcolonial sense of place.

At the outset of this chapter, I asked why, when the pastoral is such an ideologically compromised mode, should Naipaul and Walcott turn to it? This may seem a peculiar question given that Walcott himself has disclaimed the pastoral. His unsympathetic review of *Enigma* rather disapprovingly identifies English literature as the most "botanical" of national literatures and takes particular aim at Naipaul's pastoralism. Such statements would appear to distance Walcott from the pastoral, and although the term appears with some frequency in his poetry and repeatedly in *Tiepolo's Hound*, he tends to use it in a negative sense.[22] Yet Walcott's poetry is frequently punctuated by standard pastoral references to meadows, reapers, scythes, and sickles, and Wordsworthian spots of time feature prominently in *Another Life*.[23] His epic poem *Omeros* (1990), whose landscape incorporates groves of laurel trees as well as banana pastures, applies conventional pastoral description to a tropical landscape.[24]

Tiepolo's Hound, too, suggests the importance of pastoral in Walcott's poetics, not least in its inclusion of his watercolors of pastoral scenes such as "Pasture, Dry Season" (1998)—an indication that the selection of his paintings is not as random as some reviewers have suggested.[25] In *Tiepolo's Hound*, Walcott's preference for natural landscapes, the profound influence of his father's copies of European landscapes, and Pissarro's ruralism combine to produce a poem replete with pastoral imagery, as in the following lines in which the narrator describes one of his father's paintings:[26]

The precise furrows of a landscape from which a lark arrows
while, under her parted hood, a blind girl listens,

some sunlit shire behind her, all with a rainbow's
benediction, the light that brims and glistens

like tears in Millais's work were like my mother's
belief in triumph over affliction. A peasant sows

his seeds with a scything motion, the lark's good news
is beyond his hearing, striding these humped furrows

a clod trampling clods in sabots, his wooden shoes
riding the troughs of ploughed soil, these boots

my father drew from Millet.

$$(12-13)$$

While it could be argued that Walcott is here paying homage to his father
rather than to the pastoral landscape his father copied, I do not think
it accidental that he gives so much prominence to his father's pastoral
mimicry, a subject that he had treated numerous times before. Nor, more
importantly, is it by chance that the central subject of Walcott's poem is
Pissarro, the great painter of French rural life, for Pissarro's pastoralism
is intimately connected to a poetics of stillness and modesty that has great
appeal for Walcott.

Walcott's pastoral is not the idealized, luminous pastoral of Claude,
however, but the more gritty pastoral represented by Pissarro, who does
not shy away from the "raw vehemence of real weather, / snow-spattered
mud, grey gardens in grey mist" (69). In *Tiepolo's Hound*, pastoral supports a contemplative aesthetic of the everyday that Walcott privileges
over a romantic celebration of the sublime or the transcendent. In contrast to Van Gogh's sunflowers or Gauguin's glowing mangoes, Pissarro
painted "such anonymous pleasures as the glitter / of aspens in wind,
shadows on a rough road" (77). Pissarro's "paintings have the meditative
progress / of a secular pilgrim," exhibiting an "uxorious" relationship
with the landscape: "Narrative excess / had made theatrical melodrama
of great art, // but no Pissarro landscape has some rain-whipped wretch /
huddling under an oak" (64–65). Walcott's interest in Pissarro not only is
a function of his Caribbean provenance, then, but is tied to the quiet, simple pleasures of Pissarro's pastoral vision, a vision that corresponds to his
own "Methodist" preference for the plain, his "awe of the ordinary" (8).

Through Pissarro, Walcott reaffirms his long-standing commitment to a
poetry of the everyday and his devotion to the craft of writing:

> Because these virtues grow with the acceleration
> of time and the long shadows, because we hoard
>
> what others mocked as safety, in moderation
> of self, of fame, the art of being bored
>
> diminishes conceit, and cherishes the plain
> and the repetitive: light in a kitchen,
>
> cats coiled on chairs, and sunlight shot with rain,
> things without grandeur in their modest shine.
>
> (65)

As this passage about the aesthetic of simple things continues, Walcott
subtly blends his own landscape poetics with Pissarro's, inserting a comparison with Caribbean vendors on "old island wharves" and using the
plural possessive pronoun to emphasize the shared quality of their pastoral vision. And, indeed, the term "pastoral" has shifted to a more positive
register by the end of the poem, where the narrator, while teaching in St.
Thomas, imagines Pissarro drawing "those customary pastorals of the
Antilles" (140). Significantly, this shift in the usage of the term "pastoral"
coincides with its transposition to a Caribbean setting. Pastoral, then,
holds considerable appeal for Walcott as well as for Naipaul.

Naipaul's and Walcott's attraction to pastoral cannot merely be attributed to the contemplative mood and stripped-down aesthetic that characterize both *Enigma* and *Tiepolo's Hound,* however. Nor is the choice
of a pastoral setting simply a reflection of their common desire to address
the influence of European landscape representation on their early artistic
formation, although both are important motivations. Rather, pastoral
is ultimately attractive to Naipaul and Walcott because it supports their
search for a sense of place. For instead of simply providing a record of
rootlessness, the classic theme of Caribbean literature, both *Enigma* and
Tiepolo's Hound attempt to construct a new sense of place and to bring
about an end to exile.

If the exiled writer aims to heighten the impression of rootlessness and
insist on its irreparability, the urban setting may be apt. However, if he
or she wishes to articulate a sense of place, the city may not be as ideal
a setting. Accordingly, Walcott suggests that it is in rural Pontoise rather
than the urban center of Paris that Pissarro is able to find a new sense of

rootedness, to stake his plot (46). When Pissarro leaves Paris, the city of his exile, for the nearby village of Pontoise, the river Oise on which he now resides quickly becomes "the giver / of roots and swaying shade on the stone of his house" (52). This same desire for rootedness is exhibited by the narrators of *Tiepolo's Hound* and *Enigma*. Walcott's poem ends with the narrator's unequivocal declaration of the end of exile: "This is my peace, my salt, exulting acre: / there is no more Exodus, this is my Zion" (162). Similarly, in *Enigma*, Naipaul—the placeless writer par excellence—declares with some surprise that he has finally found a home. In Wiltshire, Naipaul's narrator feels that he is in tune with his landscape for the first time: it is "that setting which had given me joy of place like no other place in the world" (218).

What makes these declarations possible are the new terms upon which this sense of place is based. In *Enigma*, Naipaul's narrator's insight into the inevitability of change and the historicity of nature has important implications for his understanding of rootedness. The narrator's evolving understanding of Jack in particular is crucial to his redefinition of root-edness as constructed rather than "natural." At first, the narrator views his neighbor Jack as continuous with the landscape: "Jack himself, how-ever, I considered to be part of the view. I saw his life as genuine, rooted, fitting: man fitting the landscape. I saw him as a remnant of the past (the undoing of which my own presence portended)" (15). The narrator's initial impression of Jack as "a man in his own setting . . . , a man in tune with the seasons and his landscape" (31) bespeaks his more general tendency to understand people and architecture as "emanating" from the landscape. But ultimately he comes to see Jack as consciously choosing his lifestyle rather than as inheriting it, as having a precarious rather than a "natural" connection to the land: "Jack himself had disregarded the tenuousness of his hold on the land, just as, not seeing what others saw, he had created a garden on the edge of a swamp and a ruined farmyard; had responded to and found glory in the seasons. All around him was ruin; and all around, in a deeper way, was change, and a reminder of the brevity of the cycles of growth and creation. But he had sensed that life and man were the true mysteries; and he had asserted the primacy of these with something like religion" (93). "Tenuousness" is the key term here, indicating a relationship to place that is fragile and constantly in need of rearticulation, in keeping with the motif of the second arrival. The narrator's central insight is that Jack creates his world rather than survive as a remnant of a world that has all but been lost, just as he learns that landscapes themselves are constructed rather than "natural."

Through the narrator's evolving vision of Jack, we can trace the emergence of a new understanding of place, one that regards the idea of a natural fit between man and landscape as illusory. "So much that had looked traditional, natural, emanations of the landscape, things that country people did . . . now turned out not to have been traditional or instinctive at all, but to have been part of Jack's way" (47), the narrator notes. The narrator's neighbors the Phillipses, while initially appearing "to belong, to be part of their setting" (220), are in fact rootless people, recent arrivals at the manor with a talent for appearing settled. Both Jack and the Phillipses create a sense of home in spite of their lack of security. Indeed, Naipaul's Wiltshire turns out to be entirely populated by the displaced and the "unanchored, floating" (240), so that the narrator is merely another addition to their numbers rather than an exception. The gap between the narrator and his neighbors narrows until no one has the privilege of a "natural" relationship to place. When Walcott and others charge that Naipaul chooses the rural setting in order to artificially heighten the appearance of his exceptionalism, they overlook this important shift from the narrator's view of himself as singular to a recognition of his resemblance to others. Naipaul's choice of a rural setting in *Enigma* opens up the possibility of a deeper questioning of traditional assumptions about place and rootedness, although this inquiry—tinged as it is with nostalgia—is neither as fully developed nor as sustained as it might be.

Walcott, too, resists the myth of fixed roots through his image of the "moving trees" that appears at the conclusion of *Tiepolo's Hound*. This striking image, which is accentuated by the unusual persistence of the b-rhymes across four consecutive couplets, expresses a need for rootedness and at the same time emphasizes that place is never stable:

The soul is indivisible as air.
Supposedly, all things become a dream,

but we, as moving trees, must root somewhere,
and there our separation shows its seam,

in our attachment to the nurturing place
of earth, a buried string, a chattering stream

or still lagoon that holds our fading face,
that wrinkles from the egret's rising scream.

(160)

Like Naipaul's narrator's reassessment of Jack, Walcott's "moving trees" image signals a departure from territorially bounded conceptions of identity. The relatively static genealogical symbol of the tree has become mobile and nomadic. This questioning of myths of origin does not lessen the importance of a sense of place in these works, however; even as "moving trees," Walcott's narrator reminds us, we "must root somewhere."

While the "moving trees" image is a provocative one that is given particular prominence through its end-placement, Walcott also flirts with a more essentialist model of identity in the poem, as his reference to the buried umbilical cord in the passage cited above suggests. Similarly, his use of the language of blood and soil in a passage in which he rejects the English landscape—"Nothing blood-recollected in the soil / of water-colour country" (151)—appears to suggest that the narrator *does* bear a more essential, biological connection to the soil of his Caribbean birthplace. Walcott has Pissarro employ biological imagery to characterize his connection to St. Thomas: "'My history veins backwards / to the black soil of my birthplace'" (142). Thus, even as it disrupts genealogical motifs, Walcott's pastoral bears the traces of an essentialism that has traditionally underwritten botanical metaphors for identity.

Walcott's recourse to biological metaphors for belonging returns us to the question of the politics of the pastoral. Walcott's and especially Naipaul's pastoralism raise questions about the viability of the postcolonial pastoral, and in particular about how successfully contemporary writers are able to negotiate the ideologically conservative legacy of colonial pastoral. This legacy includes the dehistoricization of nature, the excision of labor from the New World landscape, the negation of indigenous claims to the land and the substitution of settler claims, and the location of indigenous peoples outside of history. This is a legacy that contemporary writers and artists will come up against repeatedly in the chapters that follow.

"Frescoes of the New World": Walcott's Celebration of the Caribbean Landscape

Tiepolo's Hound helps us to shift our focus from representations of European landscapes to New World settings, for the feature that most differentiates Walcott's postcolonial pastoral from Naipaul's is its insistence on the need to celebrate the local, Caribbean landscape. Ultimately, Walcott's complaint against Naipaul is not so much his pastoralism as it is his choice of landscape. Walcott ends his review of *Enigma* by relocating the reader to a Caribbean setting: "In a small hillside hotel whose back veranda looks out on a serenity of pasture, saddle ridge, grazing cattle, and a view of the Caribbean between its bushy hills, I found an appropriate blessing" (31). In marked contrast to Naipaul's narrator, Walcott's narrator in *Tiepolo's Hound* rejects the English landscape (if not English artistic influences):

> Real counties opened from that small blue book
> I cherished: *The English Topographical Draughtsmen,*
>
> . . . .
>
> but I claimed nothing. Not from this landscape,
> the ragged hedges opening Warwickshire,
>
> not in my father's name, those fields of rape,
> not even that blue patch where the sun was higher
>
> over the sodden fields. Nothing ancestral
> that I could see.
>
> (149–50)

Thus, while the encounter between the Caribbean artist and the European landscape is central to Walcott's poem, the final outcome of this encounter is not, as in *Enigma,* a more historicized understanding of the European landscape, but a turning away from Europe.

The title of chapter 10 of Walcott's *Another Life,* "Frescoes of the New World," captures both the persistent influence of European art on Walcott's aesthetics and his simultaneous devotion to the Caribbean landscape. In contrast to Naipaul's project of finding a home in Wiltshire, in *Tiepolo's Hound* Walcott lays claim to a Caribbean sense of place by insisting on the need to make the New World landscape primary. "Paint a true street in Anse La Raye, Choiseul" (156), "paint the thick flowers too poor to have a name" (157), Walcott's narrator insists toward the end of the poem. For Walcott, the importance of Pissarro and of his fellow artist Gauguin, "our creole painter of *anses, mornes,* and *savannes*" (16), is in large part that they painted the Caribbean landscape. The majority of Walcott's landscape paintings that are reproduced in *Tiepolo's Hound* appear to have a Caribbean setting, and the narrator laments Pissarro's decision to abandon the Caribbean landscape: "You could have been our pioneer," he maintains, but instead "St. Thomas stays unpainted" (142–43). While Pissarro chooses permanent exile, however, Walcott's narrator brings exile to an end: "I shall finish in a place whose only power / is the exploding spray along its coast" (162).

2 The Myth of the West in Bernard Malamud and Philip Roth

> I remember someone in a Cambridge common room pestering the self-designated "non-Jewish Jew" and Marxist historian Isaac Deutscher, himself a [Lithuanian], about his roots. "Trees have roots," he shot back, scornfully, "Jews have legs." And I thought, as yet another metaphor collapsed into ironic literalism, Well *some* Jews have both and branches and stems too.
>
> —Simon Schama, *Landscape and Memory*

IN ANZIA YEZIERSKA'S autobiographical novel *Bread Givers* (1925), the Jewish heroine's departure from the Lower East Side for the country is described as a second migration, a passage into a New World of "free space and sunshine":

> Before this, New York was all of America to me. But now I came to a town of quiet streets, shaded with green trees. No crowds, no tenements. No hurrying noise to beat the race of the hours. Only a leisured quietness whispered in the air: Peace. Be still. Eternal time is all before you.
>
> Each house had its own green grass in front, its own free space all around, and it faced the street with the calm security of being owned for generations, and not rented out by the month from a landlord. In the early twilight, it was like a picture out of fairyland to see people sitting on their porches, lazily swinging in their hammocks, or watering their own growing flowers.
>
> So these are the real Americans, I thought. (210)

This scene is organized around an opposition between the city of New York and a pastoral world that lies outside the city: urban and rural spaces that represent two distinct Americas. Before the heroine's departure, New York had been "all of America" to her. However, upon attending college in the picturesque town, she discovers an alternate world where "the real Americans" live. Unlike in New York, in the *real* America people own their own land and radiate a "calm security": "If only I could lose myself body and soul in the serenity of this new world," Yezierska's heroine thinks, "the hunger and the turmoil of my ghetto years would drop away from me, and I, too, would know the beauty of stillness and peace" (211).

Yezierska depicts the immigrant Jew's arrival in the countryside as an entrance into the real America—a second arrival. As the passage from *Bread Givers* suggests, urban centers such as New York and Chicago were often considered to be continuous with the Old World in the early-twentieth-century Jewish American imagination. Instead of a single journey from Old World to New, a second migration may be required to reach the New World. For some Jewish Americans, including the literary critic Alfred Kazin, this second journey led from the outskirts of the city back into its center. In *A Walker in the City* (1951), Kazin recalls that as a child his greatest ambition was to enter the real America, Manhattan: "We were of the city, but somehow not in it. . . . *They* were New York, the Gentiles, America; we were Brownsville" (11–12). Yet the second journey could also lead away from the city, as is the case in a number of Jewish American works ranging from the early-twentieth-century ghetto pastorals of Yezierska's era to the highly ironized postwar pastorals of Saul Bellow, Bernard Malamud, and Philip Roth.

The brief pastoral interlude that Yezierska includes in *Bread Givers* anticipates the more sustained rural idylls that would follow in postwar Jewish American writing as Jewish American protagonists became more affluent and mobile. Jewish American writing contains numerous representations of second arrivals that bring Jewish protagonists into a pastoral America, a second journey that is often couched in settlement metaphors. What remains consistent throughout the diverse Jewish American works surveyed in this chapter is their deep attraction to a rural America and to the mythic American West. These exurban spaces are appealing to the Jewish American imagination because they represent the essential America, the New World that the Jewish immigrant or descendant of immigrants has not yet discovered.

Jewish American writing is typically perceived to be fundamentally urban in both its setting and its perspective. This strong identification of Jewishness with urban life accounts for the lack of attention that pastoral strains in Jewish American literature have received. While in postwar Jewish fiction, the suburbs have become established literary territory, critics continue to consider the countryside, and nature in particular, to be outside the purview of the Jewish American literary imagination.[1] This line of argument is contravened by the two novels considered in this chapter: Bernard Malamud's *A New Life* (1961) and Philip Roth's

American Pastoral (1997). As Malamud's and Roth's novels attest, like other contemporary writers of the Americas, Jewish American writers are the inheritors of a European vision of the New World as Eden. (One has only to think of Roth's *Goodbye, Columbus* (1959), whose central image is the suburban refrigerator overflowing with forbidden fruit, to recognize Jewish American writing's engagement with this vision.) In the United States, however, the New World pastoral myth takes on a distinctive configuration, placing special emphasis on the value of shedding the past and of undergoing a spiritual rebirth of the kind that Thoreau famously describes in *Walden*. Moreover, in the American pastoral myth, the West is privileged as the space of renewal and fresh beginnings. It is in the West, where nature dominates over civilization, that American society would regenerate itself and develop its future form. The belief that the American West could enable an exhilarating escape from the strictures of social convention and familial responsibility significantly informs the Jewish American novels considered in this chapter.

Malamud's and Roth's novels demonstrate not only that pastoral myths influence Jewish American writing but also that Jewish American writers' absorption of these myths ultimately puts pressure on the myths themselves. Spatially oriented American pastoral myths and Jewish historical memory are at odds in *A New Life* and *American Pastoral,* a conflict that can be understood in terms of a pastoral tension between the ideal and the real. The uneasy blend of American myth and Jewish experiences of exclusion that *A New Life* and *American Pastoral* contain produces a double-edged and highly ironized pastoral. At the same time, a second, less self-conscious kind of tension in these novels arises from Malamud's and Roth's casting of their Jewish protagonists as modern-day pioneers, a choice whose implications I will discuss below with reference to Malamud's posthumously published novel *The People* (1989).

Such evidence of a Jewish American pastoral notwithstanding, critics have insisted that Jewish American writing is unreceptive to nature, and they have offered historical, cultural, and theological explanations for why this should be the case.[2] Irving Howe's 1979 essay "Strangers" contains one of the major statements in Jewish American letters on the incompatibility of Jewishness and nature. In his essay, Howe recalls that while Jewish immigrant children of the 1920s and 1930s found themselves increasingly distanced from the Old World stories, they were at the same time bewildered by the American writers to whom they were introduced in school. "What could Emerson mean to a boy or girl on Rivington Street in 1929, hungry for books, reading voraciously, hearing Yiddish at home, yet learning to read, write, and think in English?" he asks. "What could the tradition of American romanticism, surely our main tradition, mean to them?" (12). Howe describes the awkward fit between Old World narratives of martyrdom and endurance and the American myths of heroic individualism to which Jewish immigrant children were now being exposed. Jews were uncomfortable with the American literature they were encountering, which "spoke in tones that seemed strange and discordant." Most inaccessible and difficult to reconcile with their Old World heritage, however, writes Howe, was the American celebration of nature:

> Hardest of all to take at face value was the Emersonian celebration of nature. Nature was something about which poets wrote and therefore it merited esteem, but we could not really suppose it was as estimable as reality—the reality which we knew to be social. Americans were said to love Nature, though there wasn't much evidence of this that our eyes could take in. Our own tradition, long rutted in *shtetl* mud and urban smoke, made little allowance for nature as presence or refreshment. . . . Nothing in our upbringing could prepare us to take seriously the view that God made his home in the woods. By now we rather doubted that He was to be found anywhere, but we felt pretty certain that wherever He might keep himself, it was not in a tree, or even leaves of grass. (16)

In this influential passage, Howe defines Jewish American identity against an American romanticism that finds its inspiration in nature. Howe associates Jewishness with a social reality, which he contrasts with the American idea of nature as divine and as divorced from the social world.

Howe's analysis has been largely accepted, as critics have continued to maintain that Jewish American culture is inimical to both nature and nature writing. For example, Andrew Furman concludes that Jewish American responses to the American naturist tradition are almost wholly negative. In "No Trees Please, We're Jewish," Furman bemoans the fact that he is unable to reconcile his work as a scholar of Jewish American writing with his environmentalism: "As my passion and concern for the environment increases, I find that reading and teaching Jewish-American literature has become more and more problematic. For Jewish-American fiction writers in this century have, by and large, created a literature that either ignores, misrepresents, or, at its most extreme, vilifies the natural world" (115). Furman goes on to survey writers from Isaac Babel to Cynthia Ozick and identifies throughout a "Judaic hostility toward the natural realm" (120). According to Furman, even in more recent Jewish

American writing such as Allegra Goodman's *Kaaterskill Falls* (1998), "Nature remains a dangerous realm that ever threatens to lure Jews from Judaism" (130).

Relatedly, in his discussion of environmental literature and cultural difference in *The Environmental Imagination,* Lawrence Buell remarks that it has now become impossible to ignore the exclusionary aspects of the American nature-writing tradition, in particular its white male bias. Buell observes that this bias has not precluded women writers or minority writers from remaking this tradition to express their own concerns. Yet he suggests that because of their urban background and lack of a memory of a rural past, Jewish American intellectuals have resisted American nature writing as incompatible with Jewish experience. According to Buell, in contrast to African American and especially Native American writers for whom the pastoral presents itself as an "opportunity," for Jewish writers it constitutes "a roadblock" (18–19).[3]

Buell's assertion that Jews lack a memory of a rural past on which to draw is questionable.[4] Although restrictions on the ownership of property and other social and economic factors ensured that Jews have tended to be disproportionately urban in the modern era, Jews also have had a high degree of contact with rural life, particularly in the nineteenth-century Eastern Europe from which many Jewish immigrants to America came. The Anglo-Jewish historian Simon Schama recounts in *Landscape and Memory* that while tracing his family's roots in what are now Poland and Lithuania, he arrived at the following realization:

> I had always thought of the Jews of the Alte Land as essentially urban types, even when they lived in villages: tradesmen and artisans; tailors and carpenters and butchers and bakers; with the rebbe as the lord of the shtetl; microcosms of the great swarming communities of Wilno and Bialystok and Minsk. And so it often was, but the villages we walked through, these picture-perfect rustic cottages with their slanting timber eaves and crook-fenced gardens, had once been Jewish houses. . . . So even if they had not worked the earth with their hands or cut hay in the fields, these Jews had been country people, no less than the villagers of the Cotswolds or the peasants of the Auvergne. (27)

If, as Schama reminds us, many Eastern European Jews "had been country people," there is also considerable evidence that memories of rural experience accompanied Jews when they left Europe.[5] Together with the influence of dominant American pastoral myths, this retention of European rural memory contributes to the appeal of pastoral for Jewish American writers. It is striking that major Jewish North American writers, including Saul Bellow and Mordecai Richler as well as Bernard Malamud and Philip Roth, have given repeated and sustained consideration to pastoral themes and spaces. We might think, for instance, in postwar Jewish writing of Richler's Duddy Kravitz feverishly acquiring land in the French Canadian countryside, or of Bellow's "Squire Herzog" retreating into the Berkshires. Returning to an earlier period of Jewish American literature, we find examples of what has been termed "ghetto pastoral" in the novels of Michael Gold, Daniel Fuchs, and Henry Roth, among others.[6] In these novels, gritty, oppressive scenes of tenement life are punctuated by pastoral interludes in which the protagonists escape to the more pleasant vistas of Central Park or Bronx Park.

Thus, if there is a rejection of the natural world in Jewish American writing, there is also a countervailing attraction to American pastoral. This attraction to pastoral works on two levels: on the one hand it bespeaks a desire to gain access to the "true" America, which is envisioned as pastoral in keeping with leading national myths, and on the other it signals the Jewish American author's ambition to claim a space in the U.S. literary canon, which has tended to privilege nature writing. Most salient in Malamud and Roth, however, is not the attraction to pastoral that they exhibit, but the profoundly disruptive impact of their appropriations of the American pastoral myth on the myth itself.

Ghetto Pastoral

Before examining the function of pastoral in postwar Jewish American writing, it is worthwhile pausing to consider the early-twentieth-century ghetto pastorals that anticipate the later move out of the city of the post-immigrant generation, as well as two transitional works by Richler and Bellow that may be usefully situated in between ghetto pastoral and the more fully formed postwar pastorals of Malamud and Roth. Although this chapter is primarily devoted to Jewish American writing, I will also make reference to Jewish Canadian writers who, while negotiating different national myths, exhibit a related attraction to the rural.

Faced with the difficulties and disappointments of the immigrant experience, the protagonists of Henry Roth and Michael Gold among others long to escape to pastoral settings that they associate with life in the Old Country.[7] In Henry Roth's *Call It Sleep* (1934), the Old World (rural) past is represented by a photograph of a cornfield that hangs in the family's Brownsville apartment. When the mother purchases the photograph, her puzzled young son asks her for an explanation:

David examined it more closely. It was a picture of a small patch of ground full of tall green stalks, at the foot of which, tiny blue flowers grew.

"Yes, I like it," he said uncertainly.

"I bought in on a pushcart," she informed him with one of her curious, unaccountable sighs. "It reminded me of Austria and my home. Do you know what that is you're looking at?"

"Flowers?" he guessed, shaking his head at the same time.

"That's corn. That's how it grows. It grows out of the earth, you know, the sweet corn in the summer—it isn't made by pushcart pedlars." (172)

This dialogue establishes both the mother's attachment to the rural life that she has left behind in Europe and her son's distance from the rural; his ignorance is such that he cannot distinguish between a bull and a cow. The photograph provides one of the few reminders of the rural world with which both the father and the mother are associated in the novel. Thus, in *Call It Sleep,* the Old World is represented by symbols of a rural life that is no longer accessible to the Jewish immigrant protagonists, who find themselves trapped within the narrow confines of the urban ghetto.

Similarly, in A. M. Klein's 1948 poem "Pastoral of the City Streets," no direct experience of the rural is available. Instead, the poem superimposes a remembered rural landscape onto the streets of urban Jewish Montreal:

I

Between distorted forests, clapped into geometry,
in meadows of macadam,
heat-fluff-a-host-of-dandelions dances on the air.
Everywhere glares the sun's glare,
the asphalt shows hooves.

. . . .

II

And at twilight,
the sun like a strayed neighbourhood creature
having been chased
back to its cover
the children count a last game, or talk, or rest,
beneath the bole of the tree of the single fruit of glass
now ripening,
a last game, talk, or rest,
until mothers like evening birds call from the stoops.

(lines 1–5, 32–40)

Klein's metaphorical transformation of distinctly urban elements into features of a natural landscape—asphalt into "meadows of macadam," a streetlamp into "the tree of the single fruit of glass"—suggests a lingering memory of rural life. This rural memory lives on in the new urban environment, just as, long after the horse has gone, the image of his hoofprint remains in the asphalt that has been softened by the heat of the sun. In Klein's poem, then, the rural persists but only as a ghostly presence. By contrast, in Michael Gold's *Jews without Money* (1930), a brief escape into nature is made possible by the family's trip to Bronx Park. While in the park, the mother reconnects with her Hungarian past and with the knowledge of nature for which she has had little use since her arrival in New York: "Each new mushroom reminded her of Hungary and of things she had never told us. She talked in a low, caressing voice. She stooped to the mushrooms, and her eyes shone like a child's" (154).

Although isolated and brief, pastoral tokens of another life such as the picture of the cornfield in *Call It Sleep*—as well as pastoral episodes such as the trip to Bronx Park in *Jews without Money*, the neighborhood idyll in Klein's poem, and the college scenes in Yezierska's *Bread Givers*—occupy a privileged place in Jewish North American narratives of the first half of the twentieth century. As we move into the postwar era, novelists such as Richler and Bellow continue to introduce ghetto pastoral motifs but begin to put them to a somewhat different use, concretizing and expanding the pastoral dream of escape. While the pastoral idylls of Henry Roth and Michael Gold are characterized by their ephemerality, in Richler and Bellow a more sustained Jewish American pastoral emerges as postwar North American Jews gain greater access to spaces outside of the urban metropolis and to the promise of American belonging that they represent.

Richler's 1959 novel *The Apprenticeship of Duddy Kravitz* initially appears to conform to the conventions of ghetto pastoral, presenting the reader with one of the genre's typical scenes. Simcha Kravitz, a Jewish immigrant from Lodz, spends his spare time gardening in his urban Montreal yard: "Outside in the gritty hostile soil of his back yard, Simcha planted corn and radishes, peas, carrots, and cucumbers. Each year the corn came up scrawnier and the cucumbers yellowed before they ripened, but Simcha persisted with his planting" (45). Yet Richler moves the ghetto pastoral in a new direction when Simcha's grandson Duddy heeds his grandfather's counsel that "a man without land is nobody" and embarks on a series of schemes in order to acquire land in the Quebec countryside. Instead of presenting pastoral as a temporary escape, in *Duddy Kravitz* there is a suggestion of a more permanent move away from the city. But when Duddy finally achieves his goal and asks his grandfather to choose a plot of land for his farm, Simcha rejects the offer. Stunned by his grandfather's response, Duddy is informed that he has misunderstood his grandfather's wishes: "'Sitting in their dark cramped ghetto corners they wrote the most mawkish, school-girlish stuff about green fields and sky. Terrible poetry, but touching when you consider the circumstances under which it was written. Your grandfather doesn't want any land. He wouldn't know what to do with it'" (310). From a conventional standpoint, this rejection of the rural in *Duddy Kravitz* simply confirms the incompatibility of Jews and nature. In my reading, however, this passage suggests not a rejection of the rural so much as an anxiety about the legitimacy of a Jewish presence in the countryside, one that will feature prominently in Malamud's and Roth's pastorals as well.

Like *The Apprenticeship of Duddy Kravitz*, Bellow's *Herzog* (1961) juxtaposes ghetto scenes with a more fully realized pastoral landscape, this time moving between Herzog's childhood memories of Jewish Montreal and his adult retreat to his home in the Berkshires. Bellow's Herzog is a more mobile Jewish protagonist who moves easily between Europe and America, Chicago and rural Massachusetts, in contrast to the limited geographies of the protagonists of Henry Roth or Michael Gold. When Herzog purchases a house in Ludeyville, Massachusetts, he converts his inheritance from his father into a less portable form and styles himself "Squire Herzog. The Graf Pototsky of the Berkshires" (76). One of Herzog's defining attributes is his attraction to rural spaces: "With Madeleine, Herzog had made his second attempt to live in the country. For a big-city Jew he was peculiarly devoted to country life. He had forced Daisy to endure a freezing winter in eastern Connecticut while he was writing *Romanticism and Christianity*, in a cottage where the pipes had to be thawed with candles" (118–19). As with Duddy Kravitz, Herzog's attraction to the countryside is inspired by the immigrant generation's love of gardening. Herzog recalls his Russian-born father's "devotion to his garden, . . . how he squirted his flowers at evening with the hose and how rapt he looked, his lips quietly pleased and his straight nose relishing the odor of the soil" (242).

Notably, *Herzog* establishes a strong link between pastoralization and Americanization. Herzog describes his Berkshires house as a defiant "symbol of his Jewish struggle for a solid footing in White Anglo-Saxon Protestant America" (309). In *Herzog*, we begin to see the extent to which Jewish American pastoral not only recalls a rural European past but also looks toward an American future and greater access to American belonging. As in *Duddy Kravitz*, however, the Jew's presence in the countryside remains controversial. Herzog's attempts at pastoral assimilation are seen as misguided at best, and are attended by considerable anxiety: "'Out in the sticks? Don't be nuts. With that chick? Are you kidding? Come back to the home town. You're a West Side Jew,'" he is told (90). Nonetheless there is a strong embrace of the rural in *Herzog*, which opens and closes in the Berkshires. At the end of the novel, Herzog refuses to sell the Ludeyville house, pointing to the possibility of a more sustained Jewish American pastoral. This possibility is pursued in the pastoral novels of Bernard Malamud and Philip Roth.

"A New World, Levin": Malamud Goes West

The publication of *A New Life* marked a departure from the urban, East Coast orientation of Malamud's earlier and better-known novel *The Assistant* (1957). When *A New Life* first appeared in 1961, John Hollander wrote sympathetically in the *Partisan Review* regarding Malamud's turn to the West: "*A New Life* may . . . represent Mr. Malamud's attempt to break out of a limited, almost regional area of performance in which . . . he has been most successful. . . .[The novel's] new version of an old American pastoral encounter redeems it from the provinces of any smaller genre" (14). Perhaps more typical, however, was the accusation leveled in a *Commentary* review that Malamud was "out of his proper element" (Solotaroff 245). Critics have tended to chide Malamud for straying from a more authentically Jewish setting, and in a 1979 interview, he noted that this attitude persisted despite his long period of residence in Oregon and Vermont.[8]

The lukewarm critical reception that *A New Life* received reflects a perspective that assumes the basic incompatibility of Jews and nature. From this standpoint, Jewish American fiction must resist the pull of nature in order to maintain its Jewish character, as Cynthia Ozick does in her story "The Pagan Rabbi" (1966), in which a rabbi's obsession with nature leads to his death.[9] Yet *A New Life*'s pastoralism is more complex than this formulation would suggest. In the novel, the pastoralism of Malamud's protagonist, Seymour Levin, expresses a longing for a deeper sense of rootedness in America than he has so far achieved. On a metafictional level, Malamud's pastoralism is indicative of his desire to participate in a dominant American literary tradition.

A New Life portrays a second arrival in America, one that mimics Levin's immigrant parents' original journey from Europe to the New World.

If the Lower East Side of New York was the first point of disembarkation for many Eastern European Jews, the children of the immigrant generation, as we saw with Yezierska, often felt themselves to be still outside the mainstream of American life and believed that a second journey was required to reach the true America. S. Levin's journey west in *A New Life* is just such a journey, one that could be described as a second emigration, a repetition of his parents' crossing. This journey takes him away from the city and into the countryside, more specifically to the Pacific Northwest. Having arrived in the West, Levin feels acutely aware of his foreignness as an "Easterner," and yet he is also elated by his new surroundings because he subscribes to American pastoral myths about the possibility of starting one's life anew in the West and erasing the failures of the past. In following the trails of the pioneers, Levin hopes to gain entrance into a fresh New World. In accordance with this vision, Levin pictures himself as a heroic settler occupying a new frontier.

In *A New Life,* the Jewish immigrant reading of the departure from New York as the true departure from Europe reinvigorates the traditional American idea that the move from the East Coast to the West represents a move from Old World to New. In his seminal 1950 study *Virgin Land,* Henry Nash Smith writes that "the Atlantic seaboard after all represented the past, the shadow of Europe, cities, sophistication, a derivative and conventional life and literature. Beyond, occupying the overwhelming geographical mass of the continent, lay the West, a realm where nature loomed larger than civilization and where feudalism had never been established. There, evidently, would grow up the truly American society of the future" (45). Malamud's Levin has fully absorbed this vision of the West as the realm of a regenerative nature. He believes that moving to the wilds of the western frontier will permit him to exchange his old life for a more vital one. At the same time, in moving west he will be participating in a quintessential American experience and will achieve a more fully American identity.[10] Levin is captivated by the American myth of the possibility of self-reinvention in the West, as were many American Jews—even the urbanite Alfred Kazin could write that "*Omaha* was the most beautiful word I had ever heard, *homestead* almost as beautiful" (60).

Levin, who carries with him a sense of imperilment and "exclusion from normal life," leaves New York City in 1950 to take a teaching job at Cascadia College in the town of Easchester in an unnamed western state.[11] When Levin first arrives at Cascadia, he announces to the director of the composition program, who has come to meet his train, that he is "from the East" (7). This phrase, which is repeated several times over the course of the novel, signals the double resonance of Levin's arrival at Cascadia. The phrase references not only Levin's New York provenance but also his Jewishness. The latter connotation becomes explicit when Malamud introduces an actual Middle Easterner into the novel in the form of a Syrian boarder who shares Levin's house. Levin's Syrian doppelgänger, who has a "delicate Semitic nose," curly black hair, and "popped" black eyes, functions to amplify and racialize Levin's foreignness as well as to highlight Levin's tenuous status as an American. When the Syrian is caught urinating in the street outside a bar, the police question Levin regarding his own citizenship as well as his decision to wear a beard. The primary visual signifier of Levin's otherness is his dark beard, which provokes frequent comment and which Levin finally decides to remove. Levin is called upon repeatedly to defend his beard: "Americans have often worn them," he insists, citing the example of Abraham Lincoln (25). The problem of Levin's controversial status as an American is further highlighted by the frequent references to the House Un-American Activities Committee and McCarthyism that make up the larger historical and political background of the novel.

While Levin is "dark and nervously animated," his students at Cascadia, who "represented the America he had so often heard of, the fabulous friendly West," are "blond, tending to impassive" (80). And while Levin comes from "a vast metropolis of many-countried immigrants" (80), his students have grown up in homogeneous towns. Levin feels himself to be "of the same race as the Cascadians, true, but a distant relative" (198). Levin's Jewishness is mapped onto the traditional spatial divide between country and city, his urban background standing in for his Jewishness (which is only rarely referred to in the novel). Levin's lack of rural experience and his sense of exclusion from his rural western surroundings signal his ethnic difference, his now doubly diasporic status as both a New Yorker and a Jew: "He had never seen so many horses, sheep, pigs across fences. The heavy Herefords (he had looked them up) turned white faces to the road as he went by. He had never seen one in the open before, or a black Angus; they had never seen a Levin" (56).

If Levin's new surroundings render him acutely aware of his foreignness, he is equally enraptured by them. Levin's move away from the city and his embrace of the West is above all an embrace of nature: "Never before had he lived where inside was so close to out. In a tenement, each descent to the street was an expedition through dank caves and dreary tunnels. He enjoyed the cherry tree reaching its knotty, mildewed branches to his back window. At the side he had a view of the wooded hills. . . . He could see the mountains" (54). *A New Life* is punctuated by flashbacks to Levin's earlier life in a New York tenement, and ghetto pastoral motifs figure prominently in these flashbacks. Levin's move west makes possible the extension of these ghetto pastoral moments and the desire for nature that they express into a full-blown pastoral.

The protagonist of Malamud's later novel *Dubin's Lives* (1979), in which natural imagery also predominates, is a biographer of Thoreau, and Thoreau is a strong presence in *A New Life* as well. Levin compares himself to Thoreau twice—going so far as to suggest at one point that Easchester is his Concord—and some of the novel's most lyrical passages depict Levin entering into a Thoreauvian communion with nature. Levin carries with him a copy of *Western Birds, Trees and Flowers,* and sets out to educate himself about the natural world to which he had had only limited access in the city. Performing some outdoor chores for his landlady, Levin comes to learn the difference between a sickle and a scythe, and harvests her pear trees, but he is rather tentative in these gestures: "On a shaky ladder that left him with nervous knees he gathered yellow pears, shying away from the bees sucking the sweet wounds of fruit" (52). Malamud's depiction of his protagonist's education in nature in *A New Life* resonates with Naipaul's treatment of this theme in *The Enigma of Arrival,* which similarly embraces Thoreauvian values only to find them ultimately constraining.

Levin's pastoral fantasy culminates in an Edenic sexual encounter in the forest with the wife of one of his colleagues. Immediately preceding this thrilling episode, however, he is overcome by a sense of the illegitimacy of his presence in nature: "Here the common man rejoiced in what was naturally visible. But being where he was not supposed to be continued to trouble Levin; he turned as if forewarned someone was in the wood behind him; expecting, if not a boot in the pants, at least the forester's hard hand and gruff get the hell off private property. He would run like mad" (172). At its height, Levin's communion with nature is tempered by an anxiety about his claim to a space in a pastoral America. This anxiety links Levin's pursuit of nature and the West to his troubled pursuit of American belonging, which is also advanced through his affairs with Gentile women, his purchase of a car, and his struggles with the department in which he teaches over what constitutes "American" values. Levin's powerful attraction to nature reflects his desire for a more secure foothold in the United States and at the same time registers his profound sense of exclusion from American life.

Levin's marginality among the athletic and outdoorsy people of Easchester is exacerbated by his frustrated desire to teach American literature, including the nature-centered American literary tradition that figures so prominently in *A New Life*. Levin has diligently studied Cooper, Hawthorne, Emerson, and Thoreau, and refers to their writings throughout the novel. Yet as a composition instructor at the college, Levin is barred from teaching literature, and he has to resort to listening through the bathroom walls to his colleague lecturing on Twain and Poe. Most revealingly, Levin's credentials as a prospective teacher of American literature are challenged by his colleagues on the grounds that he lacks adequate experience of nature: "We have some of the best fishing streams in the world in Cascadia. Ernest Hemingway has fished here. How will you ever teach Thoreau, once you have your Ph.D., without ever in your life having been to a wild place?" (249). In moving west, Levin at once attempts to claim a new geographical territory for himself and a new literary territory, but he is thwarted on both counts. "You are still an outsider looking in," he is told (248).

While Levin's access to American literature as both a Jew and an urbanite is severely curtailed, in writing *A New Life*, Malamud himself successfully stakes out a larger and more ambitious territory for Jewish American writing. If the United States is "Nature's Nation,"[12] a country whose national literature has been disproportionately preoccupied with natural themes, Malamud's choice to leave the city behind represents an attempt to appropriate a more fully American space for the Jewish American novel. Moreover, this act of appropriation ultimately transforms the myth of the West itself. Leslie Fiedler observes that in *A New Life* "the West itself was reborn as . . . a Jewish West, the American West as a facet of Jewish-American culture" (149). As Fiedler's remark implies, in *A New Life* Malamud does not merely insert a Jewish presence into an established American literary genre while leaving that genre essentially intact. Rather, Malamud's appropriation of American pastoral challenges the myth of the West itself.

Some critics have argued that Levin's education in the natural world is a failure, and, indeed, the novel ends with Levin's expulsion from Eden (although not from the West).[13] It is not so much that Levin's appreciation for nature fails, however, but that his attempt to escape his past through a retreat into nature proves unsuccessful. When he initially arrives in the West, Levin views Easchester as a town without history: "During the day, Levin enjoyed the town though it seemed entirely contemporary, without visible or tangible connexion with the past. Nature was the town's true

history, the streets and park barren of fountain spray or sculpture to com-
memorate word or deed of any meaningful past event" (68–69). Yet the
more Levin tries to escape the past, the more he finds that present time is
"past-drenched": "Was the past, he asked himself, taking over in a new
land? Had the new self failed?" (111). It is not Levin's interest in nature
that must be abandoned, but the myths about American nature that he
has absorbed, in particular his belief in the possibility of spiritual rebirth
through a retreat into the natural world. Thus, Levin's Jewish presence in
Easchester begins to disturb the idea of the West itself.

It is primarily through his study of nature that Levin comes to question
the American pastoral myth. Levin's keen observation of nature reveals
not only renewal but also continuity with the past. His pleasure in nature
"was tempered by a touch of habitual sadness at the relentless rhythm of
nature; . . . change that wasn't change, in cycles eternal sameness, a repetition he was part of, so how win freedom in and from self? Was this why
his life, despite his determined effort to break away from what he had
already lived, remained so much the same?" (170). While digging up a
weedy flower garden for his landlady, he finds "last season's walnuts and
acorns, six varieties of worms, a soggy doll, and thickly-rusted screwdriver from yesteryear. The past hides but is present" (52–53). Levin's
archeological dig in his landlady's garden suggests that the division between the natural and social worlds is not as neat as the American pastoral myth would propose. Instead, *A New Life* asserts the impossibility of
the kind of rebirth traditionally envisioned by American nature writers
by pursuing a historicized, entangled reading of American nature.

Levin eventually sheds his vision of himself as a new Thoreau and
the dream of self-regeneration that this vision entails. While in *Walden*
Thoreau advocates a renunciation of the past through an engagement
with nature, Levin concludes in a key passage that the countryside is not
a refuge from the troubles of the past but simply provides more space for
their expression: "He had lived in dark small rooms in anonymous tene-
ments on grey streets amid stone buildings crowding the sky; loneliness
tracked him in the guise of strangers. In the country it dwelt in the near
distance under vast umbrella skies. In the city, compressed; spacious in
the country. Space plus whatever you feel equals more whatever you feel,
marvellous for happiness, God save you otherwise" (220). In *Walden*,
Thoreau writes that in retreating to his cabin on Walden Pond, "Both
place and time were changed, and I dwelt nearer to those parts of the
universe and to those eras in history which had most attracted me. Where
I lived was as far off as many a region viewed nightly by astronomers"

(132).[14] For Levin, by contrast, the retreat into nature provides no escape from history and the old life. Instead of embracing a life unfettered by convention, human society, and familial duty, Levin at the end of the novel takes on the responsibility of caring for his mistress and her two children, a gesture that announces his rejection of the individualistic ethos of American naturism.

Malamud unsettles the American pastoral by exposing this spatially oriented myth to the historical and familial orientation of Levin's Jewish diasporic consciousness.[15] Malamud's Levin, who is no "American Adam," cannot sustain a Thoreauvian outlook and instead significantly revises it. Easchester's reductive brand of pastoralism is one that does not admit emotional or intellectual depth, and while initially appealing, it soon collapses as Levin refuses the American pastoral myth's simplification of human experience. In Malamud's novel, the meeting of American myth and Jewish historical memory generates a complex and sharply critical pastoralism.

Roth's *American Pastoral:* "The Pastoral Is Not Your Genre"

If Malamud's quiet, meditative fiction is characterized by a deep sensitivity to nature, Philip Roth is a more restless and histrionic writer who rarely gives much attention to landscape. In contrast to Malamud's highly evocative landscape description, Roth tends to include details about his novels' natural settings solely for comic effect. Characters such as Faunia Farley, the illiterate milkmaid in Roth's *The Human Stain* (2000), provide little more than a caricature of rural life. Moreover, Roth tends to associate ruralism with the loss of Jewish identity. Thus his novel *The Plot against America* (2004) chillingly imagines World War II–era urban Jewish boys being exported to the rural heartland by the "Office of American Absorption" to be de-ethnicized.

This equation of ruralization with assimilation lies behind the denunciation of pastoral that concludes *The Counterlife* (1986). In *The Counterlife,* Roth's alter ego, the writer Nathan Zuckerman, visits his wife Maria Freshfield's native rural village of Chadleigh in Gloucestershire, England. Maria's pastoral world of beech woods, yew trees, streams, and ruined mills holds a certain charm for Zuckerman. Ultimately, however, both Zuckerman and Maria come to the conclusion that he and the pastoral are ill suited. "The last thing you want," Maria tells him, "is to make readers happy, with everything cozy and strifeless, and desire simply fulfilled. The pastoral is not your genre, and Zuckerman Domesticus now seems to you just that, too easy a solution, an idyll of the kind you hate, a fantasy of innocence in the perfect house in the perfect landscape on the banks of the perfect stretch of river" (317). Zuckerman confirms Maria's assessment, declaring: "The pastoral stops here and it stops with circumcision" (323).

Yet despite Zuckerman's unequivocal disavowal of pastoral in *The Counterlife*, Roth's next Zuckerman novel, *American Pastoral*, which like *A New Life* follows a Jewish protagonist out of the city and into the countryside, is in many ways a reprise of the pastoral themes that Malamud had explored more than thirty-five years earlier. *American Pastoral* is the fifth novel in Roth's series about the writer Nathan Zuckerman. In the first Zuckerman novel, *The Ghost Writer* (1979), the young Zuckerman had traveled from Newark to the Berkshires to sit at the feet of his literary idol, E. I. Lonoff. Lonoff, who bears a striking resemblance to Malamud,[16] lives in the "*goyish* wilderness of birds and trees where America began and long ago had ended" (4). This rural meeting proves prophetic, for by the time we reach *American Pastoral*, Zuckerman has followed Lonoff's example and has moved out of the city. In *American Pastoral* we learn that Zuckerman now lives in the hills of western Massachusetts: "Up in the woods. About ten miles from a college town called Athena. I met a famous writer there when I was just starting out. Nobody mentions him much anymore, his sense of virtue is too narrow for readers now, but he was revered back then. Lived like a hermit" (63).

Further connections between *A New Life* and *American Pastoral* are suggested by the striking similarity of the names of their respective protagonists, Seymour Levin and Seymour Levov. If the names they bear are similar, however, the two protagonists are thoroughly opposed: while Malamud's Seymour Levin is dark, bearded, and intensely cerebral, Roth's Seymour "The Swede" Levov is blond, blue-eyed, and a star athlete. In *American Pastoral*, Zuckerman moves offstage for much of the novel to shift the focus to his Newark high school classmate, the Swede, whom he idolized as a teenager and whose apparently idyllic life becomes the object of intense scrutiny of the adult Zuckerman. Unlike Malamud's Levin, the Swede is the poster boy for assimilation: as close to the Gentiles as a Jew can get. He was the boy, Zuckerman recalls, "we were all going to follow into America" (89). The Swede wears his Jewishness "lightly" and embodies an "unconscious oneness with America" that culminates in his move from Newark to the Waspy rural village of Old Rimrock, New Jersey (20). Zuckerman is awed by the Swede's apparent ability to resolve all the contradictions of assimilation, and yet he asks: "Where was the

Jew in him? You couldn't find it and yet you knew it was there. . . . What *was* the Swede's subjectivity?" (20). Like the pastoralism that Malamud's Levin encounters in the Pacific Northwest, the Swede's American pastoral seems to Zuckerman to be all surface and no depth. Unconvinced by the Swede's placid appearance, Zuckerman sets out to expose the dark underside of his pastoral existence.

While Roth's and Malamud's protagonists are in many ways dissimilar, they share a common desire to escape the city. Although the Swede insists on keeping the family business, a glove-making factory, in Newark long after the city has gone into decline, he soon moves his residence from Newark to the more rural environs of Old Rimrock. There he purchases a 170-year-old stone farmhouse on Arcady Hill Road, in which he lives with his wife, Dawn, and their daughter, Merry, surrounded by the cattle Dawn raises. Like each of the Jewish American protagonists discussed in this chapter, the Swede encounters strong resistance to his decision to move to a rural area, particularly from his father, whose refrain is "I come from the city": "'What are you going to do with all the ground,' his father asked him, 'feed the starving Armenians? You know what? You're dreaming. I wonder if you even know where this is. Let's be candid with each other about this—this is a narrow, bigoted area. The Klan thrived out here in the twenties. . . . Why did they hate Roosevelt out here, Seymour? . . . Because they didn't like the Jews and the Italians and the Irish—that's why they moved out here to begin with. . . . And this is where the haters live, out here'" (309). For the Swede's father, the rural remains off-limits to American Jews. But like Levin, the Swede sees himself as a frontiersman, conquering new territory by pushing his way into rural America. If for his father's generation, Keer Avenue in Newark was where Jews "la[id] claim like audacious pioneers to the normalizing American amenities" (10), the Swede seeks a new frontier, "commuting every morning down to Central Avenue from his home some thirty-odd miles west of Newark, out past the suburbs—a short-range pioneer living on a hundred-acre farm on a back road in the sparsely habitated hills beyond Morristown, in wealthy, rural Old Rimrock, New Jersey, a long way from the tannery floor where Grandfather Levov had begun in America" (14).

The Swede's rural property represents a claim to a kind of American space that even his family's economic successes in America have not achieved. His dream of living in the countryside is first kindled when, as a sixteen-year-old boy on his way to a baseball game, he encounters a rustic New Jersey house that "*said* 'House' to him": "The stone house was

not only engagingly ingenious-looking to his eyes . . . but it looked inde-
structible, an impregnable house that could never burn to the ground and
that had probably been standing there since the country began" (190). As
an adult, he pursues this dream of stability and permanence by purchasing the Old Rimrock house, but even more than the house, it is the land
itself that impresses him:

> The Swede couldn't get over those trees in the first years out in Old Rim-
> rock. *I own those trees*. It was more astonishing to him that he owned trees
> than that he owned factories, more astonishing that he owned trees than that
> a child of the Chancellor Avenue playing field and the unbucolic Weequahic
> streets should own this stately old stone house in the hills where Washington
> had twice made his winter camp during the Revolutionary War. It was *puz-
> zling* to own trees—they were not owned the way a business is owned or even
> a house is owned. If anything, they were held in trust. In trust. Yes, for all of
> posterity, beginning with Merry and *her* kids. (325)

The Newark factory and the glove-making business prove to be mobile
assets, but the Swede's Old Rimrock property offers a sense of permanence
and security in America that he craves, a legacy to pass down through
the generations. Like Anzia Yezierska's quiet, shaded streets with homes
that have been "owned for generations," the Swede's trees represent an
experience of belonging previously unavailable to American Jews.

While Malamud's Levin emulates Thoreau, the Swede's hero turns out
to be Johnny Appleseed, a choice that bespeaks the Swede's desire for a
deeper sense of place. In his rereading of the Johnny Appleseed legend
in *The Botany of Desire,* the environmental journalist Michael Pollan
suggests that the legend is more complex than the Disney version allows.
Johnny Appleseed (John Chapman) is for Pollan a figure of contradiction
who "lived everywhere and nowhere" and who had the "ability to freely
cross borders that other people believed to be fixed and unbreachable"
(*Botany* 33). Pollan's comments shed light on one of the few passages in
Roth's novel that gives any sustained attention to landscape: "And then
[the Swede would] turn and stride all the way back, past the white pasture
fences he loved, the rolling hay fields he loved, the corn fields, the turnip
fields, the barns, the horses, the cows, the ponds, the streams, the springs,
the falls, the watercress, the scouring rushes, the meadows, the acres
and acres of woods he loved with all of a new country dweller's puppy
love for nature, until he reached the century-old maple trees he loved
and the substantial old stone house he loved—pretending, as he went
along, to throw the apple seed everywhere" (318). For the Swede, Johnny

Appleseed embodies two key American traits: freedom of movement and an appreciation for nature. At the same time, the Swede's infatuation with Johnny Appleseed reflects his desire to be rooted, to reenact the process of settling the land in which John Chapman's orchards played such a significant role.

Just as in Bellow and Malamud pastoral is linked to an assimilationist desire to inhabit the "real America," so too in Roth, the Swede's pastoralism marks the increasing Americanization of the post-immigrant generation. In Roth's dystopian novel *The Plot against America,* this theme is pushed to its darkest and most dramatic extreme, ruralization forming part of a fascist World War II–era conspiracy to deprive American Jews of their rights of citizenship. In *American Pastoral,* however, the presentation of the Levov family's deepening pastoralization and Americanization is more open-ended. Roth's novel traces the double trajectory of ruralization and Americanization from the immigration of the Swede's grandparents to the Newark ghetto of Prince Street, to his father's rise in the glove business and the family's life in their Keer Avenue Newark neighborhood, to the Swede's own successes and his corresponding move to the rural environs of Old Rimrock. Old Rimrock is the culmination of a process of ruralization that had begun two generations before, and yet because of the Swede's daughter, Merry, the smooth progress of the family's rise in American life and of their pastoralization comes to a grinding halt. While the Swede dreams of his daughter inheriting the Old Rimrock property and the trees that he has held in trust for her, Merry has no corresponding vision. She adamantly rejects her father's pastoralism: "You just can't keep hiding out here in the woods," she tells him. "All you can deal with is c-cows. C-cows and trees. Well, there's something besides c-c-c-cows and trees" (109). As a teenager, Merry is drawn instead toward the city and the radical student politics of the 1960s, leading her to bomb the local post office and subsequently disappear. By the end of the novel she is living in an urban slum in conditions "even worse than her greenhorn great-grandparents had, fresh from steerage, in their Prince Street tenement" (237); the Levov family has come full circle.

While in *A New Life* Levin's pastoral dream is undone by McCarthyism, the Swede's pastoral fantasy is derailed by the counterforce of the Vietnam War. Merry's hatred for America and her antiwar activism fly in the face of her father's deep sense of patriotism, and her transformation into the "Rimrock bomber" effectively brings an end to her father's pastoral dream. Zuckerman recounts that Merry "transports [her father] out of the longed-for American pastoral and into everything that is its antithesis and its enemy, into the fury, the violence, and the desperation of the counterpastoral—into the indigenous American berserk" (86). After the bombing, the Swede's wife, Dawn, also abandons the pastoral dream, deciding to sell the old stone house. In the course of designing a thoroughly modern new house, Dawn begins an affair with the architect Bill Orcutt, who is the representative in *American Pastoral* of WASP America. Orcutt's family dates back to the American Revolution, and he serves as the Swede's tour guide and local historian when the Levovs first arrive in Old Rimrock. Dawn is initially irritated by Orcutt's "proprietary manner," and suspects that he is contemptuous of their "embarrassing origins." The Swede himself shares some of Dawn's anxiety when he tours Old Rimrock with Orcutt: "He couldn't remember ever in his life feeling more like his father . . . than he did marching around the graves of those Orcutts. His family couldn't compete with Orcutt's when it came to ancestors—they would have run out of ancestors in about two minutes. As soon as you got back earlier than Newark, back to the old country, no one knew anything. Earlier than Newark, they didn't know their names or anything about them. . . . But Orcutt could spin out ancestors forever. Every rung into America for the Levovs there was another rung to attain; this guy was *there*" (306). Yet Dawn is finally seduced by Orcutt's pedigree, or at least the Swede interprets her affair in these terms, viewing it as "genealogical aggression—the overpowering by origins" (382–83). In the final scene of the novel, the collapse of the Swede's pastoral, symbolized by his smashing a portrait of their prize bull, coincides with his discovery of his wife's affair with Orcutt.

The Swede's brother accuses the Swede of mimicking a life that cannot be his: "Out there with Miss America, dumbing down and dulling out. Out there playing at being Wasps, a little Mick girl from the Elizabeth docks and a Jewboy from Weequahic High. The cows. Cow society. Colonial old America. And you thought all that façade was going to come without cost. Genteel and innocent" (280). Similarly, Zuckerman's narration suggests that the Swede's pastoral fantasy—his fantasy of assimilation—is responsible for the bombing committed by the Swede's daughter, "who was neither Catholic nor Jew." As we learn in *The Counterlife*, Zuckerman's objection to pastoral is that it represents an abdication of responsibility: a desire to recover an undivided, confusion-free state. This is an unacceptable desire for Zuckerman, because to be a Jew is to be *in history*. Thus in Roth, as in Malamud, the Jew's attraction to American pastoral runs up against the problem of history. In *American Pastoral*, the Swede mistakenly thinks that by moving to Old Rimrock he can escape the uncertainties that confronted his immigrant forefathers, but like Levin, he must learn that the natural realm does not provide a refuge from the instabilities of the social world. Merry's introduction of the bomb into the placidity of Old Rimrock is Roth's version of the machine in the garden—an irreversible jolting of nature into history. The complex version of pastoral that results suggests that for Jewish American writers, pastoral is a viable mode only if it can incorporate a social and historical awareness, if it can engage the real as well as the ideal.

Malamud's and Roth's novels profoundly complicate the American pastoral myth by exposing it to the Jewish historical experience of displacement and exclusion. In bringing American pastoral into contact with Jewish diasporic consciousness, Malamud and Roth generate a sharply double-edged pastoral. Initially, S. Levin and the Swede are attracted to a simple, escapist pastoral that excludes complexity and tension. This pastoral fantasy is heavily influenced by an American nature-writing tradition that locates a redemptive natural world outside of history. Ultimately, neither protagonist is able to sustain this simple brand of pastoralism because it is incapable of expressing the full range of his Jewish diasporic experience. If Malamud's and Roth's protagonists are constrained by their reductive conception of pastoral, however, their novels themselves do not succumb to the temptations of the simple pastoral but instead expose its limitations, thereby producing a complex, critical pastoralism. The paradox of both novels is that while the protagonists' turn toward the pastoral mode is an attempt to retreat from the world, in appropriating the pastoral Malamud and Roth have just the opposite effect: they move Jewish American writing onto a more expansive canvas, while at the same time interrogating the American pastoral myth and exposing its exclusionary power.

Revisiting the Myth of the West in Malamud's *The People*

The complex brand of pastoralism that *A New Life* and *American Pastoral* advance, while profoundly critical in the ways that I have suggested, is attended by a problematic identification with settlement narratives. Levin in particular understands his move west as echoing that of the pioneers: "My God, the West, Levin thought. He imagined the pioneers in covered wagons entering this valley for the first time, and found it a moving thought" (8). Levin comes to Easchester in search of his "manifest destiny" (97), envisioning himself as a new brand of pioneer whose move from East to West will reenact the settlers' journey. First had come explorers, traders, trappers, and settlers to the West, and now—Levin.

Similarly, in *American Pastoral,* the Swede is cast as a "short-range pioneer" (14): "Everybody else who was picking up and leaving Newark was headed for one of the cozy suburban streets in Maplewood or South Orange, while they, by comparison, were out on the frontier. . . . Well, he couldn't commute from Down South but he could skip Maplewood and South Orange, leapfrog the South Mountain Reservation, and just keep going, get as far out west in New Jersey as he could while still being able to make it every day to Central Avenue in an hour" (307). As this passage attests, pioneer motifs, while less prominent here than in *A New Life,* lend a western flavor to the Swede's pastoralism. The Swede envisions himself as a frontiersman, his idolization of Johnny Appleseed underscoring his attachment to settlement narratives.

In *A New Life,* pioneer motifs overlap with allusions to New World exploration, a convergence that brings to light the colonialist subtext of the American pastoral myth. In Jewish American writing, the second migration to the New World is often associated with exploration and settlement motifs, as in the following passage from Yezierska's *Bread Givers:* "That burning day when I got ready to leave New York and start out on my journey to college! I felt like Columbus starting out for the other end of the earth. I felt like the pilgrim fathers who had left their homeland and all their kind behind them and trailed out in search of the New World" (209). Yezierska's heroine's enthusiasm for discovery narratives is matched by that of Malamud's Levin, who compares himself in *A New Life* to the Spanish conquistadors: "He saw himself as stout as Cortez—Balboa, that is—gazing down at the water in wild surprise, both eyes moist" (135). At times in *A New Life,* the exploration narrative is played straight, as when Levin alludes to the hero of Fenimore Cooper's *Leatherstocking Tales:* "The mystery of the wood, the presence of unseen life in natural time, and the feeling that few men had been where he presently was (Levin, woodsman, explorer; he now understood the soul of Natty Bumppo, formerly paper . . .)" (171). More often, however, the mock-heroic narrative is presented for comic effect, serving to underline the distance between the Jewish American protagonist and his American heroes: "Heading towards unknown mountains in voyage to the Pacific Ocean, world's greatest. Imagine, Levin from Atlantic to Pacific" (127). Roth's deployment of the settlement narrative is similarly comic in tone, the New Jersey setting rendering the pioneer metaphors even more incongruous.

While Malamud's and Roth's heavy use of irony deflates exploration and settlement narratives, it does not fundamentally disrupt them. The distinction between ironization and critique can be clarified through a comparison of two responses to the poem that Robert Frost famously read at John F. Kennedy's inauguration. The familiar first lines of Frost's "The Gift Outright" read: "The land was ours before we were the land's. / She was our land more than a hundred years / Before we were her people" (lines 1–3). One reply to this poem can be found in Saul Bellow's *Herzog*. Toward the end of the novel, Herzog declares his continuing attachment to his home in the Berkshires in defiance of the exclusionary narrative of American belonging that Frost's poem contains: "And here (his heart trembled) the house rose out of weeds, vines, trees, and blossoms. Herzog's folly! Monument to his sincere and loving idiocy, to the unrecognized evils of his character, symbol of his Jewish struggle for a solid footing in White Anglo-Saxon Protestant America ('The land was ours before we were the land's,' as that sententious old man declared at the Inauguration.) I too have done my share of social climbing, he thought" (309). This passage ironizes Frost's poem in the context of Jewish American insecurities about their status in rural America, thereby exposing its exclusionary subtext. The sense of irony in the passage stems from the reader's recognition that Herzog can make no equivalent claim to a preordained connection to the land.[17] However, the negation of indigenous land claims on which Frost's formulation depends is left unquestioned by Bellow. Similarly, when Malamud ironizes the trope of virgin territory in *A New Life*, he does so in order to call attention to Levin's sense of belatedness rather than to challenge the idea of virgin territory as such or to expose American pastoral's complicity with an ideology of conquest: "Let's admit—wherever Levin had been, someone had been before (no Chingachgook he, even in the primeval forest . . .)" (281). Thus Malamud fails to ask a question that George Handley suggests is central to a postcolonial sense of place: which peoples' claims to the American landscape have been effaced in order to make possible a reading of New World nature as pristine and empty (6)?

We can compare these passages from Bellow and Malamud to Derek Walcott's reading of "The Gift Outright" in his essay on Frost. According to Walcott, Frost's "choice of poem was not visionary so much as defensive." "This was the calm reassurance of American destiny that provoked Tonto's response to the Lone Ranger," Walcott writes. "No slavery, no colonization of Native Americans, a process of dispossession and then possession, but nothing about the dispossession of others that this destiny demanded" ("The Road Taken" 93–94). In highlighting the disinheritance of indigenous peoples upon which Frost's Americans' gift of themselves "to the land vaguely realizing westward" (line 14) is predicated, Walcott's interpretation of the poem goes much further than Bellow's in challenging the restrictive narrative of American belonging articulated by Frost. Walcott's sharply critical reading of Frost's poem enables us to locate the American myth of the West as part of a longer tradition of expansionist colonial narratives in the New World.[18]

Thus, despite Malamud's and Roth's concern with the exclusionary aspects of American pastoral myths, indigenous claims on the land go unacknowledged in *A New Life* and *American Pastoral*. When indigenous themes are introduced in *A New Life,* no link to the settlement metaphors favored by the novel is made. Instead, when Levin is called upon to defend the use of a reader that contains the Hemingway story "Ten Indians," the story merely provides an occasion for a discussion of academic freedom and censorship. Malamud adopts a markedly different approach, however, in his posthumously published novel *The People,* which proves highly sensitive to the colonialist implications of the American myth of the West. Set in 1870, Malamud's unfinished novel was to have been another Jewish western, one that like *A New Life* would insert the figure of the *schlemiel* into a western, natural setting. This time, however, instead of citing Thoreau as the Jewish protagonist's hero, Malamud's Yozip Bloom identifies almost exclusively with the perspective of the Indian.

Yozip is a Russian Jewish greenhorn with heavily accented English who inadvertently becomes the representative of an Indian tribe, the People, that is in the process of negotiating its land rights with the Commissioner of Indian Affairs in Washington. When we first meet Yozip, he is "drifting westward, a decent direction" (3), peddling dry goods and doing other odd jobs along the way. As Yozip wanders the country attempting to find a sense of purpose, he appears profoundly disoriented: "He moved into Idaho, stopping off for a while at Moscow. Nothing in Moscow reminded him of Moscow" (4). At issue throughout Malamud's manuscript is Yozip's uncertain status in the New World, his confusion as to whether he is a native or a non-native: "An officious Jew he met in Wyoming told him he spoke with a Yiddish accent. Yozip was astonished because he now considered himself to be, in effect, a native. He had put in for citizenship the day after he had arrived in the New World, five years ago, and figured he was an American by now. He would know for sure after he had looked through the two or three official documents his cousin was keeping for him for when he got back from wherever he was going" (3). As Yozip soon discovers, the members of the tribe are also profoundly disoriented. Like Yozip, the People are noncitizens who are continually threatened with dispossession, and both Yozip and the tribe struggle with the English language that they are attempting to acquire. The People are in danger of losing the land that has been granted to them, and after witnessing Yozip inadvertently commit an act of heroism, they induct him into their tribe and ask him to act as their representative in their treaty negotiations.

In *The People*, Yozip's condition of dispossession and that of the tribe serve to mutually amplify one another. Gone are the ironic settlement metaphors that characterized Levin's experience of the West in *A New Life*. Instead, Yozip identifies strongly with the tribe and its resistance to the white settlers. Indeed, Pocatello, the Idaho town in which Yozip meets the tribe, is named for the leader of the Shoshone people who led the struggle against the settlers in the late nineteenth century. At the same time, however, Malamud's achievement in the manuscript is that he maintains a constant tension with regard to Yozip's status as a "new Indian." At first, Yozip's induction into the tribe appears to remedy his problem of belonging, as he comes to learn their language and adopt their style of dress and many of their customs. Yet his Indianness is constantly being called into question by the white society, by the tribe members, and by Yozip himself. This ambiguity is heightened when the tribe is forced to flee its land and attempts to escape to Canada (recalling the 1877 flight of Chief Sitting Bull north of the border). Yozip, who has been elected chief and renamed "Jozip," is called upon to lead the tribe into safety and to determine their tactical strategy. However, his ability to do so is limited by his distinct cultural background and his politics, for he is an avowed socialist, pacifist, and vegetarian: "What kind of warrior chief was a Jew who lived among a tribe of Indians with peace raging in his heart?" (75), he asks himself. As a result, Yozip makes poor decisions on the tribe's behalf that lead to its repudiation of him: "'You were a fool to think you are the equal of an Indian,' Indian Head said. 'This trek to Canada has destroyed many of the People'" (82).

Malamud also contrasts the tribe's intimate rapport with its land, "this land that lives in our heart," as Chief Joseph puts it (13), with the immigrant Yozip's perpetual state of disconnection from his environment: "If only a man knew where to go. It shamed him still to think that one place was as good as another. What does one attach himself to?" (16). Because Yozip's relationship to the land is so dissimilar to that of the People, he is extremely uncomfortable in his role as a spokesperson for the tribe in its land negotiations. When the chief of the tribe decides to send Yozip to

Washington as his envoy, Yozip protests: "'What do I know from strange cities?' . . . 'How can I tulk with my short tongue? Where will I find the words? When I open my mouth to tulk they will laugh at me'" (27). The chief is insistent, however:

> "We are sending you to Washington to speak with your eloquence on our behalf. We send you to speak for our tribe that has chosen you to be our brother. . . ."
>
> But Yozip was still worried. "What can a greenhorn do for you in such a city as Washington? Suppose they say I am not yet a citizen and so they keep from me my citizen papers?"
>
> "None of us have citizen papers," said Indian Head. (28)

If there is sympathy and overlap between the Indian and Jewish perspectives in *The People,* then, Malamud is careful not to conflate these perspectives. Instead, Yozip continually calls attention to the distance separating him from the rest of the tribe.

By returning in *The People* to an earlier historical moment when the fate of indigenous peoples was not yet sealed, and by focusing on the Indians' point of view, Malamud approaches the myth of the West from a strikingly different angle than he had in *A New Life.* In *The People,* we gain a much deeper understanding of the exclusionary power of the myth than we had in *A New Life,* in which an indigenous perspective was entirely absent. When a colonel tells Yozip that the tribe must yield to "the manifest destiny of a young and proud nation" (45), we struggle with Yozip to decipher the colonel's expansionist discourse:

> "We must therefore affirm our right to this land in the name of our nation, and our inalienable right to direct your next move within this country. If you disregard us we will exercise the right of eminent domain and do with our land what we have to do to fulfill our destiny."
>
> "So what is eminent domain?" Jozip whispered to Indian Head.
>
> "The strong man does what he wants. The weak man listens." (45)

At the same time as presenting this more critical reading of the myth of the West, *The People,* written a good twenty-five years after *A New Life,* also testifies to the enduring appeal of American pastoral for Malamud, whose earlier critique of the myth does not result in his wholesale rejection of pastoral. Interestingly, while Yozip displays a typically Malamudian love of nature and while he is acculturated into both white and Indian societies, he never loses his distinctly Jewish identity; in fact, *The People* is much more overtly preoccupied with Jewishness than is *A New Life.* In the projected final chapter of *The People,* Malamud had planned to portray Yozip dancing a Hasidic dance in the woods. Jewishness thus continued to coexist with and complicate American pastoralism in Malamud's writing through the end of his life.

In this regard, Jewish American writing anticipates the appeal that pastoral motifs such as the West and indigeneity would hold for other diasporic New World writers. For instance, Gish Jen's *Mona in the Promised Land* (1996), which explicitly cites Jewish American precedents, briefly introduces pioneer motifs in its portrayal of the arrival of a Chinese American family in a heavily Jewish New York suburb: "Two foothills of the forsythia they are moved to address immediately with hedge clippers (feeling quite hardy and pioneering, Westward ho! and all that)" (4). Western and pastoral themes also figure prominently in two Japanese Canadian novels: Joy Kogawa's *Obasan* (1981) and Hiromi Goto's *Chorus of Mushrooms* (1994). In seeking to engage pastoral landscapes and motifs, these writers, like their Jewish American counterparts, must confront and negotiate tensions between diasporic and indigenist narratives of the land.

3 Joy Kogawa's Native Envy

> If we could ignore the awesome psychological impact of evacuation, incarceration and loss of property, life for us in Slocan was tolerable. We were buffered by our remoteness from the racism of a society at war with Japan. There was no pressure on the camp dwellers to put in long hours of work to get ahead. In the summer, everyone tended their own small gardens of vegetables. For an avid fisherman like dad, the Slocan Valley was paradise.
>
> —David Suzuki, *Metamorphosis*

CANADIAN WRITING is rarely considered in the recently emerged field of hemispheric American studies, which instead tends to be oriented southward and to tacitly exclude Canada from "America."[1] This tendency is exacerbated by Canada's own ambivalence about its relationship to the Americas. Canadian scholars have largely absented themselves from critical conversations about a hemispheric American studies, in part out of a perception that such a practice will only reinforce U.S. cultural and political hegemony.[2] They are understandably hesitant to put at risk the hard-won recognition that the field of Canadian literature has gained, questioning—as in fact a number of their colleagues in the United States have as well—whether the hemispheric turn is itself an imperializing move. Canadianists' strong participation in hemispheric American studies, however, has the potential to offset the danger that this field will maintain the United States as its default center, and may also help to broaden its mandate beyond a mere refashioning or rehabilitation of U.S. American studies. Indeed, when we extend such conversations to include Canada, it becomes possible, for example, to identify the truly hemispheric reach of certain landscape ideas and ways of seeing *despite* distinct national histories and iconographies of place.

The following reading of Joy Kogawa's *Obasan* (1981) and its sequel, *Itsuka* (1992), demonstrates that Canada is heir to and shares with the United States and the Caribbean Islands a common colonial discourse about the relationship between New World nature and belonging. A dominant strain of Canadian literary criticism has, in part out of a desire

to establish a distinct Canadian cultural identity, argued for the uniqueness of the Canadian response to nature. Against this exceptionalist
view—but recognizing significant national and regional differences—this
chapter illustrates the relevance of Canadian articulations of place to
broader inter-American discussions.

Obasan's powerfully corrective historical vision and aesthetic strengths
have been extensively discussed in the secondary literature and do not
need to be reviewed again here.[3] Instead, this chapter focuses on tensions
and ambiguities surrounding Kogawa's model of diasporic belonging. In
contrast to the common practice of reading *Obasan* under the banner of
"Japanese American" or "Asian American" writing,[4] it locates the novel
in its national context and more specifically within a Canadian nature-
writing tradition. Accordingly, the first section of the chapter situates
Obasan in relation to Canadian critical and literary responses to nature.
The second section then looks in detail at Kogawa's reliance on established New World narratives about nature and the primitive, raising further questions about the viability of the pastoral mode for contemporary
writers of the Americas.

Obasan, a fictionalized account of the persecution of Japanese Canadians during and after World War II, has met with critical acclaim for its
contribution to the Japanese Canadian redress movement as well as to
contemporary Canadian literature and culture more broadly.[5] The novel
played a key role in debunking the deeply entrenched national myth of
Canada as a benign multicultural mosaic; indeed, in 1988, when the
Canadian government belatedly agreed to make reparations for the internment of Japanese Canadians, sections of *Obasan* were read out in
the House of Commons. Perhaps because of the novel's very political and
popular success, the model of diasporic belonging upon which Kogawa
relies both in *Obasan* and *Itsuka* has received little critical attention.
Relatedly, Kogawa's participation in patterns of landscape representation
that extend across the Americas has been obscured by the nationalist orientation of studies of Canadian nature-writing traditions.

The understanding of nature and its relationship to indigeneity that
informs both *Obasan* and *Itsuka* reflects the influence of long-standing
New World representational practices. Indeed, while constructions of the
figure of the Indian have been rigorously analyzed in the context of Euro-
American writing, *Obasan* illustrates that this discussion needs to be extended to include minority writing (as some scholars of African American literature have begun to recognize). As with Malamud's and Roth's
investment in settlement narratives, however, Kogawa's construction of

the figure of the Indian is worth attending to, not primarily in order to expose the limitations of her model of belonging, but rather in order to consider what these limitations suggest about the challenges that contemporary writers confront in their attempts to reimagine the relationship between land and identity in a New World context.

"This is my own, my native land" serves as a refrain for *Obasan,* which documents the erosion of Japanese Canadians' fundamental rights of citizenship and their sense of belonging during and after World War II. In the 1940s the Canadian government attempted to depatriate Japanese Canadians by insisting that their true loyalties—regardless of where they were born—lay with Japan, the "home" to which they were encouraged to "return" after the war. *Obasan* contests this exclusion by asserting the Canadianness of its characters. "*I am Canadian,*" writes Kogawa's protagonist's Aunt Emily in a manuscript, underlining and circling the words in red so hard that the paper tears (47).

Kogawa takes the phrase "This is my own, my native land" from the sixth canto of Sir Walter Scott's Scottish romance *The Lay of the Last Minstrel* (1805). Toward the beginning of *Obasan,* Aunt Emily quotes the following lines from Scott's poem, which she had been made to memorize as a child and which had first inspired in her a feeling of identification with Canada: "Breathes there the man, with soul so dead, / Who never to himself hath said, / This is my own, my native land!" (6.1.1–3; qtd. in *Obasan* 47).⁶ Scott seems a rather unlikely reference point for Kogawa, who argues in her novels for an inclusive, multiethnic vision of Canada that would allow for a plurality of attachments. By contrast, *The Lay of the Last Minstrel* posits a more restrictive model of belonging according to which there is a homologous bond between an individual and his native landscape:

> O Caledonia! stern and wild,
> Meet nurse for a poetic child!
>
> . . . .
>
> Land of my sires! what mortal hand
> Can e'er untie the filial band,
> That knits me to thy rugged strand!
> (6.2.1–7)

Scott's Minstrel balks at the suggestion that he should settle in "the more generous southern land" of England because of the depth of his attachment to his native Scotland. The Minstrel strongly condemns exile, proclaiming instead the value of the native and of ties of birth and blood. What remains unclear in Kogawa's citation of *The Lay of the Last Minstrel* is whether she is ironizing the Minstrel's model of belonging or endorsing it. The ambiguity that the citation of Scott generates is typical, I would argue, of *Obasan* and its sequel, *Itsuka,* which flirt repeatedly with primitivist conceptions of home and belonging.

Tensions surrounding Kogawa's understanding of belonging become most acute with regard to her treatment of First Nations material, which features prominently in both *Obasan* and *Itsuka.* Both novels share in contemporary English Canada's "almost obsessive literary concern with Native people" (Fee 15). The two novels' intense identification with the Canadian landscape is accompanied by a concomitant identification with First Nations Canadians, who, Kogawa suggests, have been subject since European contact to forms of displacement and dispossession that align them with Japanese Canadians. Kogawa's alliance of her characters with First Nations Canadians reflects what Terry Goldie describes as "the impossible necessity of becoming indigenous" in settler societies such as Canada (13). Kogawa's central claim to a fully realized Canadian identity for Japanese Canadians is both historically justified and important, but her articulation of this claim through her location of First Nations peoples in the natural landscape bears further scrutiny than it has hitherto received. Her consistent linking of indigeneity, land, and nature reveals the influence of a landscape idea that understands civilization and nature as separable on the one hand, and the Indian and nature as inseparable on the other. If in the Jewish American writing of Malamud and Roth, an attachment to settlement narratives reinscribes the exclusion of a Native American perspective, in Kogawa the presence of the figure of the "natural Indian" similarly signals the persistence of colonialist ways of seeing in contemporary diasporic writing of the Americas.

Canadian Landscape Aesthetics and the Frye Thesis

While it is widely acknowledged that *Obasan* provides a deeply moving account of Japanese Canadian dispossession during and after World War II, less often remarked upon is that the novel does so by drawing heavily on botanical and arboreal motifs, a register of imagery that also featured prominently in Kogawa's early poetry collections *A Choice of Dreams* (1974) and *Woman in the Woods* (1985).[7] At first glance, the predominantly pastoral mode of nature imagery that Kogawa employs in *Obasan* and *Itsuka* would seem to distance her novels from mainstream Canadian writing, which by many accounts presents nature as menacing and indifferent. However, Kogawa's pastoralism may be more in line with mainstream Canadian writing than dominant Canadian critical traditions would acknowledge. By the same token, Canadian representations of nature also may be more continuous with other New World representations than such a perspective would allow.

Obasan is narrated by Naomi Nakane, a third-generation Japanese Canadian. Naomi is among the 23,000 British Columbians of Japanese descent who were forcibly displaced from their homes in the aftermath of the Japanese attack on Pearl Harbor in 1941 and were prevented from returning to the West Coast until 1949 as a result of Prime Minister Mackenzie King's postwar policy of geographic dispersal and resettlement.[8] Naomi and her family are exiled from Vancouver first to the ghost town of Slocan and later to the Alberta prairies, where they endure harsh working conditions on a beet farm. In the absence of both their parents—their mother visits relatives in Japan in 1941 never to return to Canada and their father dies of tuberculosis—Naomi and her brother, Stephen, are raised by their uncle and aunt (the "Obasan" to whom the title of the novel refers). Naomi, a schoolteacher in her thirties in the present time of the novel, reflects back on the series of displacements that her family has undergone and in particular on the mystery of her mother's disappearance. In the course of this reflection, Naomi's narration gives sustained and detailed attention to the series of primarily ex-urban landscapes that she and her family inhabit.

A number of works by diasporic Canadian writers such as Hiromi Goto's *Chorus of Mushrooms* (1994), Anita Rau Badami's *Tamarind Mem* (1996), and Dionne Brand's *Land to Light On* (1997) feature a snowy, inhospitable, and overwhelmingly white landscape that isolates and envelopes the nonwhite protagonist. In these works, the cold Canadian landscape is negatively contrasted with the warm, fertile, Edenic landscape of home (Japan, India, Trinidad). In Brand's poem "Islands Vanish," for example, the snow-covered scenery heightens the sense of estrangement of three blacks driving through southern Ontario:

> In this country where islands vanish, bodies submerge,
> the heart of darkness is these white roads, snow
> at our throats, and at the windshield a thick white cop
> in a blue steel windbreaker peering into our car, suspiciously,
> even in the blow and freeze of a snowstorm, or perhaps
> not suspicion but as a man looking at aliens.
>
> (lines 1–6)

In this passage, the vast, white Canadian landscape engulfs and threatens to "drown" Brand's black protagonists. A black/white contrast structures the poem, setting up an opposition between the smaller-scale island land-scape of home (the Caribbean) and the alien sea of whiteness in which the diasporic subject now finds herself (Canada).

A comparable topographical contrast is developed in Goto's *Chorus of Mushrooms*, in which refuge from the bitterly cold Alberta prairie is provided by the family's enclosed mushroom farm, whose densely moist, warm air recalls the Japan of the grandmother's memories. When in the midst of a snowstorm the Japanese-born grandmother enters the mush-room farm for the first time, she is rejuvenated. At first the snow threatens to prevent her from finding the barn: "So much snow blowing, I really can't see, but I must be getting closer. I can smell the sour compost" (82). Once inside the building, however, she is "bathed in a blanket of soil and moisture" (83), and the renewal she experiences is expressed through an extended botanical analogy: "But for the first time in decades, moisture filtered into her body. Moisture rich with peat moss and fungal breath. . . . Her skin, so dry, slowly filled, cell by cell, like a starving plant, the mushroom moisture filling her hollow body" (84).

In advancing a bleak vision of the Canadian landscape, Brand, Goto, and other diasporic writers reverse the pattern of imagery that Kogawa had established in *Obasan*. *Obasan*'s Canadian landscape is highly varied, incorporating both pastoral and antipastoral elements, but it is frequently characterized by lush vegetation and fecundity, and at key moments in the novel it provides the setting for New World pastoral idylls. Moreover, unlike in Brand or Badami or to some extent Goto, the central movement of *Obasan* is toward an identification with the adoptive landscape rather than alienation from it. This identification with the Canadian landscape supports Kogawa's overarching argument that Japanese Canadians both belong in Canada and have been wrongfully stripped of that sense of belonging. *Obasan* thus explores the theme of displacement and racial persecution against the backdrop of a benign and harmonious natural landscape.

While pastoral imagery predominates in both traditional and modern Japanese literature,[9] from the perspective of mainstream Canadian litera-ture and criticism, Kogawa's pastoralism may seem peculiar and idiosyn-cratic. Although overwhelmingly preoccupied with natural themes, Cana-dian literature—with the possible exception of the Québécois *roman de terre*—is commonly considered to be among the most antipastoral of national literatures. The standard view of representations of nature in Canadian literature—articulated by Northrop Frye in *The Bush Garden* and elsewhere, and elaborated by Margaret Atwood in *Survival* and by

Gaile McGregor in *The Wacousta Syndrome*—is that, since the contact period, Canadian writers and painters have almost universally depicted nature as unresponsive and lawless and as inducing a sense of repulsion and alienation.[10] "I have long been impressed in Canadian poetry by a tone of deep terror in regard to nature," writes Frye in a well-known formulation. "It is not a terror of the dangers or discomforts or even the mysteries of nature, but a terror of the soul at something that these things manifest" ("Conclusion" 342; see also *Bush Garden* 225). Atwood cites this same passage from Frye to preface her discussion in *Survival* of the tendency among Canadian writers to view nature as hostile and indifferent (47). The fear of nature that Frye and his followers argue typifies Canadian literature is exemplified by Atwood's own short story "Death by Landscape" (1991), in which a widow's Group of Seven paintings of the Canadian wilderness evoke a haunting childhood memory of the disappearance of a young girl in the woods during a stay at a summer camp.

While the Frye thesis has exerted considerable influence over Canadian literary criticism, several critics have also questioned and revised it. W. H. New suggests in *Land Sliding: Imagining Space, Presence, and Power in Canadian Writing* that the Frye thesis is not universally applicable to Canadian writing, but rather refers more specifically to an Anglo-Protestant tradition exemplified by Susanna Moodie and Catherine Parr Traill (80). Heather Murray and Susan Glickman go further than New, arguing that not even Susanna Moodie's classic account of Canadian settler life, *Roughing It in the Bush* (1852), is accurately represented by the twin concepts of "garrison mentality" and "survival" that Frye and Atwood popularized. As Murray and Glickman convincingly demonstrate, Moodie expresses not only aversion but also attraction to her physical surroundings; nature is a source of solace and inspiration for her as well as hardship.[11]

The strongest critical challenge to Frye has come from Glickman, who in *The Picturesque and the Sublime: A Poetics of the Canadian Landscape* argues that Frye's influential thesis has distorted our understanding of Canadian literary responses to landscape. Glickman rereads Moodie and other figures of eighteenth- and nineteenth-century Canadian literature to find evidence of a sympathy with and enthusiasm for nature, and in particular to contest the widespread view that early Canadian writing that adopted pastoral and picturesque motifs was mere colonial mimicry—an attempt to apply a European vocabulary to new Canadian surroundings, which resulted in a failure to describe them.[12] In Glickman's account, the persistence of eighteenth-century European aesthetic conventions is not necessarily in conflict with the goal of giving literary expression to the local, colonized landscape.[13]

By the same token, however, such an emphasis on colonial Canadian literature's reliance on European aesthetics also points to its participation in a broader New World nature-writing tradition that derived from a common European inheritance. Looked at from the perspective not of national difference but of a transnational colonial inheritance, Canadian representations of nature are significantly linked to those found in other literatures of the Americas. This revised account of Canadian representations of nature provides an important context for my reading of Kogawa, which seeks to trace the influence of a colonialist discourse about New World nature on her novels. *Obasan* is above all concerned with finding a sense of belonging, with claiming a space for Japanese Canadians in the Canadian nation. In pursuit of this goal, Kogawa articulates an enthusiastic and identificatory vision of Canadian nature that finds precedents in both colonial and contemporary Canadian writing.[14] *Obasan*'s deployment of pastoralism in combination with other landscape ideas does not invalidate its claim to Canadianness but rather confirms its ties to both Canadian and New World literary traditions. At the same time, *Obasan*'s and *Itsuka*'s reliance on these traditions renders them subject to important critiques that have been made of these strategies in the context of Euro-American writing.

The Landscapes of *Obasan*

Obasan's preoccupation with the problem of belonging is expressed through its consistent emphasis on landscape as well as through the botanical imagery that the novel favors. Throughout *Obasan*, both Kogawa's Japanese Canadian and Anglo-Canadian characters are compared to trees and plants. When Naomi's uncle is in the hospital, the tubes in his wrists are likened to "grafting on a tree" (16). Later, Rough Lock, a friendly neighbor, is described through an extended arboreal analogy: "He is a thin man, skinny as a tree, his face grooved like tree bark. His arm is a knobbly branch darker than mine. His hair is scraggly and covers his head like the seaweed on Vancouver beaches draped on the rocks" (170). Another neighbor, Old Man Gower, is portrayed in more ominous terms but still in a botanical register: "He is the forest full of eyes and arms. He is the tree root that trips Snow White" (76). Most significantly, Naomi herself is subject to arboreal and botanical analogies: she is an "offshoot" of the tree trunk that is her mother's leg (77). Her hair straining at the roots as the tangles are combed out is likened first to garden weeds being "plucked from the skin of the earth" and then to trees lying "uprooted by the roadside" (179).[15] As this last sequence of images suggests, the dominant inference of Kogawa's botanical imagery is that Japanese Canadians, like the plants to which they are compared, are seeking out soil willing to house and nourish them.

The most eloquent botanical image that Kogawa employs is that of her Japanese Canadian characters' fingers as roots burrowing into the earth. In the opening scene of *Obasan,* Naomi visits an Alberta coulee with her uncle, whose "rootlike fingers pok[e] the grass flat in front of him" (2). Sitting next to her uncle, Naomi's "hands rest beside his on the knotted mat of roots covering the dry earth, the hard untilled soil" (4). In these opening pages, the unanchored roots and resistant soil introduce the central theme of the novel: the deracination of Japanese Canadians and the unyielding character of the Canadian nation. As though in defiance of the hostility of the Canadian soil, Naomi too digs her fingers into the earth and embeds herself in the land: "My fingers tunnel through a tangle of roots till the grass stands up from my knuckles, making it seem that my fingers are the roots. I am part of this small forest. Like the grass, I search the earth and the sky with a thin but persistent thirst" (4). Already in this early scene, Naomi attempts to indigenize herself by "planting" her Japanese Canadian body in the Canadian soil.

Botanical motifs recur throughout *Obasan* as Naomi struggles to come to terms with the multiple displacements—not only geographical but also familial and psychological—that punctuate the novel. The full resonance of the series of isolated botanical images connecting Kogawa's Japanese Canadian characters to the Canadian soil only becomes available, however, in the context of Kogawa's presentation of the larger landscapes of Naomi's disrupted childhood, adolescence, and adulthood. Consistently, Kogawa provides detailed descriptions of the natural and physical characteristics of the sites to which Naomi and her family are displaced.[16] *Obasan* presents us with four distinct Canadian landscapes that each play an important role in relation to the novel's twofold project of exposing the oppression of Japanese Canadians and claiming a Japanese Canadian identity: the Edenic landscape of Naomi's childhood home in Vancouver, the lush forest of Slocan (a ghost town in the interior of British Columbia to which the family is displaced during World War II), the desertlike antipastoral landscape of the beet farm in Granton, Alberta (to which they are removed three years later), and the restorative coulee near Granton that Naomi visits annually with her uncle. An examination of each of these sites in turn reveals the extent to which Kogawa's novel is governed by a conventional opposition in New World discourse between the Edenic garden and the savage wilderness.

The Edenic Garden (Vancouver)

Encouraged by her aunt Emily to reconstruct her traumatic childhood, Naomi thinks back on her early years before the internment of Japanese Canadians. As one might expect of this kind of retrospective narrative, Naomi's descriptions of her prewar childhood in Vancouver are highly idealized: Vancouver is the place of plenitude and family unity that will eventually be disrupted first by the presence of a lecherous neighbor, then by the departure of Naomi's mother for Japan, and finally by the deportation of Japanese Canadians from the coastal areas of British Columbia to the interior. In *Obasan*'s sequel, *Itsuka*, Naomi describes Vancouver as a "paradise lost" (8), and indeed Naomi's Vancouver home is unmistakably paradisal, surrounded by lush and varied vegetation: "It used to have a hedge and rose bushes and flowers and cactus plants lining the sidewalk, and the front iron gate had a squeeze latch. The backyard had a sandbox and an apple tree and a swing, and I could dangle by my knees from a branch thicker than my father's arms" (61). In this passage, botanical and especially floral features such as the rose bushes contribute to the Edenic character of the description. In addition, the anthropomorphic comparison of the tree branch to the father's arm simultaneously connects the young Naomi to her parents and to the Vancouver landscape itself, signaling the sense of security, familial unity, and rootedness that attend this period of her life. Thus, Kogawa pastoralizes even the most urban setting of the novel.

One of the Vancouver house's most prominent features is a peach tree that Naomi can see from her bedroom window, a feature that once again suggests Edenic qualities of plenitude, contentment, and enchantment. The Edenic theme is continued inside the house by a picture "in muted shades of green" hanging on Naomi's bedroom wall of a girl gazing up at a bird in a tree (64), so that even indoors Naomi is not separated from nature. Significantly, a peach is also the subject of a Japanese fairy tale that Naomi's mother relates to her. In the story, a boy named Momotaro leaps out from the heart of a huge, ripe peach that an old woman has found, much to her astonishment: "The delight of it. And the wonder. Simply by existing a child is delight" (67). The luscious peach is symbolic of the comforts and pleasures of childhood, of storytelling, and of the mother-daughter relationship itself. In this way, Japanese folklore is made to harmonize with the conventional Western mapping of childhood memories onto an Edenic narrative.

Naomi's childhood idyll of wonder and delight is disrupted, however, by the unwanted sexual advances of Old Man Gower, the next door neighbor who lures her into his yard. Just outside Naomi's Eden lies the wilderness of the neighbor's backyard, which is visible from her bedroom window: "I am a small girl being carried away through the break in the shrubs where our two yards meet. Old Man Gower is taking me to the edge of his garden on the far far side away from the street. His back-yard is a jungle of bushes, flowering trees, weeds, and flowers" (74). The "jungle" that borders Naomi's Edenic garden and the loss of sexual innocence that it represents anticipate the family's impending displacement from their home, which is later described as an "expulsion into the waiting wilderness" (132).[17] Not only the Vancouver scenes, then, but also *Obasan*'s larger structure hinges on a customary distinction in New World narratives of exploration and settlement between the sheltering garden and the uninhabitable wilderness.

The Forest (Slocan, British Columbia)

The biblical allusion to the story of Exodus that announces the family's departure from Vancouver leads the reader to expect that Naomi's family will be relocated to a harsh wilderness. In fact, the town of Slocan in the British Columbian interior, a second Eden whose air is filled with butter-flies, provides the setting for another pastoral idyll. In Slocan, the family retreats deep into nature, but it is a soft, sympathetic nature that Kogawa's Japanese Canadians encounter. Naomi and her family are so much at home in nature in Slocan that their house merges with the forest: the house is the color of "sand and earth" and looks like a "giant toadstool," lending a fairy-tale quality to the Slocan scenes (142). While in Vancouver the bedroom picture of the tree brought nature inside the house, in Slocan, "home" and "land" become one. Moreover, nature provides well for her new inhabitants: the family harvests the fruits of the earth, including fid-dleheads, mushrooms, "wild strawberries the size of shirt buttons, pierc-ingly sweet, and gooseberries large as marbles" (165). Nature sustains, nurtures, and revives: "Underfoot, the mountain floor is a soft covering of pine needles, plant leaves, green growths. We breathe and are stabbed alive by the air, the sap from the trees, the slight metallic smell of cedar and pine. The rain, the warmth bring to bloom the wildflowers that hide beneath the foliage. Everywhere is the mountain's presence. Our bones are made porous" (165). In Slocan, a redemptive, benign, and fertile nature compensates for the Japanese Canadian dislocation by offering a sense of connection with the Canadian landscape.

As is suggested by the epigraph with which I opened this chapter, this vision of Slocan as paradisal is not unique to Kogawa's novel. David Suzuki, the well-known Japanese Canadian naturalist and environmental activist, recollects that the time he spent in Slocan during the war, where he was interned with Kogawa as a child, deepened his love of nature (Interview). In his autobiography, Suzuki records in vivid detail how the years of internment in Slocan were filled with not only hardship and deprivation but also gardening, hiking, and fishing trips: "All of this provided me with a base of intimate experience and knowledge of nature upon which my scientific career in biology would be built years later" (*Metamorphosis* 70). "If my formal education was suffering," he writes, "there was plenty to pick up outdoors" (69).

Similarly, Naomi's and her brother Stephen's lives in Slocan are characterized by playfulness, revelry, and above all harmony with nature. The children spend their days "arranging stones, watching chipmunks, gathering pinecones and wildflowers" (167), and they embark on a series of adventures, exploring the natural world that surrounds them with a sense of wonder and elation. On one such escapade they look down from a bluff to which they have climbed. From this height Slocan is "Lilliput," "a dizzying kingdom" (166–67). The reference to *Gulliver's Travels* is in keeping with the adventure-story quality of the Slocan scenes. At times, a more menacing face of nature shows itself, but more frequently, nature provides a refuge, proffering the acceptance and nourishment denied Kogawa's Japanese Canadians by the larger Canadian society. Yet, as in the first idyll, increasingly this idealized relationship with nature is threatened by the intrusion of the social world of racial prejudice. The novel's complex pastoral framework thus generates a tension between the ideal and the real, between the joys of nature and the trauma of dispossession.

A new potential for Japanese Canadian rootedness is apparent in Slocan, in which Naomi's uncle and aunt reconstruct the island home they had lost by planting a rock garden, a vegetable garden, and flower beds. Yet the Slocan idyll cannot be sustained for long, and once again Kogawa's Japanese Canadians are cast out of Eden. Replaying the earlier scene of exile in the Vancouver section, in Slocan paradisal and Edenic motifs are introduced to underscore the anguish of the displacement that results from the decision of the Canadian government in 1945 to prevent both their continued residence in Slocan and the return of Japanese Canadians to their prewar homes on the West Coast. At the moment of their reluctant departure from Slocan in 1945, the gardens are "spectacular": "In the spring there had been new loads of manure and fertilizer and the plants were ripening for harvest when the orders [for departure] came" (219). When the family is forced to leave Slocan, the departure and deracination of the Japanese Canadian community is likened to a forest of trees being chopped down by a "giant woodsman with his mighty ax" (215).

The Prairies (Lethbridge and Granton, Southern Alberta)

If the forest of Slocan is an Edenic garden, the beet farm in Granton where Naomi's family lives and works after its departure from Slocan is unequivocally a wilderness. Unlike the other landscapes in *Obasan*, Kogawa's rendering of the prairies as a "strange empty landscape" takes on the "tone of deep terror in regard to nature" that Frye identifies as dominant in Canadian writing. While the Slocan forests were fertile and life-sustaining, the dry, cracked, and treeless earth of Granton is deadening. Accustomed to a mountainous, moist landscape and now finding herself in a dry, flat one, Naomi complains that on the beet farm where the family works there isn't a tree within walking distance to provide shelter from the relentless sun: "The only tree here is dead. Its skeleton is a roost for a black-and-white magpie that I often see angling across the sky. I squat on the tree's dead roots in the whine of mosquitoes" (244). What little vegetation is in evidence in southern Alberta points more to the absence of life than to its continuation: the prairies are populated by skull-shaped weeds and "an army of spartan plants fighting in the wind. Every bit of plant growth here looks deliberate and fierce" (229–30).

The beet farm is the most thoroughly antipastoral landscape in the novel, providing no shade, little water, and no repose. Whereas in Slocan the fruits of the earth offered themselves up to be harvested, in Granton Naomi and her family must toil interminably, scorched and nauseated by "the maddening sun," over crops that they will not consume but rather that will benefit only their employer. If the beet farm is a landscape of labor, it is also above all a landscape of exile. In the Granton section, the biblical story of Exodus is alluded to once again when Naomi's brother Stephen is compared to an Israelite wandering in the desert (245), and indeed the prairies are a desert for Kogawa's Japanese Canadians: "We have come to the moon. We have come to the edge of the world, to a place of angry air. Was it just a breath ago that we felt the green watery fingers of the mountain air? Here, the air is a fist" (229). In Granton, Naomi and her family are "like the weeds that are left to bleach and wither in the sun" (240). The dry, resistant soil denies them the possibility of rootedness: "We are planted here in Alberta, our roots clawing the sudden prairie air" (226). The garden/wilderness contrast sharpens here to evoke the connection to place that Kogawa's Japanese Canadians have lost and to assert the need for a restoration of that broken connection.

The Coulee (Near Granton, Alberta)

The Vancouver, Slocan, and Granton sections recall the Edenic and wilderness landscapes of New World exploration and settlement narratives. Yet the site that is most densely laden with symbolic meaning in *Obasan* is the coulee near Granton. The novel opens and closes with visits to the coulee, Naomi's uncle's favorite retreat, underlining its privileged status in the novel. The coulee, like the Slocan forest or the Vancouver garden, represents a redemptive, sustaining nature, in contrast to the desert-wilderness of the beet farm. It functions as a *locus amoenus* for Naomi, incorporating the conventional pastoral features of flowers and a spring (in this case underground), and offering a place for reflection and rest.

The coulee is also a metaphysical space, a hidden cavity that holds essential, timeless truths, as is suggested by the prose poem that opens *Obasan*. The poem describes a "sensate sea," an "amniotic deep" beneath the grass containing the "freeing word" that will counteract the silence that characterizes Naomi's and Obasan's lives aboveground. Soon after, we discover that the underground stream alluded to in the prologue lies beneath the coulee. In terms of the novel's spatial logic, the coulee provides an inner core to which Naomi seeks access in her quest for a Canadian identity and an explanation of her mother's disappearance in Japan after the war. The coulee also has a primordial and ancient quality by virtue of its twin associations with nature and with First Nations peoples. In the opening scene of *Obasan,* we learn that the coulee is located near what had once been an Indian buffalo jump; fittingly, then, the coulee is the site where the bond between Japanese Canadians and First Nations Canadians is first asserted. Kogawa's reliance on a garden/wilderness binary in *Obasan* is significantly linked to her treatment of indigeneity, the coulee, and the view of nature as refuge that underpins all three.

The "Natural Indian" in *Obasan*

Previous chapters demonstrated how, in appropriating the pastoral mode, contemporary diasporic writers of the Americas have advanced an entangled view of nature as deeply imbued with history. In Kogawa's novels, however, nature is not entangled with history but instead provides a refuge from the social world and the fragmentation and displacement that characterize it.[18] In *Obasan,* Kogawa's reliance on the Eden/wilderness binary coincides with the opposition that the novel constructs between a redemptive, "pure" nature (the Slocan forest) and an antipastoral space that is contaminated by the social world (the Alberta beet farm). The nature/culture divide also governs the novel's portrayal of First Nations peoples. Kogawa tends in *Obasan* to locate First Nations peoples in the natural rather than the social world by consistently linking them to the landscape.

As has been well documented by New, representations of land in the contact and early colonial literature of Canada inscribed power relationships and rights over territory. Visual codes of the land such as those conveyed in mapping iconographies were accompanied by verbal codes—"New World," "savage wilderness," "virgin land"—that naturalized European presence on and control over the land (New, *Land Sliding,* ch. 1). The trope of virgin territory in particular contributed to the legitimation of colonization, gendering the act of exploration and emptying the Canadian landscape of an indigenous presence. When an indigenous presence was acknowledged, it tended to be seen as continuous with the landscape, a perception that persists today in the popular image of the Indian as environmentalist, or what Native American historian Philip Deloria calls "natural Indians."[19] Since European contact, First Nations peoples have been strongly identified with nature, with which they are assumed to have a privileged and harmonious relationship because, in their cosmologies, land and self are coextensive and interdependent. While this intimacy with nature is often seen as a positive trait, it derives from a colonizing vision that did not differentiate between the New World landscape and its inhabitants but instead disengaged indigenous peoples from culture and history.

If the discourse of the natural Indian has been carefully analyzed in the context of Euro-American representational practices, little attention has been given to its influence on minority and diasporic writing. Yet Kogawa's novels attest that its influence is profound. In a key dream sequence in *Obasan* that transports Naomi back to the contact period, Naomi imagines herself in a forest together with another woman and a man:

They have been here before us, forever in the forest. At what point we notice them is not clear. It is too strong to say we become aware of them. They move on a heavily treed slope that rises sharply to our right. The woman's back is bent. Slow and heavy as sleep, her arms sway and swing, front to back, back to front. For a flickering moment she appears as she once was, naked, youthful, voluptuous.

But the mirage fades. Her face is now harsh again and angular as quartz —square, a coarse golden brown. Her body, a matching squareness, is dense as earth. With a sickle she is harvesting the forest's debris, gathering the branches into piles. (34)

Naomi soon joins the woman in the laborious task of clearing the forest, while a British officer oversees their efforts: "The man is taller, thinner, and precise—a British martinet. It is evident that he is in command" (34). The martinet, too, participates in clearing the forest, first by pruning the trees with shears and later by means of a robotic beast whose "obedience is phenomenal" (35). In this scene of colonization and environmental degradation, the British officer wields absolute control over the indigenous woman,[20] Naomi, and nature itself. Both the Canadian land and its inhabitants are subjugated to patriarchal and colonial authority.

By introducing the dream into Naomi's narrative, Kogawa demonstrates an awareness of a colonial reading of New World land as virgin territory and works to undercut this reading by highlighting the historical suppression of First Nations peoples and the natural environment. However, at the same time that Kogawa challenges colonialist discourse, she reproduces certain of its features. For example, she presents the indigenous woman as timeless, as representing an ancient way of life; she has been in the forest "forever." The woman, we are told, was once "naked" and "voluptuous," a description that evokes primitivist fantasies of the eroticized indigenous female body. The indigenous woman's physical movements are apelike, as though she were half-animal: "Her arms sway and swing, front to back, back to front." Finally, Kogawa strongly identifies the indigenous woman with nature: in contrast to the martinet who maintains a marked distance from nature, the woman has a body as "dense as earth." The indigenous woman is continuous with nature; the degradation of the woman and the degradation of nature are coterminous. This brief passage from *Obasan* thus clusters together several standard tropes pertaining to "primitive" peoples, who are presented as ancient, sensual, and in tune with nature.

Kogawa's critique of European colonization in the dream scene is accompanied by her identification of her Japanese Canadian heroine with the subjugated indigenous woman. Kogawa inserts Naomi into a scene of colonial contact, anachronistically positing a Japanese Canadian presence in the Canadian wilderness in the contact period. Like the indigenous woman, Naomi is under the martinet's command. Naomi is further linked to the indigenous woman by virtue of their gender, which separates both women from the decidedly masculine martinet. Most saliently, through this association with the indigenous woman, Kogawa identifies Naomi with nature and the less alienated way of life that the indigenous woman represents. Kogawa's alignment of Japanese Canadians, indigeneity, and nature in the dream scene introduces a nexus of associations that will be central to *Obasan*'s articulation of a Japanese Canadian sense of belonging.

Kogawa continues to link First Nations peoples with nature as well as to draw parallels between the persecution of Japanese Canadians and First Nations Canadians throughout *Obasan*. The most explicit example of this strategy comes in the opening scene of the novel, which takes place on the privileged site of the coulee. In this passage, Kogawa compares Naomi's uncle to Chief Sitting Bull:

> Everything in front of us is virgin land. From the beginning of time, the grass along this stretch of prairie has not been cut. About a mile east is a spot which was once an Indian buffalo jump, a high steep cliff where the buffalo were stampeded and fell to their deaths. All the bones are still there, some sticking right out of the side of a fresh landslide.
>
> Uncle could be Chief Sitting Bull squatting here. He has the same prairie-baked skin, the deep brown furrows like dry riverbeds creasing his cheeks. All he needs is a feather headdress, and he would be perfect for a picture postcard—"Indian Chief from Canadian Prairie"—souvenir of Alberta, made in Japan. (2–3)

While in the dream scene the indigenous woman was presented as timeless, here the landscape itself takes on primordial qualities: it is "virgin land," untouched since "the beginning of time." The construction of nature as virgin territory is one of the most pervasive tropes of New World discourse. Accordingly, Kogawa promptly deflates the twin notions of virgin land and the timeless natural Indian by referring in the second paragraph of the Sitting Bull passage to the touristic and commodified image of the Indian chief. The reference to Japanese-made souvenirs updates the theme of the exploitation of First Nations peoples and gives the passage a more critical edge. However, while more parodic in tone than the dream scene discussed above, the Sitting Bull passage continues to assert a connection between First Nations peoples and nature as well as a basic parallelism between Japanese Canadian and First Nations historical experiences: both Uncle Isamu and Chief Sitting Bull are victims of

Euro-Canadian oppression. A tension is generated, then, by Kogawa's simultaneous critique of conventional images of First Nations peoples and reliance on those conventions.

In the Sitting Bull passage, Japanese Canadians are initially associated with First Nations peoples on the basis of their physical appearance. Yet this resemblance is more than skin-deep, for Uncle Isamu's physical features connect him both to First Nations peoples and to nature. Uncle Isamu has "prairie-baked skin" and "furrows like dry riverbeds creasing his cheeks," features that suggest an intimate relationship with the land. Later in the same chapter, Kogawa pursues the theme of a physical resemblance between Japanese Canadians and First Nations peoples when the adult Naomi describes her First Nations students at the Alberta school in which she teaches: "Some of the Native children I've had in my classes over the years could almost pass for Japanese, and vice versa. There's something in the animal-like shyness I recognize in the dark eyes. A quickness to look away. I remember, when I was a child in Slocan, seeing the same swift flick-of-a-cat's tail look in the eyes of my friends" (3). Once again, Kogawa's initial emphasis on a physical resemblance points to a behavioral one—here, self-effacement and timidity. In a related passage, Kogawa puts a more positive spin on the taciturn quality that Naomi is told she shares with First Nations Canadians: "'But smart people don't talk too much. Redskins know that. The King bird warned them a long time ago'" (174). In general, Kogawa calls attention to the difficulty the two groups have in finding a sense of belonging, as when Naomi recalls how both she and a First Nations classmate wanted to anglicize their foreign-sounding names as a means of assimilating.

The initial parallelism between First Nations and Japanese Canadians that Kogawa introduces in the Sitting Bull passage finds its fullest articulation in the Slocan section of the novel. Here, the young Naomi learns that Slocan, where the Japanese Canadians find shelter from the disruptions of World War II, had originally been a place of refuge for First Nations peoples fleeing smallpox and other ills. Slocan thereby supplies Kogawa's Japanese Canadians with a significant link to an earlier First Nations presence, indicating that the subjugation of First Nations Canadians since colonization and the persecution of Japanese Canadians during World War II belong to a historical continuum of Euro-Canadian oppression. This perspective derives from Kogawa's basic emphasis on a universal human experience, as she suggests in an interview: "The Japanese Canadian community is only one small pebble on the beach of human experience but there is a universal element in our struggling political endeavour."

We feel some sort of solidarity with the world's communities in their effort to speak" (Interview 462). If Kogawa is interested in "the world's communities," however, in *Obasan* it is First Nations peoples in particular who attract her attention.

The Figure of the Indian in Diasporic Writing of the Americas

Kogawa's allusion to Chief Sitting Bull at the opening of *Obasan* affiliates her novel with other diasporic writing of the Americas that exhibits an attraction to indigenous themes and motifs.[21] For example, in his poem "Indian Reservation: Caughnawaga" (1948), the Jewish Canadian poet A. M. Klein portrays the immigrant child's envy of the Indian's ostensible freedom and closeness to nature:

> Childhood, that wished me Indian, hoped that
> one afterschool I'd leave the classroom chalk,
> the varnish smell, the watered dust of the street,
> to join the clean outdoors and the Iroquois track.
>
> (lines 8–11)

Moreover, Sitting Bull himself reappears in Derek Walcott's play *The Ghost Dance* (1989) and his epic poem *Omeros* (1990), which alludes to indigenous histories of dispossession that span the Caribbean and the United States—"one elegy from Aruac to Sioux," as a memorable line of the poem asserts (164).

In part, the prominence of Native North American themes in diasporic writing of the Americas reflects the impact of the genre of the western. Indeed, the influence of the myth of the American West that I traced in chapter 2 in the context of Jewish American writing is also evident in Canadian diasporic writing. We might think of Michael Ondaatje's *The Collected Works of Billy the Kid* (1970), or of films such as Srinivas Krishna's *Masala* (1991) which cite the myth of the West as the place of self-reinvention.[22] Imagery and stock figures drawn from the Hollywood western appear in Goto's *Chorus of Mushrooms*, which is set in the Canadian West and features a Japanese-speaking cowboy.[23] The appeal of the myth of the West often translates into an attraction to the figure of the Indian, as for instance in Barbadian Canadian author Austin Clarke's autobiographical essay "In the Semi-Colon of the North" (1982). In his essay, Clarke draws on the schoolboy's romance of the West even as he describes a journey to the Canadian North:

> I am sitting in a crowded coach of this CNR train, surrounded by women and by men who look like trappers out of the adventure books of the West I had read in Barbados. . . .
>
> The men sitting around me on the slow-moving train making up its mind on a divorce from Toronto where I had lived for five years, all looked like miners and prospectors. . . .
>
> I was myself like a prospector, travelling light and lightened by the uncertainty of expectation. (30)

As the essay continues, Clarke increasingly relies on the conventional image of the Indian as a silent, noble, enigmatic figure: two First Nations men sitting across from him on the train "did not talk, nor blink, nor smile. They were mysterious masks" (33). Clarke's essay attests to the dissemination of the genre of the western and attendant images of the Indian across the Americas. Notably, although one might expect members of marginalized groups to identify with the Indian rather than with the white man, Clarke reverses this pattern when he likens himself to a prospector "travelling light." Similarly, Gish Jen and Richard Rodriguez introduce playful pioneer analogies, and as we saw in chapter 2, Jewish American writers Anzia Yezierska and Philip Roth associate their protagonists with New World explorers and pioneers.[24]

James Clifford observes in his essay "Diasporas" that diasporic and indigenous peoples tend to employ diverging narrative strategies, strategies that often conflict sharply:

> Diaspora exists in practical, and at time principled, tension with nativist identity formations. . . . What are the historical and/or indigenous rights of *relative* newcomers—fourth-generation Indians in Fiji or even Mexicans in southwestern United States . . . ? How long does it take to become "indigenous"? Lines too strictly drawn between "original" inhabitants (who often themselves replaced prior populations) and subsequent immigrants risk ahistoricism. With all these qualifications, however, it is clear that the claims to political legitimacy made by peoples who have inhabited a territory since before recorded history and those who arrived by steamboat or airplane will be founded on very different principles. (308–9)

Clifford's nuanced account points to areas of both overlap and difference between diasporic and indigenous narratives of land and identity, which exist in tension with one another. Such tensions are highlighted by Walcott's *Omeros* and Malamud's *The People* as well as by images from Jin-me Yoon's photographic works *A Group of Sixty-Seven* (1996) and *Touring Home from Away* (1998–99), in which the potential for solidarity between First Nations and Korean Canadians is at once introduced and called into question (see chapter 6). Yet in *Obasan*, Kogawa emphasizes areas of overlap to the exclusion of an acknowledgment of the points of difference that Clifford identifies. And while a number of the above-mentioned texts exploit the comic and ironic potential of the diasporic subject's identification with the Indian, Kogawa's presentation of this theme is largely unselfconscious.[25]

The need for a more attentive reading of the slippage between the indigenous and the diasporic in Kogawa's writing is illustrated by a passage in *Obasan* that develops a contrasting identification. Upon arriving in the ghost town of Slocan, Naomi describes Japanese Canadians in altogether different terms: "We are those pioneers who cleared the bush and the forest with our hands, the gardeners tending and attending the soil with our tenderness, the fishermen who are flung from the sea to flounder in the dust of the prairies" (132). Here, Kogawa's Japanese Canadians are assigned the role of settler rather than native, and a heroic narrative of exploration and settlement is referenced. In the southern Alberta sections of the novel in particular, Kogawa's Japanese Canadians tend to be cast in the role of settler.

As though Kogawa is aware of the contradictory nature of these alternative identifications, the settler allusion in this passage is immediately softened by the gardener analogy and by a reference to the displacement of Japanese fishermen from coastal British Columbia. Nonetheless, the settler motif clearly holds some attraction for Kogawa. It resurfaces in *Obasan*'s sequel, *Itsuka*, in which Kogawa evokes the heroic dimensions of the pioneer narrative to highlight the injustice of the dispossession of Japanese Canadian strawberry farmers: "Dan's father and other issei pioneers cleared the Fraser Valley with horses and their bare hands, and their strawberries were large and luscious. The burgeoning berry industry, lands, equipment—all were taken by the government and turned over to returning war veterans. White war veterans. . . . Dan fought for his farm. He lost. Then he became ill" (151). Later in *Itsuka*, Naomi uses a settlement metaphor to describe the efforts of the Japanese Canadian redress movement: "Here in the mid-1980s, we're still hacking our way through the wild woods, struggling to better the human condition" (214). These examples testify that it is possible within the symbolic economy of the two novels to represent Japanese Canadians as settlers as well as natives and expose ambiguities surrounding Kogawa's attempt to ally Japanese Canadians with First Nations peoples as fellow victims of oppression.

Kogawa briefly acknowledges this tension in a passage in *Obasan* that concerns the story of Goldilocks. While in Slocan, the young Naomi puzzles over whether she and her family are the bears who live in the woods or Goldilocks who breaks into the house, eats Baby Bear's food, and sleeps in Baby Bear's bed. However, the riddle of how Japanese Canadians can be both foreign and native, "both the enemy and not the enemy" (84), as her brother Stephen puts it, tends to be introduced by Kogawa in order to point to contradictions in the Canadian government's treatment of its citizens as well as to highlight the Japanese Canadians' sense of internal exile. The novel's political goal of establishing the Canadianness of Japanese Canadians presses it to resolve rather than to explore such ambiguities, and, in general, Kogawa is unwilling to allow her Japanese Canadian characters to slide between the two poles of settler and native, instead aligning them firmly with First Nations Canadians. This desire to assert the indigeneity of Japanese Canadians has significant implications for Kogawa's resolution to the problem of belonging.

The Persistence of Primitivism in *Itsuka*

In *Gone Primitive*, Marianna Torgovnick makes the suggestive argument through readings of figures such as Conrad, Lawrence, Lévi-Strauss, and Freud that a primary impetus of primitivism in the modern age is the condition of "transcendental homelessness." Primitivism alleviates modern alienation by offering a return to origins and to a simpler, easier time unencumbered by the anxieties of modern urban life. A central feature of primitivism is thus its "hominess": "Going primitive is trying to 'go home' to a place that feels comfortable and balanced, where full acceptance comes freely and easily. . . . Whatever form the primitive's hominess takes, its strangeness salves our estrangement from ourselves and our culture" (185).

The desire to recover a sense of belonging that Torgovnick identifies as central to Euro-American modernist and postmodernist primitivism motivates Kogawa's primitivism as well, testifying that primitivism is not the exclusive purview of Euro-Americans. One of the markers of the influence of primitivist discourse on Kogawa is her tendency to associate First Nations peoples with the natural environment. The European primitivist tradition, which "postulated people dwelling in nature according to nature" (Berkhofer 72), produced both negative and idealized views of First Nations peoples. But whether primitivism constructed the Indian as savage irrationality or as living in harmony with the natural landscape, it maintained a vision of indigenous peoples as "natural."

The purported intimacy between First Nations people and the land has been both exploited and parodied by First Nations writers. Some draw on it, identifying a parallel between the oppression of the environment and that of First Nations peoples, as do many of the poems and stories by members of the Native Women's Writing Circle collected in *Into the Moon* (edited by Leonore Keeshig-Tobias, 1996). Similarly, Okanagan writer Jeannette Armstrong's novel *Whispering in Shadows* (2000) advances a narrative of reconnection with the earth in its alliance of First Nations and ecological concerns. Armstrong's novel culminates in a scene in which the protagonist, a First Nations painter and activist for indigenous and environmental causes, communes with the spirit of a tree, much to the envy of her non–First Nations companion who has no access to this experience. Armstrong's heroine discovers that the tree "is speaking a language" that her body "has known for the thousands of years of [her] various ancestors" (101). Cree writer Tomson Highway's *Kiss of the Fur Queen* (2000) and Cherokee writer Thomas King's *Truth and Bright Water* (1999), on the other hand, are novels that heavily ironize the trope of the Indian's privileged relationship with nature in comic episodes in which First Nations characters display various degrees of ineptitude and lack of enthusiasm on camping trips. King's young protagonist in *Truth and Bright Water* had hoped to spend his vacation at the West Edmonton Mall: "But my mother wanted to go camping, to get into nature and see stuff like animals and scenery. I told her we saw that all the time, but she said the mountains were different" (78).

Lacking any such ironic overtones, Kogawa's alliance of Japanese Canadians and First Nations peoples in *Obasan* enables her to effect a rapprochement between Japanese Canadians and Canadian nature, which in turn bolsters her protagonists' claim to a full Canadian identity. This strategy becomes more pronounced in *Itsuka*, Kogawa's sequel to *Obasan*. In *Itsuka*, Naomi has fallen deeper into spinsterhood and an isolation that is only exacerbated by her move from southern Alberta to Toronto. Yet in Toronto, she finally finds a lover in the unlikely person of a French Canadian priest, Father Cedric, who is working with Naomi's Aunt Emily to lobby for the compensation of Japanese Canadians by the federal government. Cedric is described as having "earth-coloured hair," recalling the indigenous woman from Naomi's dream in *Obasan* whose body was "dense as earth." And indeed, it subsequently emerges that Cedric is part Métis: "His mother, he says, was swarthy and small. . . . Her thick black hair was in one long braid to her waist. She was, he believes, the great-granddaughter of a Métis woman" (107). Cedric tells

Naomi that "we have so much to learn from trees" (206) and woos her by taking her out of the city and into the wilderness of the Laurentian Shield—a gesture that puts an end to any doubts regarding the authenticity of his Métis identity: "He brings the car to a stop beneath a large tree. 'The place of my great-great-grandmother,' he says lightly. He picks up the rattle from the dashboard and taps his cheeks. 'You see these high cheekbones? They come from here. When I go back in my mind, it isn't to France. It's here. I begin here'" (133). Cedric thus affirms his indigeneity by demonstrating a powerful intimacy with the Canadian landscape.

Although *Itsuka* is set in urban Canada rather than in the rural landscapes of *Obasan*, Naomi finds relief from her new Toronto life through periodic retreats into nature, as Father Cedric takes her to the woods of the Laurentian Shield, a snowy ravine in Toronto, the Bruce Trail, and Toronto Island. These nature idylls are linked to the theme of the primitive by virtue of Cedric's indigenous credentials. Cedric brings Naomi out of the city to the banks of the Muskoka River, telling her tales of dryads along the way. "Such a specific sense of place he has—this bright woodland of boulders and trees" (134), Naomi marvels. Walking through the woods with Cedric, Naomi senses "the touch . . . , not so much of history as of prehistory" as well as "the breath of his ancestors" (134). In a series of scenes that contain her characteristic blend of fairy-tale and Edenic imagery, Kogawa presents nature as the primordial dwelling place of the spirit of First Nations peoples: "[Cedric] is released, he tells me, from the political by the personal and the primitive. His mother's gift to him was a capacity to sense sentience. . . . It's the breath of his ancestors that comes of this air. A soft-footed breeze. They breathed here where we are, and infused their lungs with these living seasons" (134).

In *Itsuka,* the emblem of the Japanese connection to First Nations Canadians is the "Japanese Haida rattle" that Cedric inherits from his father and later gives to Naomi, symbolically conferring on her an (indigenous) Canadian identity.[26] At one point in the novel, Cedric relates the rattle's history:

> Back in the early 1900s, Japanese miners and fishermen had settled on the Queen Charlotte Islands. At the time of the Japanese Canadian round-up in 1942, a few of the men fled to the more remote islands and were sheltered by the Haida. . . .
> The isseis and their protectors ate the same food—seaweed, herring roe, young ferns, berries. The sun and sea joined them. Children were born. Moon-faced children. Babies with Japanese eyes. And there were dark-skinned children

on the islands as well—offspring of slaves in flight from the south. One of the issei fathers carved this rattle for his child. (108)

This Japanese Canadian creation myth highlights cooperation between First Nations peoples and Japanese Canadians at the moment at which Japanese Canadian need was greatest. It literalizes the symbolic alliance of First Nations and Japanese Canadians that Kogawa had introduced in *Obasan* and extends it further by alluding to mixed Japanese-Haida relationships that result in births of Japanese Haida children. Thus, the narrative of the rattle supplies a myth of origin and a sense of belonging that had previously eluded Kogawa's Japanese Canadians.

The story of the rattle also anticipates Naomi's sexual union with Cedric. In a scene of lovemaking in the wilderness that recalls similar scenes in Malamud's *A New Life* and Haitian writer Jacques Roumain's *Masters of the Dew* (1944) (see chapter 5), Naomi recovers the connection with nature and with Canada that her family's forced removal from Vancouver and Slocan had severed. After the lovemaking scene, Naomi declares herself "found" (208), conforming to a well-established model in anglophone Canadian literature of the white protagonist who gains a sense of vitality and rootedness through sexual contact with the Indian. In broader North American terms, Kogawa's novels are a contemporary version of what Deloria calls "playing Indian," in which Indian guise and an affiliation with Indianness are adopted as a means of gaining a sense of national belonging.[27]

If the scenes involving Father Cedric and the narrative of the Japanese Haida rattle are informed by a primitivist desire for origins and belonging, this desire is at its most intense in the Hawaiian episode in *Itsuka*. At one point in the novel, Naomi accompanies her Aunt Emily to Hawaii, a "nisei paradise" of communal togetherness. Hawaii is presented in *Itsuka* as a luscious, primordial natural retreat: "The extravagant moist air on this island is thick with the sweet scent of fruit and flowers and there are ferns and fringe trees, fronds, fat grass, skinny velvety moss grass, trees with fan-shaped leaves as high as a house. Mynah birds chatter in trees. Little grey-brown robin-size doves with turquoise beaks go bob-bobbing along the floors of indoor-outdoor restaurants. On the streets, in the stores, we blend into a collage of races. We're both tanning quickly and beginning to look like the 'locals.' If belongingness was all that mattered in life, Aunt Emily says, she'd move to Hawaii in a flash" (85). Kogawa's idealized depiction of Hawaii as a place of harmony with nature and of uncomplicated belonging is reminiscent of the European primitivist fantasy of the ideal other place (often located to the south) that alleviates modern alienation. As with the protagonist of Carpentier's *The Lost Steps* who travels deep into the Latin American jungle to salve his anomie, Naomi's journey south relieves her sense of unbelonging, at least for a time. In stark contrast to the alienated condition of Kogawa's Japanese Canadians, the Japanese Hawaiians are fully at home in their landscape: "Hawaii's niseis, Aunt Emily says, are as unbent as free-standing trees. Unlike us crippled bonsai in Canada, they've retained community here" (85).

It is in the natural paradise of Hawaii that Naomi experiences the most complete sensation of belonging; she has never before "felt so comfortable" as she does there (85). While reveling in the exotic delights of Hawaii, Naomi has a "deep-sea dream" that echoes European fantasies of gaining access to a pre-linguistic and unified self through a retreat into nature: "Somewhere in this no longer physical, no longer visible world is the moment of discovery. . . . There's a quality of knowing that is completely unchanged as I slide down the stream of deeper disappearing, and during some pre-dawn of speech I'm aware of music, of song. . . . Then again in a seamless shift, I'm past sound, into thought. I'm a single waft of thought and I know that I, the thought and the person, am one, indivisibly, consciously and utterly myself" (87). By traveling to the exotic other place, Naomi recaptures a sense of herself as whole and achieves a less alienated state. Yet because it relies on a fantasy of escape and return to a simpler, less complicated existence, this primitivist solution to the problem of belonging is difficult to sustain. Naomi's Hawaiian idyll is soon ended and she must once again confront the more complex realities of her Canadian life. After her sojourn in Hawaii, Naomi returns to Toronto to continue her work on behalf of the cause of Japanese Canadian redress. The culminating event of *Itsuka* is the Canadian government's capitulation in 1988 to the Japanese Canadians' demands for compensation. Naomi's quest for belonging is fulfilled both by this political victory and by her joint union with the Métis (Cedric) and the Canadian land, with which Cedric has brought her into closer contact.

Botanical and Biological Metaphors for Belonging

In both *Obasan* and *Itsuka*, Kogawa attempts to indigenize Japanese Canadians by linking them to the natural Indian and to a Canadian landscape that lies outside of time. If this vision of nature as refuge perpetuates a dubious division between the natural and the social worlds, Kogawa's occasional recourse to biological metaphors for identity also raises questions about her model of Japanese Canadian belonging. One of the virtues of the botanical register of imagery that Kogawa favors is that unlike the more insistently biological imagery of bloodlines, it does not necessarily posit an essential, fixed connection to place. However, in accordance with her reading of nature as outside of history and her attraction to indigenizing narratives, Kogawa's botanical imagery tends to slide into the biological. The Canadian landscape and the mother's body are linked throughout *Obasan* so that the characters' connection to land and nature is often expressed in biological terms. In the opening passage of the novel, the underground stream at the coulee is likened to "amniotic" fluid. In addition, the tree image is used to express Naomi's relationship both to the land and to the mother in passages in which botanical and biological imagery overlap:

> I am clinging to my mother's leg, a flesh shaft that grows from the ground, a tree trunk of which I am an offshoot—a young branch attached by right of flesh and blood. Where she is rooted, I am rooted. . . . Her blood is whispering through my veins. The shaft of her leg is the shaft of my body and I am her thoughts. (77)

> Your leg is a tree trunk and I am branch, vine, butterfly. I am joined to your limbs by right of birth, child of your flesh, leaf of your bough. (291)

Another of Kogawa's favored images is that of bones embedded in the land, in particular the bones of Japanese Canadian fishermen and buffalo buried in the prairies. This strain of imagery also tends toward the biological, merging body and land and naturalizing the Japanese presence in the Canadian landscape. The slippage between the botanical and the biological in *Obasan* signals a longing for a native landscape to which one is fundamentally bound as Scott's minstrel is to Scotland in *The Lay of the Last Minstrel*.

In a culminating passage in *Obasan,* Naomi locates Canadian identity in the Canadian soil: "Where do any of us come from in this cold country? Oh, Canada, whether it is admitted or not, we come from you we come from you. From the same soil, the slugs and slime and bogs and twigs and roots" (271). Here again is Kogawa's characteristic insistence on a universal, undifferentiated Canadian identity based on a relationship to land and nature. Kogawa's belief in a universal humanity leads her to emphasize sameness rather than difference: all Canadians are alike in their fundamental connection to the Canadian soil. Rejecting Margaret Atwood's maxim that "we are all immigrants to this place even if we were born here: the country is too big to inhabit completely" (*Journals of Susanna Moodie*, n.p.), Kogawa suggests instead in this anthemic passage that we are all natives, rooted in the soil, whether we were born here or not. While this strategy has certain advantages, particularly in highlighting the exclusion of some Canadians from their full rights of citizenship, it also tends to collapse together distinct forms of oppression as well as to perpetuate what Clifford calls "nativist identity formations." Yet as the passage continues, Kogawa's botanical imagery begins to hint at an alternative model of belonging: "We come from the country that plucks its people out like weeds and flings them into the roadside. . . . We erupt in the valleys and mountainsides, in small towns and back alleys, sprouting upside down on the prairies, our hair wild as spider's legs, our feet rooted nowhere. We grow where we are not seen, we flourish where we are not heard, the thick undergrowth of an unlikely planting" (271). In contrast to the earlier lines, these images of chaotic and unlikely plantings and of rootless and itinerant weeds suggest a far more accidental, contingent, and provisional connection between a landscape and its people than the one that Kogawa had previously evoked. In this second set of images, plant life is not exempt from the disruptions and displacements that characterize the social world but instead nature comes to embody these displacements. Thus, in this alternative reading of botanical metaphors for identity, nature is very much entangled with the social world.

Obasan's brand of pastoralism generates significant tensions by virtue of its construction of nature as a refuge from the social world, its reinscription of the figure of the natural Indian, and its reliance on a primitivist solution to the problem of belonging. These tensions are worth acknowledging because they point to obstacles contemporary writers of the Americas face in their attempts to construct new narratives about land and belonging. They also indicate the limitations of the pastoral mode itself, which, even when deployed in a complex and critical form, bears the traces of ways of seeing New World landscapes and peoples that were popularized by colonial discourses of contact and settlement. How might a New World sense of place be expressed without relying on those formulations introduced by exploration and settlement narratives? Is the pastoral mode finally too heavily implicated in these narratives to support alternative models of belonging? Part II will consider what advantages other landscape ideas—as well as other genres and media—may have to offer contemporary writers and artists of the Americas.

Marvelous Gardens and Gothic Wildernesses

4 Jamaica Kincaid's and Michael Pollan's New World Garden Writing

> There was a rubber tree in this botanical garden. . . . When first seen by any of us . . . , it was a curiosity; eventually we accepted its presence in our midst, even as we accepted our own presence in our midst, for we, too, were not native to the place we were in.
> —Jamaica Kincaid, *My Garden (Book):*

> Gardening is an exploration of a place close to home.
> —Michael Pollan, *Second Nature*

As we saw in Part I, the pastoral mode has considerable appeal for diasporic writers in the Americas because of its unique capacity to register simultaneously the attachment to place and the anguish of dispossession. In its complex form, pastoral is sharply double-edged, bringing into tension the ideal and the real, nature and history. Yet pastoral is only one of a number of landscape ideas—including the marvelous, the sublime, and the gothic—that have influenced the meaning of place in the Americas. Moreover, nonfiction genres of writing as well as alternative expressive media make possible innovative treatments of landscape and its relationship to belonging that complement those found in fiction and poetry. Accordingly, I turn in this chapter to garden writing, a nonfiction genre that may be productively compared with fictional treatments of the garden. Although on the surface, garden writing may appear to be benign and apolitical, Jamaica Kincaid and Michael Pollan demonstrate the genre's capacity for political and postcolonial critique, confirming "the often overlooked truth that the best garden writing is both social and horticultural document" (Marranca 12).

At first glance, the garden seems an unlikely candidate for a site in which to think through contemporary debates surrounding place and identity. Deeply implicated in both European and New World myths of origins, the garden is neither readily assimilable to a postmodern reading of space, nor is it looked upon particularly favorably in diaspora studies. A special issue of the *South Atlantic Quarterly* entitled "After the Garden?" asks whether the garden may be a hopelessly old-fashioned metaphor that has outlived its usefulness. In his introduction to the issue, Michael Crozier notes that while "for many cultures across time the garden has been both site and object of what would now be called cultural reflexivity" (626–27), the advent of an era of time-space compression and the contemporary maxim that "place is out" would appear to obviate the garden as a meaningful symbolic site. Indeed, the garden is not easily reconciled with postmodern readings of space, which tend to be couched in metaphors of vacancy and blankness. In contrast to "non-places" such as airport lounges and theme parks, which are characterized by their ephemerality and lack of concern with identity (Augé 77–78), the garden suggests fullness and density, foundations and origins. Unlike the borderlands, another favorite of current criticism, the garden points toward interiority and enclosure as well as edges and margins; the garden is a "closed" rather than an "open" spatial metaphor. Similarly, the garden indicates a stronger attachment to place than either the technological metaphor of the circuit, with its unending and dynamic flow, or the rhizome, Deleuze and Guattari's botanical metaphor for a dispersed and fragmented nomadic identity.[1]

If the garden is seen as outmoded, botanical imagery more broadly has also come under attack. The case against botanical imagery is compellingly presented by the anthropologist Liisa Malkki, who argues that the metaphors of "soil," "roots," and "transplantation" that pervade our everyday language perpetuate the often harmful myths of identity as territorially bounded and nations as segmented, discrete spaces that many are now trying to debunk. In her article "National Geographic," Malkki observes that botanical metaphors typically naturalize the relationship between a people and a place, and she worries about the exclusionary implications of such metaphors for those who become "uprooted." "Conceiving the relationships that people have to places in the naturalizing and botanical terms described above leads, then," she concludes, "to a peculiar sedentarism that is reflected in language and in social practice" and that "enables a vision of territorial displacement as pathological" (31). Thus, Malkki exposes the oppressive implications of seemingly benign commonsense botanical metaphors relating to identity and origins.

Malkki is clearly correct to be concerned about the unreflective usage of botanical metaphors, but such a critique may also be misleading when it implies that botanical imagery *necessarily* functions to inscribe a nostalgic or exclusionary politics of place. Moreover, one might question how feasible it would be to abandon a vocabulary that, as Malkki shows, continues to be so deeply ingrained in contemporary thinking about identity. For these reasons, it may be useful to acknowledge the flexibility as well as the limitations of botanical imagery and to consider how, when it is approached critically, botanical imagery may function to interrogate exclusionary models of identity as well as to perpetuate them. Glissant's adoption of Deleuze and Guattari's rhizome metaphor is evidence of this flexibility, as are the reimaginations of the garden that I discuss below and in chapter 5.

Indeed, looked at from another angle, the very history of associations that makes the garden appear so outdated and suspect might also be seen to be an advantage. The garden as a place of cultivation has etymological ties to both "culture" and "colonization," and thus invites reflection on two concepts that are of particular concern to theorists of diaspora and postcoloniality. The garden also has significant connections to hybridity, both metaphorically as a figure for the hybridization of cultures and historically in that nineteenth-century theories of racial hybridity drew on the science of botany.[2] In addition, because of its associations with the biblical Garden of Eden, the garden recalls the original exile and displacement, as well as the myths of origin upon which our understanding of identity so often depends. Finally, the garden's associations with regeneration and femininity draw attention to the spatial organization of foundationalist narratives and the gendering of space.

Gardens—real and imagined—have traditionally functioned as sites of self-reflection and as spaces in which to express social, economic, and power relationships as well as values and belief systems. Both literary and visual images of the garden and the design of actual gardens have served to convey ideological commitments and political ambitions. Garden historian John Dixon Hunt reminds us that gardens were traditionally considered to be a representational art form, a system of signs. Hunt argues in "The Garden as Cultural Object" that societies tend to invent new garden traditions at times of dramatic social and political transformation, citing the Italian Renaissance villa garden and the nineteenth-century English bourgeois private garden as two examples. If, as has been proposed by Arjun Appadurai and others, globalization constitutes another such moment of transformation, might not the garden emerge once again as a site in which to register some of the paradigm shifts that are currently taking place?

In his discussion, Hunt underlines the conservative "political and cultural motives" that have informed invented garden traditions—their tendency to "seek to establish continuity with a suitable historic past" (19). Yet other commentators, such as the nature writer Michael Pollan, advance an alternative reading of the garden as "a place to experiment, to try out new hybrids and mutations" (*Botany of Desire* 185). Jill H. Casid concludes her *Sowing Empire* by arguing that, as tempting as it may be, we should not "just disavow the botanical": "The landscape garden may seem like hopelessly colonized terrain better left behind. Those marked as 'Other' or who refuse to align themselves with an imagined 'center' may dream of charting out into the promise of formless space anxious that a landscape of resistance or revolution may ultimately be a contradiction in terms. However, we cannot afford to cede the ground through which hegemony refashions itself as the order of nature. What we need, instead, are counterlandscaping practices of resignification and transformation" (241). In keeping with this imperative to reclaim the heavily colonized territory of the garden, the present chapter and the chapter that follows consider whether the garden may also accommodate a more radical representational practice.

In the New World Garden with Jamaica Kincaid and Michael Pollan

In their garden writing, Jamaica Kincaid and Michael Pollan interrogate traditional inscriptions of botanical metaphors for identity in order to reimagine the terms of New World emplacement. In so doing, they capitalize on the genre's openness to history—both personal and social. Although sharply contrasting in tone, and while informed by distinct cultural backgrounds and life experiences, their garden writing is united by a common premise: that, as Kincaid insists, "the world cannot be left out of the garden" (*My Garden* 82), or, as Pollan puts it, "The garden . . . [is] better approached as an arena than a refuge" ("Introduction" x). For both authors, gardens cannot be understood without reference to social and power relations.

Kincaid's and Pollan's rejection of the more conventional reading of the garden as a place of refuge and repose, as *hortus conclusus,* serves as the point of departure for their respective contributions to the genre. They emphasize the relations of power and the histories of dislocation (both human and botanical) that are encoded in New World landscapes and thus establish garden writing as a genre that supports the articulation of a postcolonial sense of place. At the same time, both authors make use of the

genre to explore the diasporic subject's relationship to American belonging, calling attention to the extent to which the activity of gardening is
itself "a painstaking exploration of place" (Pollan, *Second Nature* 75).

Kincaid's gardening essays, the majority of which were originally written as installments in the *New Yorker's* gardening column, have been collected in *My Garden (Book):* (1999). Although they have received considerably less attention than her fiction,[3] Kincaid's gardening essays offer
a rich and compelling commentary on several of her hallmark themes:
colonialism, history, and diasporic subjectivity. The essays cover a wide
geographical territory, from the botanical garden of Kincaid's Antiguan
childhood, to the Vermont garden that Kincaid tends as an adult, to her
travels to flower shows and on "plant-hunting" expeditions to such far-
flung sites as Kew Gardens, England, and Yunnan Province, China.

Pollan's *Second Nature: A Gardener's Education* (1991) is more nar-
rowly circumscribed within the geography of the U.S. Northeast and
locates itself more directly within a U.S. nature-writing and gardening
tradition. Its primary setting is the rural Connecticut dairy farm that
Pollan, an environmental journalist and the editor of the Modern Library
Gardening series, purchases as a Thoreauvian escape from his Manhattan
apartment. Yet Pollan's garden writing, too, has significant temporal
scope and autobiographical dimension, reflecting back on his childhood
relationship to landscape, and in particular on the postwar suburban
setting of his Jewish family's assimilation into American society. Pollan
observes in *Second Nature* that "much of gardening is a return, an effort
at recovering remembered landscapes" (40). This mnemonic function of
the garden contributes to the articulation of a diasporic identity in both
Kincaid's and Pollan's New World garden writing.

Kincaid's and Pollan's innovative approach to the genre is recognized
in *American Garden Writing: An Anthology,* which excerpts both authors
in a section that was newly added to the 2003 edition. In her preface to
the expanded edition, Bonnie Marranca remarks that she incorporated
this additional material to reflect new directions in the world of gardening and in the genre of garden writing: "Poetic reveries of the garden have
drifted naturally toward politics and culture, without denying the sheer
pleasure of gardening as an activity with often deeply spiritual attachments. Garden writers have simply become more aware of the global implications of local life and increasingly activist in their concerns. But that
just means that they are reconnecting to the ancient tradition which joins
culture and horticulture in a more worldly historical perspective" (xx).
Marranca's preface to the original 1988 edition theorized the garden as

a document of social history, stressing the need to integrate natural and human history into a common framework and suggesting that "horticulture . . . is one more historical portrait of a nation" (xxii). The expanded edition of *American Garden Writing* continues this emphasis on the intimate relationship of natural and social history but suggests that, in part due to the popularity of the personal essay, garden writing has begun to address a greater variety of social and political concerns.

In keeping with these developments, both Kincaid's *My Garden (Book):* and Pollan's *Second Nature* are strongly autobiographical in character as well as deeply preoccupied with history, indicating some of the larger areas of experience that may be effectively engaged by the genre of garden writing. Moreover, Pollan and Kincaid exploit several features of the genre that support a postcolonial reading of New World place. Foremost among these is the garden's capacity to engage the fault line between nature and culture, which as Pollan observes in his introduction to the Modern Library Gardening series, "is always an interesting place for a writer to stand" (xi–xii). For in contrast to wilderness settings such as the forest or the desert, the garden foregrounds rather than suppresses the human presence in nature.

In his garden writing, Pollan interrogates the American belief in wilderness as cure, as well as the assumption of a divide between nature and culture that underpins it. Pollan's *Second Nature* takes aim at two cherished American landscapes, the wilderness and the suburban lawn, proposing the garden as an alternative paradigm. He recalls in *Second Nature* that "like most Americans out-of-doors, I was a child of Thoreau. But the ways of seeing nature I'd inherited from him, and the whole tradition of nature writing he inspired, seemed not to fit my experiences" (3).[4] Deeply influenced by a U.S. nature-writing tradition that posits nature as the cure for culture, Pollan initially attempts to create a wild garden that minimizes evidence of man's interference in nature. When this approach fails, Pollan comes to understand that the ideal of wildness is a false one and instead plants a geometrically-ordered garden. "I guess by now I am more turned off by romantic conceits about nature than by a bit of artifice in the garden," he confesses (*Second Nature* 137).

Pollan complains of the American tendency to privilege observed and untouched landscapes over man-made ones, emphasizing instead the degree to which the natural and social worlds are always intertwined. He notes in *Second Nature* that while the wilderness ideal suggests that nature lies outside of history, "gardens keep throwing us back on the past" (284). In fact, Pollan insists, there is no pure nature or escape from history in an America whose landscape was dramatically transformed by the importation of European plants during the colonial era. On a walk near his rural Connecticut home, Pollan stumbles upon the remains of an abandoned nineteenth-century town which lie "like shadows on the landscape" (*Second Nature* 54). As with Seymour Levin's unearthing of a rusty screwdriver in his landlady's flower garden in Malamud's *A New Life,* or V. S. Naipaul's revelation that there is slavery in Caribbean vegetation, Pollan's discovery of the Connecticut town's remains suggests the irrevocable presence of history in the natural world.

Similarly, Kincaid asserts that, far from being "natural," "The garden is an invention, the garden is an awareness, a self-consciousness, an artifice" (*Among Flowers* 188). In her gardening essays, Kincaid rejects the conventional reading of the garden as an escape from the social world. Instead, she poses the question: "Why must people insist that the garden is a place of rest and repose, a place to forget the cares of the world, a place in which to distance yourself from the painful responsibility that comes with being a human being?" ("Sowers and Reapers" 41). Echoing Pollan's view that gardens invite contemplation of the past, Kincaid's *My Garden (Book):* opens with the declaration that the garden is "an exercise in memory" (8). In Kincaid's reading of it, the garden provides access both to a personal past (her childhood in Antigua) and to a broader historical past (the role of the science of botany in imperial conquest). Thus, she proclaims that "memory is a gardener's real palette; memory as it summons up the past, memory as it shapes the present, memory as it dictates the future" (*My Favorite Plant* xvi).

According to Kincaid, botanical gardens such as that which she frequented as a child in Antigua were subtle agents of colonization: "The botanical garden reinforced for me how powerful were the people who had conquered me; they could bring to me the botany of the world they owned" (*My Garden* 120).[5] The botanical garden, in which the presence of foreign plants in a Caribbean setting was made to seem appropriate, is in her reading a means of naturalizing colonial rule: "To us it was an unusual idea: a garden in which were gathered specimens of plants from various parts of the British Empire; but we soon absorbed it, got used to it, took it for granted, the way we had with another European idea, that of leaving your own native (European) climate and living in places native to other people whom you cannot stand" (143). The botanical garden in turn exposes the closely interconnected trajectories of natural science and colonial expansion. These intersecting histories are embodied in the careers of such "botany thieves" as Carolus Linnaeus, Andreas Dahl, and

Joseph Banks, to whom Kincaid refers in essays such as "In History" and "To Name Is to Possess." Kincaid associates the botanists' activity of collecting plants with colonial rule itself, identifying them as part of one and the same "need to isolate, name, objectify, possess various parts, people, and things in the world" (*My Garden* 143).

Kincaid's investigation of the connections between gardening and conquest resonates with the work of literary critic Mary Louise Pratt and of scholars of colonial botany and landscape design such as historian Richard Drayton and art historian Jill H. Casid. Pratt's and Drayton's studies identify key developments in the history of the natural sciences in order to document the reciprocal relationship between science and empire and to show how the sciences patterned colonial expansion. For example, Pratt's *Imperial Eyes* considers the impact of the globalizing aspirations of Linnaeus's system of plant nomenclature and emphasizes the "transformative, appropriative dimensions" of natural history, which were all the more forceful because they were veiled by its appearance of neutrality and passivity.[6] In her analysis of eighteenth- and nineteenth-century travel narratives, Pratt traces the movement of the naturalist's "imperial eye" as it authoritatively scans the landscape, emptying it of both its inhabitants and its history, while at the same time appearing not to wield any power over that landscape.

Drayton's *Nature's Government* also addresses the role of botany in empire building, revealing how scientific discourses naturalized the exercise of British colonial power and highlighting the role of gardens in the aestheticization of power.[7] Drayton argues that botany played a key role in legitimating colonial rule at the end of the eighteenth century, when the state adopted a new ideology of agricultural improvement. In her discussion of "imperial georgic," Casid makes the related argument that eighteenth-century landscaping practice must be approached as a "technique of empire." Her *Sowing Empire* proposes that "georgic forms of landscape, the picturesque landscape garden, the *ferme ornée* (ornamented farm), and the colonial plantation justified and glorified patriarchally organized and controlled agricultural production and heterosexual reproduction as the necessary bases for family and for national *and imperial* stability" (xxii). Such studies thus echo Kincaid in their suggestion that through the story of the colonial garden "we may explore the history of the world" (Drayton xii).

As both Kincaid and Pollan show, in engaging the fault line between nature and culture and foregrounding the human presence in nature, garden writing proves uniquely suited to the task of registering the historical dimensions of natural phenomena. The nonfiction essay form allows for an extensive consideration of the historical relationships among humans, nature, and science; witness the frequent digressions into colonial New World history that characterize Kincaid's and Pollan's garden writing. In particular, Kincaid's discussion of the botanical garden illustrates the genre's openness to both personal and public history, complementing revisionary academic histories of colonial botany such as Drayton's. Indeed, one of Kincaid's central aims is to situate the garden in the context of colonial history. She does so by presenting the botanical garden and its plant inhabitants as a kind of analogue of the human colony, emphasizing how both plants and humans become subject to the colonizer's will to classify and possess.

Gardening in the Diaspora

The heavily autobiographical character of Kincaid's and Pollan's prose combines with memories of immigration (direct and inherited) to produce a mode of garden writing that exploits the garden's deep associations with rootedness and transplantation, thereby renegotiating the terms of diasporic emplacement. One of the primary means by which Kincaid and Pollan stress the embeddedness of nature in the social world is by pursuing an analogy between human and plant migration. In *The Botany of Desire* (2001), Pollan likens the adaptive capacity of apples to that of successful immigrants to the United States: "Like generations of other immigrants before and after, the apple has made itself at home here. In fact, the apple did such a convincing job of this that most of us wrongly assume the plant is a native" (5–6). Pollan's apples undergo a transformation that parallels that of the Puritans: "Much like the Puritans, who regarded their crossing to America as a kind of baptism or rebirth, the apple couldn't cross the Atlantic without changing its identity—a fact that encouraged generations of Americans to hear echoes of their own story in the story of this fruit" (12). Similarly, Kincaid compares her own migratory propensities to that of a flower in her garden, while also subtly calling attention to race as a contributing factor to the dynamics of mobility: "I moved the *Scabiosa ochroleuca* into the yellow bed—it is yellowish and tall and airy and wants to go everywhere it feels will be susceptible to its presence (I am reminded of myself, except for the yellowish part)" (*My Garden* 27).

In Kincaid's essay "The Glasshouse," the botanical garden of her childhood becomes deeply expressive of the sense of dislocation from which she and other Antiguans suffer. Kincaid associates her childhood encounter with foreign plants in the colonial botanical garden with her own condition as a member of an uprooted and colonized people. In particular, the botanical garden's rubber tree stands out in her memory: "The rubber tree was a massive twist of trunks and roots all coiled up and turned in and out of each other. When first seen by any of us . . . , it was a curiosity; eventually we accepted its presence in our midst, even as we accepted our own presence in our midst, for we, too, were not native to the place we were in" (*My Garden* 145). Fittingly, it is while sitting in the shade of this rubber tree that Kincaid's stepfather tells her of his mother's permanent exile in England and of his father's work on the Panama Canal. Thus, in "The Glasshouse," the botanical garden's transcolonial collection of plants echoes the multiple dislocations to which the Antiguan people have been subjected, even as the botanical garden's exclusion of native Antiguan plants exacerbates the young Kincaid's alienation from her childhood landscape.

In Kincaid's and Pollan's rendering of it, the garden is a space of becoming rather than of being. Kincaid insists that "a garden, no matter how good it is, must never completely satisfy" (Introduction xix). A garden is always a work in progress that can only ever approximate the ideal garden that the gardener envisions in her mind; analogously, the process of diasporic rerooting is always incomplete. Accordingly, a final feature of the genre of garden writing that Kincaid and Pollan exploit is its built-in emphasis on the active and the processual.

Pollan notes that "gardening . . . engages us with the natural world, as actors rather than passive spectators" (Introduction xi). This statement suggests a significant distinction between genres of writing that construct humans as observers of nature and those that construct humans as actively engaged with the landscape. The protagonists of V. S. Naipaul, Derek Walcott, Bernard Malamud, and Philip Roth encounter an observed, rather than acted-upon, landscape. Rarely do these characters interact directly with the landscape, and when they do, their actions are generally ineffectual and comic. Where, by contrast, landscapes are not so much observed as they are landscapes of labor, as in the more politically engaged writing of Joy Kogawa, the protagonists are frequently depicted toiling on the unforgiving land. But Kincaid's and Pollan's garden writing foregrounds labor of a different kind: the labor of identity- and place making. In their writing, the landscape is continually being transformed by human agents in their effort to construct a sense of place. This shift from an observed to an acted-upon landscape is key to their rereading of the garden, and it coincides with the redefinition of identity as processual that we will see in chapter 5 as well. In Kincaid and Pollan, the garden is no static idyll or Eternal Spring awaiting recovery, but instead is the site of ongoing activity and experimentation.

In my reading, one of the primary activities that transpires in Pollan's and especially Kincaid's gardens is the articulation of a diasporic sense of place. In the opening chapter of *Second Nature,* Pollan traces the varying relationships to the land of three successive generations of his Jewish American family. Pollan begins by recounting his Russian Jewish immigrant grandfather's rise in America as a story that revolves around agriculture and land: "Starting out with nothing, selling vegetables from a horse wagon, he eventually built a fortune, first in the produce business and later in real estate" (12). Pollan attributes his maternal grandfather's "obsession" with land to his immigrant desire for financial security: "Grandpa loved land as a reliable if somewhat mystical source of private wealth. No matter what happened in the world, no matter what folly the government perpetrated, land could be counted on to hold and multiply its value" (13). At the same time, his grandfather displayed a farmer's genuine tenderness for the land that coexisted incongruously with his developer's capitalist instincts.

In one of the many autobiographical passages that punctuate *Second Nature,* Pollan recalls his childhood visits to his grandfather's garden in Long Island, which he "judged a paradise." His grandfather's proudest achievement was his vegetable garden, where the young Pollan first experienced "the vegetable sublime": "The vegetable garden in summer made an enchanted landscape, mined with hidden surprises, dabs of unexpected color and unlikely forms that my grandfather had taught me to regard as treasures" (22). While his grandfather's appreciation of his garden was largely utilitarian, Pollan gleaned from his grandfather's garden a lesson in "the hospitality of nature to human habitation": "If I could look at it and see Candyland, he probably saw Monopoly; in both our eyes, this was a landscape full of meaning, one that answered to wishes and somehow spoke in a human language" (22).

For his part, Pollan's father participated in a subsequent phase in evolving Jewish American relationships with the land: postwar suburbanization. Pollan's father's discomfort with the suburban lifestyle revealed itself in his unusual approach to lawn care. While Pollan was growing up in Long Island, his father failed to conform to one of the sacrosanct rules of suburban life: "A single unmowed lawn ruins the whole effect, announcing to the world that all is not well here in utopia. My father couldn't have cared less. He owned the land; he could do whatever he wanted with it. As for the neighbors, he felt he owed them nothing. Ours was virtually the only Jewish family in a largely Catholic neighborhood, and with one or two exceptions, the neighbors had always treated us cooly. Why should he pretend to share their values? If they considered our lawn a dissent from the common will, that was a fair interpretation" (24). Pollan recalls neighbors slowing down as they drove by the offending lawn and then "hitting the gas angrily" in "the sort of move that is second nature to a Klansman" (25). When the neighbors' disapproval became too voluble to ignore, Pollan's father finally took out the lawnmower and proceeded not to tame the lawn, but to carve his initials into it with the mower—after which he retired the mower forever. Pollan's father expressed his ethnic difference through his interaction with the suburban landscape, signing his name upon the lawn in defiance of both suburban etiquette and the Catholic majority. By choosing this particular form of dissent, his father resisted the homogenizing force of the quintessential American landscaping form: the suburban lawn.

Building on both his grandfather's devotion to gardening and his father's nonconformism, Pollan's own garden similarly resists the American lawn's intolerance of difference and insensitivity to the local. His Connecticut garden is a place of unprecedented "juxtapositions and conjoinings": "This place come summer'll be more like a buzzing marketplace, a teeming, polyglot free port city where all manner of diverse and sundry characters—immigrants drawn from near and far, past and present, East and West, upstairs and down—will meet and mingle and fuse in heretofore unimaginable combinations" (*Second Nature* 267). Pollan imagines his garden as a heterogeneous meeting ground that will "brin[g] together far-flung genes in fresh combinations" (268), generating new forms of hybridization. Fundamentally, then, Pollan's garden is a garden of the diaspora. In contrast to the American attachment to pure wilderness or the uniformity of the American lawn, Pollan's New World garden is "a kind of blooming archive, a multicultural, transhistorical crossroad" (265).

It is in this context that we can interpret the discussion of "bloodlines" that accompanies Pollan's survey of the various gardening catalogs, which range from patrician, to mainstream, to radically environmentalist. Pollan expresses a particular dislike for the White Flower gardening catalog, which is Waspy and conservative, and which prefers old pure strains to new hybrids: "Modern hybrids are the garden world's parvenus, the offspring of dubious unions that threaten to dilute the bloodlines of plant society" (249). Indeed, he suspects that "something more than good taste is at stake" in this aversion to hybrids, citing the catalogs' preference for white flowers, which stand at the top of the color hierarchy, as well their obsession with purity and pedigree. In one particularly vivid passage, Pollan fantasizes about the White Flower Farms' annual Open House being crashed by Abbie Hoffman or the Marx Brothers. Thus, for Pollan, the snobbishness of gardening catalogs "sometimes . . . is really just a mask for a much less benign snobbishness about human bloodlines and society" (245). Although Pollan makes no explicit reference in these passages to his Jewishness, his discomfort with the exclusionary racial and class subtext of the gardening catalogs clearly stems from his own family's immigrant history.

Like Pollan's family's gardens and suburban lawns, Kincaid's Vermont garden functions as an arena in which to construct a diasporic identity. At the opening of *My Garden (Book):*, Kincaid recalls "the most peculiar ungardenlike shapes" (7) that her Vermont flowerbeds took on when she first created them, shapes that ultimately came to "resembl[e] a map of the Caribbean and the sea that surrounds it" (8). In an interview, she elaborates on the idiosyncratic process through which she made a garden out of her childhood geography lessons: "Every time I would tell somebody helping me in the garden what I wanted them to do in the garden they would get very upset because you can see the shapes I wanted are odd. The landscape looks like a map. I've made a map: this is an isthmus, this is a peninsula, this is an island, and this is a continent. If you look at it, it's strange. This bed, I call Hispanola: part is Haiti, part is the Dominican Republic" (Interview 793). When Kincaid transforms her Vermont garden into a map of the Caribbean, she defiantly inscribes her identity onto a diasporic landscape in much the same way that Pollan's father had when he carved his initials onto his suburban lawn. As the mapping motif signals, Kincaid's gardening is an act of memory. The Vermont garden can only ever partially approximate the remembered landscape of the Caribbean, however. Rather than reproducing the Caribbean, it generates a hybrid landscape that merges past and present. As with Pollan, then, Kincaid's gardening contributes to her self-fashioning and diasporic emplacement.

If the motif of mapping with which Kincaid opens *My Garden (Book):* is one that speaks to the question of diasporic emplacement, so too is the discussion of the "wild garden" that concludes the book. The theory of the wild garden, developed by the nineteenth-century garden writer William Robinson, appeals to Kincaid because in contrast to formal and rigidly structured garden design, it allows for "the luxury of stating and enjoying the results of your own will, your own idea of how the things in front of you ought to be" (228). More importantly, Robinson rejects the presentation of foreign plants as exotic specimens, instead incorporating only those foreign plants that are well suited to their new environment. "*The idea of the* wild garden," Robinson wrote in 1895, "*is placing plants of other countries, as hardy as our hardiest wild flowers, in places where they will* flourish without further care or costs" (Robinson xix; qtd. in Kincaid 228).

Kincaid is particularly struck by Robinson's belief in foreign plants' capacity for naturalization, noting that the "hardy exotic" plants that Robinson lists have now been so thoroughly indigenized as to have become entirely ordinary.[8] Her discussion of the wild garden reveals that the landscape of England is populated by nonindigenous plants such as the daylily and the marshmallow that now appear quite commonplace. Kincaid celebrates the theory of the wild garden because it rejects conventional gardening practice, which would value a foreign plant solely for its exotic character and insist on its essential difference. Instead, Robinson's model testifies to the possibility of new forms of rerooting. Robinson maintains that "the essential thing to bear in mind is that the plants that go to form [the flora of the northern or temperate regions of vast continents] *are hardy, and will thrive in our climate as well as native plants*" (4).

In her introduction to her edited anthology *My Favorite Plant: Writers and Gardeners on the Plants They Love* (1998), Kincaid recalls the *Meconopsis betonicifolia* that she had seen growing in the garden of gardening consultant Wayne Winterrowd. Kincaid remembers the plant as "growing comfortably in the mountains of Vermont, so far away from the place to which it is endemic, so far away from the place in which it was natural, unnoticed, and so going about its own peculiar ways of perpetuating itself (perennial, biannual, monocarpic or not)" (xvii–xviii). She confesses that she herself never has been able to successfully grow the *Meconopsis betonicifolia*: "It sits there, a green rosette of leaves, looking at me with no bloom. I look back at it myself, without a pleasing countenance" (xvii). And yet despite her frustrations, the *Meconopsis betonicifolia* remains a symbol for Kincaid of the possibility of indigenizing that which is not native to the landscape as well as the unlikely and idiosyncratic forms that this rerooting may take.

Kincaid's discussion of the wild garden and of "diasporic" plants such as the *Meconopsis betonificifolia* indicates the extent to which her garden writing functions to assert her sense of *location* in her adoptive home in Vermont. In Kincaid's novel *Lucy* (1990), botanical imagery primarily serves to express postcolonial alienation, as is indicated by the familiar reference to Wordsworth's infamous daffodils.[9] Yet elsewhere Kincaid's botanical imagery becomes more affirmative, suggesting a capacity for successful transplantation and rerooting. In her essay "Wisteria," for example, she asserts her desire to insert herself into new settings by comparing herself to the *Scabiosa ochroleuca* that "wants to go everywhere it feels will be susceptible to its presence" (*My Garden* 27). In keeping with this desire for rerooting, Kincaid's garden writing not only incorporates numerous travel narratives but also devotes a striking amount of space to questions of house building and home making. In her essay "The House," Kincaid describes her habit of imagining herself living in other people's houses. She is careful, however, to note the identity of the previous owners of her houses in Vermont, as though to call attention to the discontinuity that her own presence signals.

Just as Kincaid's garden is always incomplete, then, so her sense of place is always tenuous. Her foregrounding of her inadequacies as a gardener, of the imperfect nature of the gardening process which is full of doubts, runs contrary to a conception of place as a birthright to be inherited or recovered. Instead of constructing foundational myths that would posit a fixed relationship between a people and a landscape, her consistent emphasis on the anxieties of gardening suggests that creating a sense of belonging is an active and ongoing process. Even as Kincaid affirms the potential for rerooting, her aim is to unsettle: "I am in a state of constant discomfort and I like this state so much I would like to share it" (*My Garden* 229).

Plant Hunting with Jamaica Kincaid

At the moments in which Kincaid seems most secure in her sense of place, she challenges her reader to question this complacency. In particular, her plant-hunting writing, which parodies New World exploration narratives, powerfully exposes the contradictions that attend a postcolonial sense of place. As many of the excerpts included in the anthology *American Garden Writing* attest, the genre of garden writing has strong historical ties to travel and exploration writing. The eighteenth-, nineteenth-, and early-twentieth-century texts that are excerpted in a section of the anthology entitled "Travelers and the Travels of Plants" combine natural history with travel and exploration narrative and establish garden writing as a significant subgenre of colonial New World writing. In tracing this literary tradition, the editor of the anthology celebrates the achievements of such figures as the early-twentieth-century naturalist Ernest K. Wilson, "one of the last of the great, bold plant hunters" (Marranca 209). Kincaid's appropriation of the plant-hunting narrative is, by contrast, much more politically charged.[10]

In her preface to *In the Land of the Blue Poppies: The Collected Plant-Hunting Writings of Frank Kingdon Ward,* Kincaid identifies a genre that she terms "the literature of discovery and description of the new landscape" (xiii). Reading this canon of literature, which extends from Columbus to Lewis and Clark, Joseph Dalton, and Kingdon Ward, she experiences "pleasurable disturbances" (Preface xiii). In her own plant-hunting writing, Kincaid both joins in and disrupts this literary tradition. In her essay "Plant Hunting in China," which details a seed-collecting expedition, Kincaid alludes to the tradition of botanical exploration narratives. Throughout the essay, Kincaid distances herself from the plant-hunting narrative by repeatedly referring to other members of the plant-hunting expedition as "the botanists." She documents their behavioral patterns as though she were conducting a sociological study: "In Zhongdian, . . . I noticed this about the botanists: wherever they found themselves, they looked forward to the next place" (*My Garden* 201). Yet at the same time that she is differentiating herself from the botanists, as a member of the expedition Kincaid is necessarily implicated in the plant-hunting narrative and comes to embody the figure of the "botany thief" whom she so frequently attacks in her garden writing. The series of nervous breakdowns that she suffers over the course of the expedition may be read as symptomatic of her discomfort with her participation in this narrative.

Kincaid's breakdowns also bespeak the acute alienation that she experiences in China. Increasingly, over the course of "Plant Hunting in China," Kincaid strategically exaggerates her sense of estrangement in China in order to assert the depth of her rootedness in Vermont, to which she longs to return: "A week passed by after I left my family and I missed them and I missed my surroundings in Vermont; I was almost on the edge of the world (the world as I have come to know it); I could still speak to them directly through a telephone, but I was beginning to think that everything I had known, everyone I had known, was very far away and I might not be able to get back to them" (*My Garden* 200). Kincaid's overpowering homesickness would seem to confirm her status as an American who rightfully belongs with her family and her garden in Vermont, where her presence is sorely missed. Yet her unflattering portrayal of herself as an insensitive American tourist who complains about the food and the bathrooms in China and in general exhibits "monumentally rude and truly insulting behavior" (*My Garden* 200) implies that the cost of her successful Americanization may be an arrogance that attends this new-found sense of security. Thus, while claiming a sense of place, "Plant Hunting in China" also registers the tensions surrounding Kincaid's ambiguous status as both colonized Caribbean subject and privileged American garden owner. By casting herself in the role of the overbearing "plant appropriator" whom she has so often reproached, Kincaid at once proclaims that she has successfully rerooted herself in Vermont and signals the troubling implications of her diasporic emplacement.[11]

Kincaid continues to foreground these contradictions in *Among Flowers: A Walk in the Himalaya* (2005), her contribution to National Geographic's travel-writing series. In this memoir of her month-long seed-collecting expedition to Nepal, Kincaid inhabits the plant-hunting narrative yet more fully than she had done in "Plant Hunting in China." At the same time, her participation in this narrative remains something of an anomaly. As a member of the plant-hunting expedition to Nepal, Kincaid is both a figure of privilege and a curiosity: "They were used to seeing people who looked like Bleddyn, Sue, and Dan, people of European descent. They were not used to seeing people like me, someone of African descent, but they knew of our existence" (28). During the expedition, Kincaid attracts more attention than do her companions; one Nepalese woman is fascinated by her hair, while another insists to Kincaid that she is wearing a mask, that her face is not her true face. Throughout, Kincaid remains conscious of the inequalities that underlie the comforts that she has come to expect as an American: "It was the created injustices that led to me being here, dependent on Sherpas, for without this original injustice, I would not be in Nepal and the Sherpas would be doing something not related to me" (84). And yet in the same breath, she confesses her desire to maintain her privileged position: "They should bend to our demands, among which was to make us comfortable when we wanted to be comfortable" (84).

Among Flowers, like Kincaid's earlier plant-hunting and gardening essays, suggests that journeys such as her trek in the Himalayas are inextricably bound up with the literary tradition of natural history exploration narrative that precedes them. Kincaid's journey to Nepal begins with a visit to a bookstore in Kathmandu that specializes in the literature of exploration. There she purchases *The Kanchenjunga Adventure,* an account of the mountaineer Frank Smythe's 1930 climbing expedition that she reads throughout the trip: "Among the thrills of reading it was becoming familiar with some people and a terrain between the pages of his book and outside the book, this at the same time" (104). Thus, for

Kincaid the terrain of plant hunting does not exist independently of its literary representations but rather is coextensive with them, an insight that gives added weight to her own contributions to the genre.[12]

Kincaid's primary intervention into the plant-hunting narrative in "Plant Hunting in China" and *Among Flowers* is to call attention both to its strong appeal and to its troubling reliance on structures of power that make the Nepalese and Chinese landscapes available for consumption by Western tourists, mountaineers, botanists, and prosperous gardeners such as herself. One of the plant-hunting narrative's key moves, she recognizes, is to transform the everyday realities and routines of ordinary people into a "spectacle" for the benefit of "people from rich countries" (*Among Flowers* 185–86). In *Among Flowers,* Kincaid resists reproducing these structures: "I saw the people and took them in, but I made no notes on them, no description of their physical being since I could see that they could not do the same to me" (77). Yet at the same time, she revels in the pleasures of travel and eagerly anticipates how the plants that she has collected in Nepal will flourish in her Vermont garden. The photographs included in *Among Flowers* alternate between ethnographic images of Nepalese villagers and mock-heroic scenes of Kincaid negotiating the dramatic landscape. These photographs, which at once perpetuate the standard visual language of exploration narratives and disturb this language by drawing attention to Kincaid's racial difference, heighten the sense of ambiguity surrounding her participation in the expedition.[13]

In one of her garden essays, Kincaid complains of "the absence of this admission, this contradiction: perhaps every good thing that stands before us comes at a great cost to someone else" (*My Garden* 152). In another essay, she implicates herself more directly in this critique: "And I thought how I had crossed a line; but at whose expense? I cannot begin to look, because what if it is someone I know? I have joined the conquering class; who else could afford this garden—a garden in which I grow things that it would be much cheaper to buy at the store?" (*My Garden* 123). In such statements, Kincaid alludes to the asymmetrical power relations that have made tropical plants available for Western appropriation and consumption as well as the land, labor, wealth, and leisure time necessary to sustain a garden such as her own. But in the context of Kincaid's larger awareness of the extent to which human and botanical displacement historically have gone hand in hand in the Americas, such ethical qualms also would seem to apply to prior human presences on the land that have been expropriated in order that she might occupy her Vermont garden.[14]

Garden Writing and Ecocriticism

One of the striking features of Kincaid's and Pollan's garden writing is the extent to which it incorporates a historical awareness of the patterns of ecological change that accompanied the human colonization of the New World. Pollan's entangled reading of American nature in particular emphasizes that human settlement always goes hand in hand with botanical dispersion and transformation. In *Second Nature,* he points out (as do Naipaul and Kincaid in a Caribbean context) that many plants often thought to be indigenous to the United States were in fact imported by Europeans: "Working in concert, European weeds and European humans proved formidable ecological imperialists, rapidly driving out native species and altering the land to suit themselves. The new plant species thrived because they were consummate cosmopolitans, opportunists superbly adapted to travel and change. In a sense, the invading species had less in common with the retiring, provincial plants they ousted than with the Europeans themselves" (133). The domestication of the American frontier was facilitated by the distribution of apple seeds, which Pollan presents from the "plant's-eye view" as having a kind of intentionality. It is in this spirit that Pollan refers in his chapter on the apple in *The Botany of Desire* to the "biological settlement of the West": "Everyone knows that the settlement of the West depended on the rifle and the ax, yet the seed was no less instrumental in guaranteeing Europeans' success in the New World" (42). Such observations generate a more critical reading of the West and of American nature than the dehistoricized one that Seymour Levin initially espouses in *A New Life* or that Seymour Levov pursues through his admiration for Johnny Appleseed in *American Pastoral.* Pollan's garden writing powerfully debunks the American vision of nature—and of the West in particular—as a refuge from history and as the space of new beginnings.

Pollan's interest in "ecological imperialism"[15] and his keen awareness of how European colonization transformed both the ecological and the human landscapes of North America indicate that garden writing may be a genre that is amenable to an ecocritical or environmentalist reading. In *Second Nature,* however, Pollan is sharply critical of the tendency among U.S. environmentalists to privilege nature over culture and to conceive of wilderness as hallowed: "Thoreau, and his many heirs among contemporary naturalists and radical environmentalists, assume that human culture is the problem, not the solution. So they urge us to shed our anthropocentrism and learn to live among other species as equals. This sounds like a fine, ecological idea, until you realize that the earth would be even worse off if we started behaving any more like animals than we already do" (135–36). The lesson that Pollan learns in the garden—"to be less afraid to exercise human power in nature, to do what is necessary to make the land conform to our designs and supply our needs" (147)—must sound nothing short of blasphemous to an environmentalist's ears. And yet it is precisely in this revelation about the appropriateness of human intervention in nature that Pollan locates his environmental philosophy, a philosophy based on the idea of the garden rather than the wilderness. Pollan's "garden ethic" posits that culture and nature are deeply entangled rather than sharply opposed. Rejecting the dualistic character of some environmentalist thought, Pollan emphasizes that there is no wilderness that lies beyond the reach of history. His is an environmental ethic that is unromantic, focused on the local, and "frankly anthropocentric" in situating man in, rather than outside of, nature.

In *The Botany of Desire,* Pollan continues to trouble the nature/culture opposition by tracing "the social history of . . . plants" and the "natural history of the human imagination" (xviii). Here, however, Pollan departs somewhat from the anthropocentric perspective that he had embraced in *Second Nature* by placing new emphasis on plant agency—on "the plant's point of view" (xvi). This revised framework is one in which plants and humans evolve as partners "in a coevolutionary relationship [in which] every subject is also an object, every object a subject" (xxi). Notably, it is only when Pollan takes some distance from the garden and the genre of garden writing, as he does in *The Botany of Desire,* that his nature writing becomes more "biocentric" and more compatible with ecocriticism. By contrast, Pollan's meditations on the garden in *Second Nature* exhibit a strained relationship to U.S. environmentalist movements.

Ecocriticism, while a field that is still taking shape, may be understood as having two basic aims: to expose the fallacious notion that there is no "nature" outside the text, and to encourage a shift from an anthropocentric to an "earth-centered" perspective that acknowledges the current global environmental crisis.[16] The genre of garden writing tends to work against the latter agenda, privileging the realm of culture and celebrating human participation in (and control over) nature. Garden writing has received little attention in the growing body of ecocritical scholarship, indicating that if nonfiction nature writing has been the focus of ecocriticism, it would seem that only *certain* genres of nature writing favor an ecocritical approach. As Dominic Head points out, the novel also may be a difficult genre to harness to an ecocritical project by virtue of its built-in emphasis on textuality and human subjectivity.[17] Indeed, the human-centered pastoralism of the novels discussed in previous chapters does not readily invite an ecocritical reading. And while the Caribbean novels that I will consider in chapter 5 conceive of the marvelous landscape as dynamic rather than as the passive object of human control, they nonetheless also tend to retain an anthropocentric viewpoint. From an ecocritical perspective, then, both the garden writing and the fiction and poetry considered in this study may appear hopelessly anthropocentric despite their profound preoccupation with landscape.

Genre may not be the only impediment to the application of an ecocritical reading to these texts, however. Susie O'Brien suggests in a provocative discussion of Kincaid's gardening essays that Kincaid's resistance to ecocritical approaches is symptomatic of larger tensions between postcolonialism and ecocriticism, tensions that ecocritics have tended to elide in their increasing efforts to render their discussions more inclusive of multicultural voices (O'Brien, "The Garden and the World").[18] A number of volumes have aimed to "internationalize" the predominantly U.S.-centered field of ecocriticism and to embrace ethnic minority literatures as well as to move away from ecocriticism's traditional emphasis on nonfiction. For example, in their introduction to their edited book *Beyond Nature Writing*, Karla Armbruster and Kathleen R. Wallace maintain that "if ecocriticism limits itself to the study of one genre—the personal narratives of the Anglo-American nature writing tradition—or to one physical landscape—the ostensibly untrammeled American wilderness—it risks seriously misrepresenting the significance of multiple natural and built environments to writers with other ethnic, national, or racial affiliations. If such limits are accepted, ecocritics risk ghettoizing ecocriticism within literary and cultural studies generally" (7). Yet, from another corner, ecocritics who are more hostile to postmodernism and more skeptical of constructivist views of nature may be inclined to frame the question of multicultural literatures rather differently. Ecocritics sometimes seem to see their project as being in competition with postcolonial and gender studies, or at least as having diverging theoretical investments.[19] Accordingly, in *Practical Ecocriticism*, Glen A. Love intimates that a multicultural agenda may be at odds with the interests of ecocriticism when he writes that postmodernism "has done much to raise our awareness of the national, ethnic, racial, gender, and other lenses through which we interpret reality. But it cannot long be ignored that our constructions occur always within the overarching context of an autonomously existing system that we call nature" (26).

Responding to these debates within ecocriticism itself, O'Brien argues that the assumption on the part of many ecocritics that ecocritical and postcolonial projects will necessarily be aligned needs to be reconsidered in light of their conflicting conceptions of the relationship between nature and culture. For where ecocritics tend to privilege the realm of nature, postcolonial critics are more apt to put their emphasis on the cultural sphere, often to the exclusion of any consideration of the physical environment. If postcolonial critics need to pay more attention to the physical world, then "ecocritics need to acknowledge the possibility that literary theory and ecology are not compatible" (O'Brien, "The Garden and the World" 182). Indeed while ecocriticism's call for more direct contact with the physical world produces a mode of criticism that tends to reinforce a nature/culture dualism, the garden writing of Pollan and Kincaid privileges the realm of culture in order to insist upon the indivisibility of the natural and social worlds. As we have seen, Pollan's and Kincaid's garden writing advances a postcolonial sense of place by calling attention to the profound presence of human culture in the natural world and to our heavily mediated relationship with the physical environment.

One might have thought that ecocriticism and postcolonialism would find a meeting ground in Kincaid, whose garden writing is uniquely informed by a postcolonial sensibility. Instead, as O'Brien convincingly argues, contemporary ecocriticism's indebtedness to an American wilderness ideology that divorces nature and culture perplexes the relationship of postcolonial garden writing such as Kincaid's to environmental movements. Kincaid's garden writing gives little overt consideration to environmental concerns,[20] which may account for her absence from even those ecocritical discussions that engage multicultural and postcolonial literatures. As O'Brien notes, Kincaid's admittedly bourgeois gardening practice—gardening for pleasure rather than sustenance—is difficult to reconcile with the ecological imperative to exploit nature only according to necessity.[21] And like Pollan, she expresses an attitude toward the nonhuman world that is far from reverential. When her gardening efforts are spoiled by raccoons and rabbits, Kincaid gleefully plots their demise, desisting only when "three whining pacifists" (her husband and her two children) voice their objections.

Perhaps most revealing, however, is Kincaid's self-presentation as a privileged plant hunter. Mimicking the "thefts" carried out by colonial botanists, Kincaid denies the possibility of innocent contact with nature unmediated by the relationships of power that resulted in the creation of botanical gardens in the colonial Caribbean of her childhood. Rather than breaking out of these power structures, Kincaid ironically reproduces them, as though rehearsing the botanical conquest of the New World. Far from embracing a biocentric perspective, Kincaid insistently draws attention to her participation as a gardener in the conquest of nature in order to expose the contested character of all New World emplacements. Thus, the very features that tend to make Kincaid's garden writing unreceptive to an ecocritical reading—its built-in anthropocentrism and emphasis on the primacy of culture—are also the features that enable her exploration of the often vexed relationship between landscape and postcolonial belonging.

5 Marvelous and Gothic Gardens in Shani Mootoo, Gisèle Pineau, and Maryse Condé

I remember the lingering fragrances that lay thick in my childhood world. I feel that then all the surrounding land was rich with these perfumes that never left you: the ethereal smell of magnolias, the essence of tuberoses, the discreet stubbornness of dahlias, the dreamy penetration of gladioli. All these flowers have disappeared, or almost. . . . The land has lost its smells. Like almost everywhere else in the world.

—Edouard Glissant, *Caribbean Discourse*

IN THE epigraph to this chapter, Edouard Glissant muses on the flowers of his childhood landscape, conjuring up a vision of the Caribbean island as an Edenic garden. Yet as the passage continues, Glissant rejects this paradisal vision, insisting that "these thoughts on flowers are not a matter of lamenting a vanished idyll in the past" (*Caribbean Discourse* 52). While renouncing the search for a lost paradise, however, he continues to locate future Caribbean visions within the natural realm: "We dream of what we will cultivate in the future, and we wonder vaguely what the new hybrid that is already being prepared for us will look like, since in any case we will not rediscover them as they were, the magnolias of former times" (52).[1] This chapter examines some of the "new hybrids" that are currently being cultivated by contemporary Caribbean women writers who, like Glissant, maintain a strong attachment to landscape while at the same time interrogating the Caribbean literary traditions, both colonial and postcolonial, that have relied so heavily on botanical registers of imagery. In the rural Caribbean novels of Shani Mootoo, Gisèle Pineau, and Maryse Condé, Edenic motifs intermingle with gothic, dystopian landscape imagery, as well as with natural scientific, ethnographic, and touristic discourses about island nature. These contrasting landscape ideas are deployed in Mootoo's *Cereus Blooms at Night* (1996), Pineau's *The Drifting of Spirits* (*La Grande Drive des esprits*, 1993) and Condé's *Crossing the Mangrove* (*Traversée de la mangrove*, 1989) within a marvelous framework that calls attention to their discursive status.

Mootoo, Pineau, and Condé expose the limitations of inherited landscape ideas that inform established models of Caribbean identity, but do so without as a consequence abandoning the rural in favor of the city.[2] Instead, they elaborate an alternative Caribbean landscape aesthetics that reimagines identity as conditioned by a dynamic interaction between place and displacement. Because their interest lies in reterritorialization as well as deterritorialization, emplacement as well as displacement, they focus their attention on rural spaces, which in their novels become sites in which to explore the mutual interdependence of roots and routes. In so doing, they engage a wide variety of discourses and landscape ideas that historically have been brought to bear on the Caribbean landscape, taking as their primary reference point the master narrative of the Caribbean garden as the site of the recovery of a prelapsarian identity. Mootoo, Pineau, and Condé disrupt this master narrative by reframing the relationship between the garden and exile and by challenging the conventional gendering of the garden narrative.

In all three novels, marvelous motifs combine with gothic elements to undermine the truth claims of realist narratives, including exploration, scientific, and ethnographic discourses. The novels present semi-fantastical worlds, folk fables of love and suffering that take place against a vivid natural setting. They privilege extrarational orders of experience: Pineau's Léonce possesses supernatural powers as a result of the caul with which he is born, and he converses with the ghost of his dead grandmother who appears before him in his garden. Condé's Mama Sonson sees into the future, and several characters seek or make contact with ancestral spirits over the course of her novel. Mootoo's protagonist Mala appears to be more in touch with vegetable life than with human society and engages in an "uncanny communion" with the plants that surround her (163). Moreover, if marvelous motifs of clairvoyance and spirits shape the action of *Spirits* and *Mangrove*, in *Cereus* the magical powers of transformation that both plants and people exhibit coincide with the novel's interest in the transgression of borders.

While signaling the three novels' investment in the marvelous, the presence of supernatural forces also evokes gothic literary traditions. The gothic, which has connections to the sublime as well as the marvelous, exposes the limits of realist narrative by drawing attention to extrarational

dimensions of experience. The gothic performs its critique of Enlightenment rationalism in part by excavating a past that will not be laid to rest.
In the gothic discourses surrounding the U.S. South and the Caribbean,
the suppressed history that resurfaces tends to revolve around the institution of slavery and its violent distortion of the family structure (as Toni
Morrison's *Beloved* [1987] notably attests). In keeping with this gothic
New World tradition, the landscapes of *Spirits* and *Mangrove* in particular are haunted by the ghosts of the slavery past.

The marvelous and gothic Caribbean landscapes that Pineau, Mootoo,
and Condé present encourage the reader to question the assumptions
about identity and place that inform New World landscape representation.
In contrast to Kogawa's unselfconscious primitivism or Malamud's and
Roth's uncritical perpetuation of settlement narratives, Pineau, Mootoo,
and Condé invite scrutiny of the narrative conventions and landscape
ideas they deploy by presenting them within a marvelous framework that
problematizes the status of "reality." Similarly, the gothic motifs that they
incorporate challenge the forms and categories of rationality that colonial
discourses about the Caribbean landscape inscribe, unsettling received
ideas through their estranging quality. At the same time, their novels reference a range of lenses through which the colonial landscape has been
viewed, not only literary but also historical and scientific, so that no single
image of the Caribbean Islands can obtain a stable authority.

The first section of this chapter traces the motif of the redemptive retreat
into island nature as it is exemplified in a foundational Caribbean novel
by Jacques Roumain and subsequently revised by Maryse Condé. While
Condé alludes to various Caribbean literary programs and the representations of nature upon which they draw (including Roumain's brand
of primitivism), Pineau and Mootoo mimic nineteenth- and twentieth-
century travel and scientific discourses. Accordingly, in the following
sections, I show how the proliferation of landscape ideas in the three
novels, including natural and social scientific discourses as well as the
overlapping discourses of the marvelous and the gothic, signals the con-
structedness of all images of Caribbean nature. Finally, the remaining
portions of this chapter consider the garden as a site of regeneration and
emplacement, in order to illustrate how, like the Caribbean and North
American authors considered in previous chapters, Condé, Pineau, and
Mootoo contest exclusionary representations of New World landscape.
They do so, however, by simultaneously engaging a variety of discourses
about nature, their wide-ranging approach making possible a profound

critique of Caribbean landscape ideas and the constructions of identity that these landscape ideas promote.

The Caribbean Garden Narrative in Roumain and Condé

Caribbean writers come to the landscape and to the garden in particular bearing a considerable historical burden. The figure of the Caribbean garden is deeply embedded in the European paradisal vision of the Americas that fueled colonial exploration in the sixteenth and seventeenth centuries.[3] While the early explorers' hopes of recovering the original Garden of Eden in the New World were eventually abandoned, paradisal associations with the Caribbean persisted, shifting by the beginning of the eighteenth century to accommodate the taste for cultivated, pastoral landscapes, and then in the late eighteenth century to reflect an emerging interest in wild, sublime scenes. Thus, as Mimi Sheller and Ileana Rodríguez have shown, Edenic and pastoral motifs were increasingly superseded by romantic and sublime descriptions of the Caribbean landscape, which circulated in natural scientific and travel literatures and the illustrations that accompanied them.[4]

At the same time that it recalls this set of paradisal and sublime associations, the figure of the garden in a Caribbean context necessarily evokes its dark underside: the plantation. Accordingly, in contemporary Caribbean writing, the paradisal landscape often is haunted by the historical legacy of plantation agriculture and the slave labor that sustained the plantation economy. In addition, the figure of the Caribbean garden recalls the kitchen and provision gardens that were sometimes allotted to slaves, and which potentially offered slaves the possibility of greater independence and control over their physical and financial well-being.[5] Finally, as the garden writing of Jamaica Kincaid testifies, the Caribbean botanical garden bears witness to the historical participation of the natural sciences in the colonial project and, more fundamentally, to the reciprocal relationship of science and empire (see chapter 4).

The persistence of paradisal and natural scientific readings of New World nature and the historical aftermath of the plantation combine to ensure the continued reliance of twentieth-century Caribbean writing on the trope of the regenerative Edenic garden that promises sanctuary from history and a return to origins. Indeed, the search for precolonial and preslavery origins through a retreat into nature is one of the dominant motifs of Caribbean and New World writing.[6] This impulse is particularly strong among Negritude writers, who appropriated the European narrative of the New World as the place of lost origins that could be recovered through renewed contact with nature, but, as this chapter attests, the influence of what I am terming the "garden narrative" can also be traced across anglophone and francophone Caribbean writing more broadly.[7]

One particularly instructive and influential example of the garden narrative is Haitian novelist Jacques Roumain's *Masters of the Dew* (*Gouverneurs de la rosée* [1944]).[8] *Masters of the Dew* portrays the return of a Haitian peasant to his native island after a fifteen-year period of exile in Cuba and his role in healing the community that he had left behind, which has been torn apart by a feud and devastated by a terrible drought. As a heroic figure, Manuel displays above all a fealty to place. In Roumain's novel, the strength of the bond between humans and nature is emphasized through repeated comparisons of the characters to plants, flowers, and trees, and Manuel is depicted as having a strong connection to the earth. Not only are the characters likened to nature but nature is also given human attributes (veins, kidneys, hands, skin), this reciprocity of imagery further underscoring the link between the human and the natural worlds. The severity of the crime of betraying one's roots is illustrated symbolically in *Masters of the Dew* when the peasants' inadvertent erosion of the roots of their crops leads to hunger and impoverishment. As Manuel pointedly asks: "Can a man desert the soil? Can he turn his back on it? Can he divorce it without losing the very reason for his existence, the use of his hands, the taste for life?" (107). The garden narrative as it is elaborated by Roumain inscribes an opposition between the garden and exile that also informs not only other foundational Caribbean novels such as Simone Schwarz-Bart's *The Bridge of Beyond* (*Pluie et vent sur Telumée miracle* [1972]) but more recent Caribbean writing such as Michelle Cliff's *No Telephone to Heaven* (1987).

In *Masters of the Dew*, Manuel seeks an end to exile by retreating deeper into the mountains, as he looks for a source of water to irrigate the fields of his village. His movement away from the coast and the plantations into the remote areas of the hinterland mimics the maroon trajectories to which he is heir. According to the spatial logic of the novel, the garden functions as a refuge from corrupting outside forces. Manuel brings his lover Annaïse to a secret spot in the mountains where he has discovered a spring, and the pair are transformed into a Caribbean Adam and Eve: "We're far away, Manuel, we're at the very end of the world," Annaïse declares. "At the beginning of the world, you mean," Manuel corrects her. "Because at the beginning of beginnings, there were a woman and a man like you and me. The first spring flowed at their feet, and the woman and the man entered the spring and bathed in life" (117). In this Edenic scene, Roumain constructs a myth of origins, as Manuel and Annaïse's sexual union coincides with the discovery of the water source that is also the life source of the peasantry. It is by recovering this magical Eden that Manuel will ensure the renewal of his people and bring about the genesis of a new Haitian peasantry. Thus, Roumain reproduces the European vision of the New World as the site of origins, as a Garden of Eden awaiting recovery.

Maryse Condé's *Mangrove* replies to Roumain's novel and the garden narrative it embodies both by explicitly citing *Masters of the Dew* and through its broader reinterpretation of the Caribbean landscape.[9] In addition, Césairean poetics and the Créolité movement become the target of Condé's highly irreverent satire over the course of the novel. The action of the novel unfolds against the backdrop of the dense and twisting forest surrounding the remote Guadeloupean village of Rivière au Sel. The villagers have gathered for the wake of Francis Sancher, the mysterious and tormented stranger who has died "no natural death" (10).[10] The members of the community take turns narrating from their diverging perspectives the events surrounding Francis Sancher's brief period of residence in Rivière au Sel. In addition to Sancher's disruptive presence, numerous other creolized and displaced figures, such as the part-Chinese Moïse the Postman, the Indo-Caribbean Ramsaran family, and several Haitian migrant laborers, come together to create a highly heterogeneous community.

As its title suggests, Condé's novel relies heavily on landscape and botanical imagery to advance an inclusive and pluralistic vision of Caribbean society. Critics have noted that *Mangrove* signals a return to Antillean space on the part of an author who has long exhibited a marked ambivalence toward the nativist project of constructing a Caribbean identity. Indeed, with this novel Condé returns not only to the Caribbean but to the rural Caribbean, joining in a tradition of Caribbean peasant literature.[11] Yet in so doing, Condé significantly revises the meaning of the rural, eschewing the ethnographic impulse to locate an authentic folk culture as well as the discourse of origins and reconnection favored by Roumain. Instead, in her rendering of it, the Caribbean countryside becomes a dynamic and heterogeneous space, while the Guadeloupean peasantry are revealed to be plural and hybridized rather than authentic embodiments of a static localized culture.

As is indicated by the novel's title, its central image is the mangrove. The tangled mangrove typifies the larger landscape of Rivière au Sel, which is distinguished by its density, opacity, and twisting depths. As the members of the community gather at the wake of the mysterious stranger Francis Sancher to describe their encounters with him, in the course of the series of stories that each character tells about Sancher, his or her particular relationship to this landscape emerges. Rosa Ramsaran, who, like so many members of the community, is a relative newcomer to Rivière au Sel, recounts that she had at first reacted unfavorably to the "dark green tangled mass of trees, creepers and parasites" and "formidable mountains," which contrasted with the open, flat landscape of her childhood in the Grands-Fonds. However, she is eventually won over by the deep woods of Rivière au Sel, wandering its paths or choosing to "sit between [the trees'] roots and stay there for hours on end" (132). Throughout the novel, Condé's characters walk the forest's winding paths or commune with specific features of the landscape. Condé's protagonists tend to locate themselves in relation to the landscape in their narratives; most strikingly, Francis Sancher with his mysterious origins is repeatedly depicted sitting on a tree trunk, symbol of an abortive genealogy. But many others seek refuge in the landscape as well: Mira in the Gully, Aristide in the mountains, Dodose Pélagie in the Bois l'Etang, Xantippe in his Creole garden.

While the motif of nature as refuge suggests a separation of the natural and social worlds, Rivière au Sel's landscape is significantly marked by its contact with modernity. Moreover, Rivière au Sel's physical landscape is deeply expressive of the dislocations that characterize its social landscape. Two prominent families of Rivière au Sel, the Lameaulnes and the Ramsarans, are each engaged in exploiting the landscape for profit. Loulou Lameaulnes fantasizes that his flower nursery will become the royal purveyor of flowers to the Queen of England, while his son attends a flower show in the United States and anticipates charging tourists admission to view his Guadeloupean garden. For their part, the Ramsarans reap profits from breeding artificial crayfish and various crops that recall the agriculture of the plantation. The Lameaulnes and the Ramsaran dynasties, founded by a white Creole from Martinique and a laborer of Indian extraction, respectively, are both mixed-race families who remain somewhat apart from their adoptive community. The Ramsarans' slogan "Buy local. Buy Ramsaran crayfish" (9) takes on a particular poignancy in the context of the taunt of "Kouli malaba isi dan pa peyiw!" ("Coolie malabar, this country's not yours!") that greets Ti-Tor Ramsaran when he purchases four acres of land in Rivière au Sel (7–8). For the Ramsarans to describe their product—and by extension themselves—as "local" is to assert their connection to the landscape in defiance of the xenophobia that they encounter. Over the course of the novel, the Ramsarans are joined by many other outsiders who struggle to find acceptance in Rivière au Sel, so that their predicament comes to seem more typical than not of this heterogeneous community.

In a chapter entitled "Carmélien," Condé explicitly parodies Roumain's simpler solution to the problem of origins in *Masters of the Dew*. After reading Roumain's novel in school, Carmélien Ramsaran mimics Roumain's hero's search for the spring that will save his people, but his adolescent male fantasy of mastering nature is thwarted: "At night he dreamed he too was master of the water, irrigating the grateful soil, ordering the pumpkins and eggplants to grow, and he would wake up in surprise in a pool of urine that would bring down Rosa's wrath in the morning, so that he would try to make up his bed on the sly" (143–44). Thus, the heroic masculinity of Roumain's Manuel, which Carmélien attempts to mimic, is quickly deflated, just as Xantippe's Césairean fantasy of wielding an Adamic power over nature will later be undercut. So too Carmélien's interracial desire for Mira Lameaulnes (who stands in for Roumain's Annaïse) is frustrated by Mira's racial intolerance. Mira staves off Carmélien's romantic overtures with the familiar taunt of "Kouli malaba!" (147). The interracial romance between the Indo-Caribbean Carmélien and the light-skinned Mira (while remaining unrealized) runs contrary to Roumain's organizing metaphor of the spring, which suggests a single and fixed source of Haitian identity.

In Condé's rewriting of Roumain's novel, Caribbean nature is not a bounded space tied to a single identity but instead opens itself up to a variety of diasporic perspectives—Indian, Chinese, Haitian, white Creole, as well as African. The rural is marked in Condé's rendering as much by mobility as it is by stasis, as much by the gesture of wandering the forests' paths as by sitting on the trees' roots. At the same time, the landscape remains highly localized, the characters exhibiting a strong attachment to the land. In Condé's reading, then, botanical imagery does not support an ideology of stable, singular roots but rather one of diversity and mixture. Place and identity are presented as processual in Condé's novel; crossing the mangrove is an act that can never be completed, as one character memorably points out. Yet the novel's insight into the instability of place and its relationship to identity does not result in a denial of nature's capacity to comfort and to nourish: "Only there, among the giant trees, the marbri, châtaignier, candlewood, mastwood and Caribbean pines, did

[Aristide] feel at home" (46). If Condé's model of identity is processual and dynamic, her reading of the Caribbean globalized rather than insular, place nonetheless remains a meaningful category.

Feminist geographer Doreen Massey has called for a more progressive sense of place that would acknowledge the need for an attachment to place but would be "adequate to this era of time-space compression" (237). "The question," Massey writes, "is how to hold on to that notion of geographical difference, of uniqueness, even of rootedness if people want that, without it being reactionary" (241). Her answer is to develop an alternative model that would envision place as processual rather than static, as linked to the global rather than bounded, as having multiple rather than single, unique identities, and as retaining at the same time both meaning and specificity (244–45). Condé's *Mangrove* articulates such a vision of place, but in contrast to Massey's urban focus as well as to anthropologist Liisa Malkki's suspicion of botanical metaphors (see chapter 4), Condé does so by retaining, rather than jettisoning, botanical and landscape imagery. Indeed, it is Condé's presentation of the landscape that enables her to accomplish this reimagination of place and identity.

Natural and Social Scientific Discourses in Mootoo and Pineau

While Condé targets twentieth-century Caribbean aesthetic programs, Mootoo and Pineau thematize the conventions of the colonial exploration and scientific narratives that have so heavily influenced New World landscape representation. In his study *Myth and Archive,* Roberto González Echevarría traces the impact of the rhetorical conventions of scientific discourse on Latin American narrative. According to González Echevarría, while natural scientific writing holds sway in the nineteenth century, in the twentieth century anthropology comes to take its place as the shaping force behind representations of Latin American nature and experience.[12] Mootoo and Pineau write out of anglophone and francophone rather than hispanophone New World traditions, but their respective preoccupations with natural scientific and anthropological discourse suggest that González Echevarría's comments have resonance in other New World contexts as well. Mootoo's and Pineau's novels register the profound influence of natural and social scientific discourses even as they disrupt them.

Mootoo's *Cereus* is set in the fictional Caribbean island of Lantanacamara, apparently in the early twentieth century, among a community of Indian indentured laborers and their descendants. It revolves around the relationship between Tyler, a male nurse recently returned from studying abroad in the "Shivering Northern Wetlands," and his elderly patient Mala Ramchandin, who had once been the proprietor of a mysterious and rather sinister garden. As Tyler cares for Mala at the Paradise Alms House, he gradually uncovers the story of her troubled childhood, her mother's abandonment of her, and the abuse she suffered at the hands of her father.

A marvelous garden serves as the backdrop for the narrative action, as the young Mala retreats into the decaying family home that is increasingly enveloped by the grotesque plants that surround it. Scenes of Nurse Tyler attempting to rehabilitate his patient are intermingled with flashbacks to Mala's childhood and teenage years when she was left at the mercy of her sexually abusive father by the departure of her mother, Sarah, who flees to the Shivering Northern Wetlands with her white lover, Lavinia. During this period, Mala's refuge becomes the garden adjoining her house, which stands at the center of the novel and is also linked to several other gardens. Mala's garden is a magical space that provokes both wonder and repulsion among those who encounter it.

The action of *Cereus* begins in the late nineteenth century, and an important reference point for the novel is the literature of nineteenth-century scientific exploration, as well as its Renaissance antecedents. The names of two key sites in the novel, El Dorado Park and the town of Paradise, recall European exploration narratives and the Renaissance vision of the New World as a lost paradise and a source of fantastic wealth. Moreover, in Mootoo's novel the fabulous world of Mala's garden lies at the center of a problematic exploration narrative.

Reinterpretations of the relationship between botany, gardening, and empire such as Jamaica Kincaid's, which I discussed in chapter 4, help to account for the prominence of the natural sciences in *Cereus,* and in particular for the novel's desire to expose natural science's complicity with the economic and political interests of empire. At various points in the novel, Mootoo draws attention to the colonial practice of exporting plants from the colonies to botanical gardens in the Mother Country. Upon first encountering the cereus plant at the almshouse, Tyler instantly recognizes it from "the Exotic Items Collection of the SNW [Shivering Northern Wetlands] National Botanical Gardens" that he had visited while studying in the Wetlands (23). When the young Mala learns of what she believes to be her impending departure for the Wetlands, she sets about collecting seeds and cuttings from the garden to take with her, mimicking the activities of colonial botanists who exported exotic plants from the New World to the Old. The figure of the naturalist is represented in *Cereus* by Mala's lover, Ambrose Mohanty, who has recently returned from studying entomology abroad. In addition, small line drawings of various species of insects scattered throughout the text playfully evoke the illustrations that nineteenth-century naturalists habitually included in their diaries and publications.

Canadian writer George Bowering's novel *Burning Water* (1980) also highlights the role of the naturalist in eighteenth-century British colonial exploration, depicting the Scottish botanist Archibald Menzies as a more enlightened and benevolent foil to British explorer George Vancouver, whose imperialistic ambition is insatiable. Bowering's Vancouver and Menzies are bitter enemies, so much so that the novel ends with the naturalist's (historically inaccurate) murder of the British naval officer. In *Cereus,* by contrast, the interests of colonial power and the natural sciences are allied. Indeed, Ambrose Mohanty, who becomes a naturalist while studying in the Wetlands, is one of the most thoroughly colonized of Mootoo's characters. Later when Ambrose's son Otoh takes up the scientific exploration narrative, Otoh's intrusion into Mala's garden leads directly to its seizure and her institutionalization, exposing the destructive potential of colonial science. Mala is deemed insane by a community that is lacking in both compassion and understanding, and after being sedated she is sent away to the almshouse where she is strapped down to her bed. Only Tyler, who is himself ostracized by the community of Paradise because of his sexual orientation, is able to communicate with Mala and interpret her gestures.

In *Cereus,* the scientific exploration narrative holds the promise of financial gain: the "discovery" of Mala's garden results in the capture and sale of the rare birds that inhabit it. Thus, Mootoo exhibits a historical awareness that scientific ventures in the colonial period were far from disinterested. Mootoo updates the theme of the commercial interests of colonial science when she has Ambrose consider working in ecotourism: "I am thinking . . . of purchasing a pirogue, a small boat, to take foreign visitors who come in search of nature's tropical wonders up the river and out to the vast swamplands on the eastern coast. The swamp is the home of magnificent birds, so colourful and varied in size, with fantastic appendages that make them appear to have escaped the pages of a fairy tale. . . . Those foreign naturalists would give their arm and a leg to see what lives in that swamp" (217). This passage identifies continuities between natural scientific discourse and the tourist gaze, in particular their reliance on the rhetoric of wonder. So too in Pineau's *Spirits,* the restaurant Exotic Delight, with its "leafy ambience dense with a magical greenness" and its naïve Haitian paintings of Edenic scenes, lures American vacationers to its tables by appealing to the tourists' appetite for the marvelous (148).

While referencing nineteenth-century natural science narratives, Mootoo's novel also alludes to the modern ethnographic account through its presentation of Tyler's relationship to his patient Mala. Mala is cast in the conventional role of the grandmother figure who is the repository of ancient knowledge, with Tyler as her interlocutor and interpreter. Tyler attempts throughout the novel to extricate the full story of Mala's dark past, but he proves to be a rather unreliable and self-involved narrator. He confesses in the preface: "Might I add that my own intention, as the relater of this story, is not to bring notice to myself or my own plight. However, I cannot escape myself, and being a narrator who also existed on the periphery of the events, I am bound to be present. I have my own laments and much to tell about myself. It is my intent, however, to refrain from inserting myself too forcefully" (3). Despite his claims to the contrary, Tyler has difficulty maintaining control of his narrative and must repeatedly remind himself to keep his focus on Mala's story rather than becoming distracted by his own concerns about his sexual identity and his budding romance.

Similarly, in *Spirits,* Pineau foregrounds the act of narration to draw attention to the role of the narrator's mediating presence in the production of the ethnographic account. The relationship between Pineau's narrator-protagonist and her subjects conforms in many respects to the structure of the ethnographic narrative, as she makes contact with informants whose stories she relates to the reader. Yet Pineau casts significant doubt on her narrator's ability to comprehend the world of the garden and its inhabitants whom she claims to represent. Because the narrator is not allowed to fully disappear into the narrative, the legitimating and regenerative function of the ethnographic plot—its ability to recover timeless New World origins—is undermined.[13]

Spirits is set in Guadeloupe and moves between rural and urban spaces as its photographer-narrator returns from her studies in France and travels into the countryside in search of ethnographic material. Pineau's novel relates the story of the Guadeloupean peasant Léonce and his garden, whose relative state of fecundity registers the rise and fall of his and his family's fortunes. The novel charts the births and deaths in Léonce's family as well as Léonce's attempts to recreate the Edenic garden that he glimpses in a vision. The story of Léonce's family saga is continually interrupted, however, by scenes from the narrator's life that reveal her increasingly troubled relationship to the characters whose lives she is narrating, and in particular her contempt for their belief in the supernatural.

The narrator, who as a student in Paris had considered becoming an ethnologist, travels into the countryside to interview and photograph informants whose stories she subsequently relates to the reader. *Spirits* again introduces a grandmother figure, Barnabé, who transmits the story of Léonce and his magical garden to the narrator. Yet, as with Tyler and Mala in *Cereus*, the transmission is often hostile and reluctant. Upon first meeting Barnabé, the narrator finds that her authority and legitimacy are called into question when Barnabé angrily asks her who has given her permission to photograph the house:

> One morning, I decided to go even deeper into the countryside. There I discovered—pure heaven for a budding photographer!—a cabin more than a hundred years old clinging like a maddened bat to the side of a green hill. Superb contrast! Powerful symbolism! Life and death united in a struggle to the death. I adjusted my Rolex, set the shutter. Snap! Snap! I made this uplifting yet depressing vision my own. At that very moment, behind me, an angry voice suddenly arose.
>
> "Who are you? Whose permission did you ask for, eh? You've got it into your head to imitate the whites who come around to photograph the falls up there! You have no family! Where are you from? Who is your mama?" (36)[14]

On her second visit, the narrator obtains her material under false pretenses when Barnabé mistakes the narrator for her daughter, and toward the end of the novel, Léonce's daughter upbraids him for allowing his story to be appropriated by the narrator.

The grandmother figure had earlier appeared in the work of Guadeloupean author Simone Schwarz-Bart, whom Pineau frequently cites in interviews as an influence on her own writing.[15] In Schwarz-Bart's *The Bridge of Beyond,* the heroine, Télumée, reconnects with the folk wisdom of her people by retreating into her grandmother's remote Guadeloupean village, which is set in opposition in the novel to the inauthentic, Europeanized towns of Point-à-Pitre and Basse-Terre. After having suffered repeated displacements, Télumée eventually begins to feel that she "is no longer a stranger on the earth" (83). At the end of the novel, she is firmly located in her garden, declaring: "But I shall die here, where I am, standing in my little garden. What happiness!" (173).[16] While Schwarz-Bart subscribes to the narrative of reconnection, however, in Pineau's hands this narrative becomes more tenuous and more difficult to sustain.

Pineau's narrator's technique as a photographer calls her credibility into question by exposing her propensity for distorting her material and exploiting her informants. In one scene that raises doubts regarding her integrity, the narrator retouches a photograph of one of her characters, and later in the novel she gains celebrity by photographing the plight of people displaced by the eruption of a volcano. Over the course of the novel, our mistrust of the narrator deepens as we become aware of her condescending attitude toward her characters and their "superstitions": "When Célestina began to tell me her stories of evil, devils, sorcerers and Satan's followers," she recalls, "I had no desire to listen. I told her that it was that kind of nonsense that put black people behind like the balls of a pig. I urged her to open her eyes, tear away the veil, to abandon the well of superstition. I threatened her with ending our friendship" (163). Formed by her metropolitan education, the narrator is incapable of accepting the alternative logic of her characters' way of seeing. Instead, the narrator's dismissive attitude signals the limitations of the realist conventions upon which her ethnographic narrative relies.

Over the course of the novel, however, the narrative distance between the narrator and her informants decreases. Pineau blurs the line between the ethnographic "frame" and the "story" of Léonce's garden, integrating her narrator unevenly into the novel to call attention to her role as medium of the characters' stories. Initially, the narrator's presence is muted—she does not appear until thirty pages into the novel—but she soon becomes an obtrusive presence. The narrator, an outsider who by virtue of her metropolitan education occupies the role of the European ethnographer, is gradually brought inside the narrative frame so that her scientific objectivity is compromised; by the end of the novel the frame and the internal narrative have merged completely. The narrator reaches a turning point when she attends the funeral of Léonce's wife, Myrtha, experiences a breakdown of sorts, and gains new respect for her characters' magical belief systems.

Pineau thus problematizes realist narrative conventions through her rendering of the ethnographic plot. The truth claims and explanatory power of such "reasonable" discourses as those advanced by the natural and social sciences are challenged as her novel exposes their economic investments as well as their limited capacity to grasp human relationships to the supernatural. In *Spirits*, rather than the narrator's erudition authorizing her narrative, her increasingly obvious limitations as a cultural interpreter threaten to jeopardize the ethnographic plot itself. To put it more broadly, by undermining the division between story and frame or inside and outside, Pineau suggests that, contrary to the garden narrative's regenerative claims, her restless narrator's wanderings in the countryside fail to supply her with a sense of origins or alleviate her feelings of alienation. For if there is no stable division between home and exile, the search for primitive origins as an antidote to exile—what Marianna Torgovnick calls the "hominess" of the primitive—cannot succeed.

Marvelous and Gothic Landscapes in Mootoo, Pineau, and Condé

In his classic essays "On the Marvelous Real in America" and "The Baroque and the Marvelous Real," Alejo Carpentier identifies a specifically New World aesthetic that results from historical, cultural, religious and geographic particularities that combine to generate a marvelous way of seeing. In the latter essay, Carpentier argues that the marvelous is more akin to the strange than to the beautiful: "Everything strange, everything amazing, everything that eludes established norms is marvelous" (101). Subsequent discussions of marvelous or magical realism have also emphasized the mode's unsettling quality, its capacity to destabilize entrenched categories of knowledge and experience and to "distur[b] received ideas about time, space, and identity" (Faris 7).[17] It is in this power to estrange that we may identify a point of intersection between the marvelous and gothic modes. Although, unlike the gothic, the marvelous integrates the extrarational as commonplace rather than as menacing, both modes point to the limits of realist representation.[18]

If gothic in general is concerned with a troubling past and its relationship to the present, postcolonial gothic uncovers repressed histories expressly in order to unsettle the dominant political and social order. Thus, in *Spirits*, the spirits of slaves inhabit the banana plantation and prevent Prospère from pursuing a career in banana cultivation. In *Mangrove*, Francis Sancher is haunted by his slaveholding European ancestors' sins, which have been punished by a curse that he cannot escape. Because indentured labor rather than African slavery makes up the historical background to *Cereus*, Mootoo's novel is less obviously preoccupied with the ghosts of slavery. Yet it too is concerned with the secrets of the past, centering around a desperate crime committed by a heroine seeking to free herself from the tyranny of her father. Marvelous and gothic modes overlap in each of the three novels, with the gothic contributing an emphasis on a repressed and troubling past.

None of the three novels considered in this chapter is thoroughly gothic in the manner of Jean Rhys's *Wide Sargasso Sea* (1966) or even

Condé's own *Windward Heights* (1995) (which rewrite the Brontë sisters' *Jane Eyre* and *Wuthering Heights*, respectively). Instead, the three novels wear their gothic conventions lightly and juxtapose them with contrasting landscape ideas such as the paradisal and the scientific. Ultimately, these juxtapositions have the effect of unsettling the colonial gothic mode, which becomes simply one among an array of landscape ideas that have been persistently and problematically projected onto colonial settings. Yet while all three authors ironically recast a long-standing literary tradition that Lizabeth Paravisini-Gebert terms the "Caribbean Gothic," Condé takes her critique one step further, raising doubts with regard to the contestatory and revelatory power of the postcolonial gothic itself.

From Marvelous to Gothic in Cereus Blooms at Night

As we have seen, Mala and her garden become the objects of a scientific expedition when Ambrose returns from studying entomology abroad and ventures onto Mala's property to court her. Yet, eventually, it is Ambrose's son Otoh who takes up the scientific exploration narrative and dares to enter Mala's garden, which is depicted as a primordial world containing rare and exotic flora and fauna. When Otoh first crosses over the fence into Mala's yard, it is as though he has entered a prehistoric world: "On this side of the fence, the world seemed quieter, as though time had slowed down. . . . As Otoh went further into the yard, sounds that he took for granted—the pounding of hammers, the swish of cars and barking of dogs—receded. Rather there was the buzzing of insects, the flutter of wings and the sounds of a breeze circulating earthy odours" (161). Upon gaining access to the garden, Otoh's response is the conventional one of wonder: "Otoh marvelled at the sight of the magnificent mudra, knowing that such a specimen might be seen only in the heart of an old-growth forest on the other side of the island" (166). The unusual peekoplat birds contained in the garden are an extraordinary sight, as are the cereus plants whose heads are "larger than any flower he had ever seen before" (165).

In keeping with Stephen Greenblatt's characterization of the discourse of the marvelous as it developed in the literature of Renaissance exploration, Otoh's reaction of wonder serves as a means of negotiating and normalizing that which exceeds his understanding. According to Greenblatt, in an act of "ideological forgetting" that elides the violence of conquest and legitimates his claims on the New World, Columbus produces a discourse of the marvelous that "has little or nothing to do with the grotesque or outlandish. It denotes, to be sure, some departure, displacement, or surpassing of the normal or the probable, but in the direction of delicious variety and loveliness" (76). Otoh's exploration narrative, however, does not remain contained within the confines of the Renaissance discourse of the marvelous, which emphasizes delight rather than the monstrous or the strange. Instead, it comes to resemble more closely Carpentier's view of the marvelous as encompassing "ugliness, deformity, all that is terrible" ("Baroque" 102). For rather than the sweet-smelling, idyllic landscape that Otoh expects to encounter in Mala's garden, he is confronted by oppressive, foul odors and repulsive vegetation.

As Otoh's exploration narrative becomes more troubled, so that "he suddenly felt himself a trespasser, an awkward voyeur" (167), the landscape description shifts into a gothic register. Moving deeper into the yard and then finally into the collapsing house, Otoh uncovers the nauseating smell and horrifying sight of the decomposing corpse of Mala's father:

> Farther into the room, through the haze of dust, Otoh made out a high platform the size of a single bed. A long, uneven bundle of clothes lay upon it. Something black protruded here and there. Mala walked right up to the bed frame and stared at the indecipherable mass. Otoh looked at her.
>
> . . . "Look, come and see." Otoh walked closer, sick to his stomach from the smell and terrified at what he was about to see. She held the light high above the bed frame so he could get a good look. (175–76)

The decaying vegetation, ruined house, and Otoh's descent down musty, dark stairs into the chamber that contains the corpse are all elements that serve to establish the scene's gothic character. Otoh is finally unable to normalize and explain his experience of Mala's garden through the relatively reassuring Renaissance language of wonder. Instead, he is overtaken by a far less pleasurable gothic encounter with an alien environment that is repulsive and threatening, and he flees Mala's house.

Although sensual Edenic gardens form the backdrop to idyllic love scenes between Lavinia and Sarah and Otoh and Tyler, over the course of *Cereus,* Mootoo's botanical imagery increasingly slides into an antipastoral, dystopian register, so that the frame of reference shifts from Renaissance and eighteenth-century arcadian imagery of the tropics to the nineteenth-century imperial gothic. Early in the novel, Tyler's first glimpse of Mala Ramchandin, with her peculiar vegetable smell and skeletal appearance, hints at the uncanny. At the almshouse, Mala's eerie, "mournful wailing" frightens the other nurses and patients: "The wailing halted abruptly, only to be replaced with breathless gasps of fright. Miss Ramchandin's hair was damp, pasted to her face and neck. . . . She stared ahead, past me" (19). Yet, for the more sympathetic and curious Tyler, Mala does not so much inspire fear as raise questions about where to locate the boundaries between sanity and insanity, between human and plant life.

Despite being situated in the town of Paradise, Mala's garden and house present a largely gothic landscape: overripe fruit, decaying vegetation and corpses, pungent odors of decay and deterioration. Mala's garden is a space of refuge, but one that resists the imposition of human control: "She did not intervene in nature's business. When it came time for one creature to succumb to another, she retreated. Flora and fauna left her to her own devices and in return she left them to theirs" (137).[19] The garden is a graveyard, filled with rotting vegetable and animal life, and, as we have seen, the decomposing corpse of her abusive father lies buried in the house, which is collapsing into the garden that surrounds it.

The ruined house that is the scene of the crime of incest in *Cereus* is a version of the dilapidated manor house that features in such postcolonial gothic works as Rhys's *Wide Sargasso Sea* and Derek Walcott's poem "Ruins of a Great House" (1962).[20] The collapsing walls of the Ramchandins' house are an architectural figure for the trauma of incest that will forever haunt Mala as well as the declining empire that helped to create the conditions for her father's abuse of her. The gothic plot reaches its climax toward the end of the novel with the graphic description of the immediate aftermath of Mala's violent confrontation with her father: "Suddenly [Ambrose] heard a dreadful crashing. Mala was calling out his name. He ran back up the stairs as though jolted by a cord. In the kitchen he saw, instead of the woman he had made love to the day before, an unrecognizable wild creature with a blood-stained face, frothing at the mouth and hacking uncontrollably at the furniture in the drawing room" (246). In this scene, in an ironic replaying of *Jane Eyre*, Mala is a beastlike Bertha to Ambrose's Rochester, subhuman in her violent frenzy. Thus, Mootoo both cites the trope of the Caribbean as a paradise in her novel and at the same time juxtaposes it with a contrasting but equally conventional dystopian vision of the tropics, complete with the madwoman of the West Indies. Yet in Mootoo's version it is not Mala who is monstrous so much as her father and the colonial society that formed him.

The Ghosts of the Slavery Past in The Drifting of Spirits
and Crossing the Mangrove

While Pineau, Mootoo, and Condé challenge various assumptions that
underpin the narrative of the search for the Edenic garden, their most
significant intervention may be their historicization of the garden, their
incorporation of temporal as well as spatial dimensions into their readings of the Caribbean landscape. González Echevarría observes in *Myth
and Archive* that nineteenth-century scientific accounts supplied New
World narrative with a particular conception of time which he summarizes as the belief that "time . . . is not the same in every place" (109).
Both scientific and ethnographic travelogues suggested that by traveling
across space, usually southward, one could move back in time to find the
origins of evolution and the beginnings of human and natural history—a
narrative that is vividly dramatized in Carpentier's *The Lost Steps,* in
which the narrator's journey into the Latin American jungle leads him
back through the stages of human history until he reaches Genesis itself.
Pineau, Mootoo, and Condé call into question the search for a site of
origins that lies outside of time. Accordingly, they also reject the claim
that history can be escaped from or erased through a retreat into the
garden. Instead, a history of displacement, enslavement, and colonization
continually intrudes into the Caribbean landscape, thwarting any desire
to cleanse the Caribbean of the ills of the past. Mootoo brings the garden
into dialogue with history by alluding to the significant contribution of
the natural sciences to the project of colonial expansion. Pineau introduces history into the garden by setting her novel against the backdrop
of World War II and by converting the garden into a symbolic battlefield. Condé punctuates her novel with references to markers of Caribbean modernity such as Toyota pickups, Télé-Guadeloupe, and the Single
European Market. In all three novels, the Caribbean landscape is at once
paradisal and a landscape of labor and of history. By self-consciously and
rigorously historicizing their gardens, Pineau, Mootoo, and Condé undermine the nature/culture opposition inscribed by the garden narrative
and pursue an entangled reading of Caribbean nature.

In Pineau and Condé, this entangled reading of nature is enhanced by
gothic motifs, which, combined with realist forms of historicization, enable them to open up their Caribbean landscapes yet more deeply to the
past. As I suggested in Part I, pastoral is a mode that, in its sentimental
versions, strains to incorporate a historical awareness. Gothic, on the
other hand, has the advantage of a built-in preoccupation with the past

so that its engagement with history is intrinsic rather than forced. More-over, as David Punter and Glennis Byron emphasize, "Gothic represents a specific view of history," one that insists upon "the impossibility of escape from history, with the recurrent sense in Gothic fiction that the past can never be left behind, that it will reappear and exact a necessary price" (55). We have already seen how *Cereus* is informed by this view of history as the return of the repressed crimes of colonial society. Whereas European exploration narratives sought out the Edenic garden located outside of time, Mootoo's garden foregrounds processes of decay, change, and transformation, and instead of containing the key that can unlock the mystery of human origins, it holds the dark secret of parental abuse. In Pineau's and Condé's novels, by contrast, the return of the repressed is directly tied to the slavery past, which refuses to be laid to rest.

In keeping with her ethnographic approach to narration, Pineau's nar-rator in *Spirits* declares that her aim as a portraitist is "to lay it bare. To scrape off the terrible shell deposited by the passage of time. To touch the essential self. And restore the timelessness that was there at the be-ginning" (156). However, Pineau continually undercuts such a project by providing dates that locate the fable in a specific historical context, and by moving back and forth between the village of Haute-Terre and the city of Point-à-Pitre, as well as Europe. Chapter 1 in the second part of the novel contains a lengthy description of the impact of the Euro-pean war on the French Caribbean and emphasizes that "the war was very much here, just off the coast of Guadeloupe" (130). The landscape of Guadeloupe is transformed by the experience of the World War II: "When the war came to an end, over there in France, the monuments to the war dead sprang up out of the earth in the same dazzling way as these banana trees today, over-fertilised, which eat their way through the Guadeloupean countryside" (131). The garden now explicitly becomes the site of history: chapter 2 of the second part of the novel opens with Léonce looking at a small garden in which a monument to the war dead has been erected.

Thus, although it initially appears so, Pineau's garden is not a refuge from the world nor from history, but instead is a medium for expressing the impact of historical events on the protagonists' lives. The second half of the novel reveals that Léonce had originally planted his garden be-cause of his grandmother's ghost's prophecy of the rise of Hitler and her insistence that he produce and store crops to sustain his family through the war. From this point on, rather than existing as an isolated space, the garden becomes tied to the war and to events in Europe. The club-footed

Léonce expresses his frustration at not being able to enlist by working on his garden, the motion of his machete mimicking that of the soldier's rifle and the garden becoming a surrogate battlefield. His grief at not being able to serve the Mother Country is such that he falls into despair, his garden mirroring his decline: "The marvellous Garden of Eden produced nothing but sickly fruit" (139).

Pineau historicizes her rural Guadeloupean garden by situating it within the context of World War II. At the same time, *Spirits* also points to a deeper presence of history in nature. In keeping with Glissant's assertion that the Caribbean landscape "is all history," Pineau's Caribbean landscape retains memories of the slave economy that had conditioned relations with the land in the not-so-distant past.[21] As the novel's title suggests, the landscape is ridden with ghosts and spirits, both benevolent and malevolent. References abound to obeahmen (*sorciers*) and voodoo priests (*houngans*) as well as to supernatural beings—and staples of the Caribbean gothic—such as zombies, werewolves, succubi, and devils. Léonce has the gift, and his daughter Gertie is also invested in the supernatural, as is signaled by her fascination with Victor Hugo, a contributor to the French gothic tradition: "Hugo was truly the new prophet, the unheeded visionary whose divinely inspired writings guided blind mankind toward the Word. Hugo knew and took into account the existence of spirits" (210–11). In Pineau's novel, Hugo becomes "the worst obeahman in all of Haute-Terre" (226).[22]

Curses pile up in Pineau's novel. Late in the novel we learn that Léonce's father is suffering from a curse that accounts for not only his phenomenal promiscuity but also the myriad symptoms exhibited by his children and grandchildren, including Léonce's club foot, Célestina's stammer, and Paul's "abominable crimes" (191) and seizures. The narrator, hearing of these supernatural phenomena from her informants, is initially skeptical and dismissive. Meeting Myrna for the first time, she complains that she "had come upon a pristine, unadulterated kind of lunacy" (37). The narrator's often strained interactions with her characters dramatize the conflict between realist and marvelous worldviews. On one level, then, *Spirits* is the story of a Europeanized Guadeloupean woman who resists but then ultimately gains an appreciation of marvelous ways of seeing, in part through her friendship with Léonce's daughter Célestina. The turning point for the narrator comes with the death of Léonce's wife: "When her mother died, I gave up speaking logic and reason to her. I no longer challenged her beliefs. I simply listened to her, curious about these tales that opened extraordinary pathways for me" (190).

In *Spirits,* cultivated landscapes including the garden are strongly associated with spirits. It is in Léonce's garden that his grandmother's ghost appears to convey her instructions and prophecies to him. In the aftermath of the war, Léonce's garden loses its paradisal character, instead becoming sinister and threatening: "Eaten at by blight, the trees stretched out dead branches like the arms of drowning men. . . . It was as if a great period of mourning had descended on his Eden of days gone by. When night fell on the hill, the trees became menacing, taking on the look of dishevelled ghosts, the shapes of monkeys, and crowded fiercely around our friend. Then he would shake off his apathy, grab his machete, which he wielded above his head, and, pursued by the ghosts of the evening, he ran and ran, breathless up to his cabin" (140). As in *Cereus,* the marvelous descriptions of the landscape in *Spirits* have a tendency to slide into gothic registers of imagery. Léonce's "lost Eden" becomes a "frightening spectacle" (152) after the war. This association of the garden with spirits anticipates a later scene in which the landscape bears ghostly traces of the plantation. When Léonce's grandson Prospère is told that banana cultivation is the future of Guadeloupe, he finds he cannot bring himself to engage in such an enterprise, for to him the banana fields are "plantations of ghosts": "Alas, Prospère did not have what it takes to be a cultivator of bananas. The vision of those extended fields, with their rows of future banana trees, . . . brought to mind a deep sense of unease, the whiff of a past not quite put away, a feeling to vomit. In each banana tree, he saw ebony wood, a soul in agony rising from another century, a spirit rooted in this earth, imprisoned for all time. Terrified, he realised one day that the banana plantations were fields of slaves imploring the strongest of the gods in the universe to send a great wind which would take them back to the land of their ancestors. Fields of lamentation. Fields of tears" (223–24). Pineau's spectral landscape unearths the presence of the ghosts of slavery in nature itself: in "plantations of ghosts" and "fields of tears." In *Spirits,* the haunted landscape recalls the days of slavery, "the whiff of a past not quite put away."

Pineau's landscape is thoroughly entangled with history, with a past that refuses to be put to rest. In contrast to Kincaid's discussion of colonial botany in her garden writing or Naipaul's and Walcott's postcolonial pastoralism, Pineau pursues an entangled reading of the landscape by evoking supernatural dimensions of Caribbean experience and by dispensing with realist narrative conventions. Pineau's gothic is confined to a few scenes and is less sustained than that of either Mootoo or Condé. Nonetheless, the gothic joins with the marvelous in *Spirits* to destabilize the ethnographic narrative to which the narrator is so problematically wedded and to open up an important avenue through which the past can make itself felt in the present.

Condé's more extensive—and ultimately more provocative—engagement with the gothic mode in *Mangrove* also thematizes tensions between rational and nonrational ways of seeing. The novel opens with the discovery of the decaying corpse of the mysterious stranger Francis Sancher, around whom the gothic plot revolves. Once again, marvelous and gothic motifs such as spirits, curses, howling dogs, secret crimes, and transgressive desires punctuate the novel. An abandoned estate is haunted by "an unknown force" that gives visitors "the feeling the evil eye of an invisible beast or spirit had bored into them," a force that apparently results in the deaths of three Haitian field-workers (16). The highly atmospheric descriptions of the dense, labyrinthine rainforest—the "dark green tangled mass of trees, creepers and parasites" (131)—that surrounds Rivière au Sel contribute to the ominous mood of the novel. More specifically Caribbean supernatural elements such as zombies, *soucouyants,* and the ghosts of slaves are introduced over the course of the novel so that the Caribbean gothic becomes yet another item in the catalog of colonial and postcolonial Caribbean literary programs—including Negritude and the Créolité movement—that are satirized by Condé.

Condé's protagonist, Francis Sancher, is tormented by a mysterious curse from which he believes he cannot escape. He wakes in the middle of the night "with a shriek that could make your blood curdle, followed by gasping and groans" (24), and rants enigmatically to his friend Moïse: "Hardly have we swallowed our first breath of air than we already have to account for every original sin, every sin through deed and omission, every venial and mortal sin committed by men and women who have long returned to dust, but leave their crimes intact within us. I believed I could escape punishment! I couldn't!" (24). The nature of Sancher's crime and the question of his origins are the mysteries that the novel slowly unravels through its multiperspectival narrative structure. Sancher's "mysterious wanderings" and "terror of the night" are eventually revealed to be tied to the slavery past. Sancher proves to be the descendant of a "sinister lineage" of white Creole planters and believes himself to be under a curse placed on his family by the slaves. "History's my nightmare," Sancher tells the resident historian Emile Etienne (196).

Xantippe, who shadows Francis Sancher on his tormented wanderings through the forest, is the other key figure in *Mangrove*'s postcolonial gothic plot. Likened at one point to a zombie and elsewhere described as a *soucouyant,* Xantippe creates a sense of "malaise" not only for Sancher but for the rest of the inhabitants of Rivière au Sel as well. Rivière au Sel and especially such sites as the Gully and the Bois l'Etang are frequented by spirits of the past and of those who were buried during slavery. Dodose Pélagie recounts that the Bois l'Etang "is supposed to be haunted by the spirits of our ancestors, who died and were buried during slavery. The sky is always gray and inked out by the knife-edge ridges of the mountain. Water lilies, duckweed and stiff tufts of grass carpet the dead eye of the pond, and the air is full of whispers, whistling noises and twittering. People avoid the place and I never meet anyone, except for that wretched Xantippe" (176). Xantippe more than any other character is attuned to the slavery past, and it is for this reason that Sancher is so distressed by him. Xantippe knows the "entire history" of Rivière au Sel and holds Sancher responsible: "Every time I meet him my eyes burn into his, and he lowers his head, for this is his crime" (205).

Notably, Xantippe is a highly parodic figure. Like his comic mimicry of the potent Adamic hero, Xantippe's exaggerated gothic haunting of Sancher contains elements of the ridiculous, and by the end of *Mangrove,* Xantippe has abandoned his vigil, declaring: "I won't touch him. The time for revenge is over" (205). In fact, from the outset Condé introduces a note of skepticism with regard to the gothic motifs that she exploits. For example, when the villagers recount that the first night Sancher spent in Rivière au Sel a violent windstorm rose up in revolt against his presence, their belief is immediately deflated by the comment: "But people will say anything" (18). Thus, while Xantippe's gothic haunting of Sancher makes the slavery past felt in the present, the parodic character of this haunting at the same time calls into question the viability of the postcolonial gothic itself (in contrast, for example, to Condé's more somber treatment of the supernatural in *I, Tituba, Black Witch of Salem* (1986) and *Windward Heights*). If such literary movements as Negritude and Créolité are the targets of Condé's satire, her treatment of postcolonial gothic also needs to be understood in the broader context of her irreverent attitude toward all rigidly conceived Caribbean literary programs. Like Mootoo and Pineau, Condé exploits gothic conventions to advance a postcolonial critique that reveals the landscape to be thoroughly imbued with history. At the same time, in Condé's novel the postcolonial gothic becomes as much subject to question as are scientific narrative in Mootoo and ethnographic narrative in Pineau.

The Garden, Gender, and Genealogy

As part of their project of interrogating established representations of Caribbean nature and their restrictive construction of origins, Pineau, Condé, and Mootoo question the gendering of narratives of the Caribbean landscape. Traditionally, the garden narrative suggests the possibility of regeneration and the foundation of a new Caribbean society cleansed of the ills of the past. Moreover, because a stable relationship between identity and place is assumed, the garden is the fixed site where such a regeneration must take place. In Roumain's *Masters of the Dew,* for instance, the hero returns to Haiti from exile and makes love with his beloved next to the Edenic spring that he has discovered, the blood coursing through Annaïse's veins becoming the water flowing in the spring: "She was stretched out on the ground and the low rumble of the water echoed within her in a sound that was the tumult of her own blood" (118). Roumain collapses together the woman's body and the land, fixing the renewed Haitian identity that is being generated to the site of the spring and inscribing the fundamental connection of the Haitians to the land they inhabit. Roumain's novel thus evinces the longing Glissant suggests "composite" cultures have for the foundational creation myths found among "atavistic" cultures, myths that legitimize the people's relationship to the land they occupy. Pineau, Condé, and Mootoo engage this foundationalist narrative by questioning whether such a regeneration is possible, how images of nature are gendered, and what constitutes normative sexuality.

Pineau's *Spirits* is replete with gendered descriptions of landscape, so much so that the effect is quite jarring. Pineau references the *femme-jardin* motif[23] in her descriptions of Léonce's wife, Myrtha, who has a "slender body which displayed for all to see its hills and valleys, contours in a landscape never before seen under heaven" (4). Léonce's garden is presented as the arena of masculine desire and male potency, particularly at the beginning of the novel when Léonce's labor in the garden compensates for a physical handicap and restores his manhood: "Wiping their brows, they would say: 'Kochi, you are really and truly strong! Damn, you make the earth cry out for mercy! Your yams are more beautiful than young black virgins!'" (9). Léonce's father's promiscuity is also described in botanical terms: "Was he to blame because his seed would always fall on distressingly fertile fields?" Sosthène complains, as the women he has impregnated take their revenge by defiling and trampling his garden (7). The effect of Pineau's exaggerated, hyperbolic use of gendered landscape imagery is to call attention to and cast doubt on the garden narrative's emphasis on male potency and its ability to bring about regeneration.

Léonce's garden in *Spirits* is strongly associated with the genealogical focus of the novel—the charting of births, death, family lineage—which is underscored when one of Sosthène's lovers becomes obsessed with tracing his family tree. In a key scene, Léonce has a vision in which the ghost of his grandmother appears in his garden to foretell how many children he and Myrtha will have. In his vision, the formerly barren garden is suddenly transformed into a fantastic Eden "bursting with fruitfulness": "Unbelievable! Ah! Ah! Greenery aplenty, heralding a miraculous harvest, with flowers twining around poles. Who could have said that those seedlings were so very few months old?" (81). Yet when Léonce awakes, he finds that "the garden had no story to tell, revealed no trace of feeling, bore the mark of no memory. . . . The garden was waiting, patiently . . . waiting for him to begin tilling. The garden just stood there, motionless, docile, dumb, distant like a woman who allows herself to be taken but feels no love and shows it" (85). Léonce's garden is full of symbolic meaning only for the duration of the dream, after which it is reduced to its mere physical existence. At the same time, the comparison of the garden to the female body is deflated, and the fertility motif is exposed as patriarchal and oppressive.

The impact of this scene recalls Condé's treatment of male sexuality in *Mangrove*. As we saw earlier, Condé's rewriting of *Masters of the Dew* parodies Manuel's mastery of both nature and the female body, with Manuel replaced by Carmélien Ramsaran, a hero who dreams of commanding vegetable life and of securing Mira's affections but who succeeds only in wetting his bed. Francis Sancher's prolific sexuality is for the most part a liability; he attempts to avoid impregnating his lovers for fear of perpetuating the curse that afflicts his family. The character of Xantippe, a Maroon figure who retains a connection to the African past in his forest hideaway, also serves to parody this hypermasculine sexuality and command of nature. In a passage that recalls the Adamic motifs and gendered landscape imagery of Aimé Césaire's *Notebook of the Return to the Native Land* (1939), Xantippe proclaims: "I named the gullies, gaping vaginas at the bottom of the earth. I named the rocks at the bottom of the water, and the fish, as gray as the rocks. In a word, I named this land. It spurted from my loins in a jet of sperm" (202). Xantippe preserves "the old ways" as he tends his Creole garden using traditional agricultural methods, and he advances an animistic perspective: "The trees are our only friends. They have taken care of our bodies and souls since we lived in Africa" (201). Condé's parodic treatment of Xantippe's Adamic relationship to nature—his awesome power to create through language and naming—casts doubt on a mode favored by a previous generation of male Caribbean writers.

Cereus advances an even more forceful critique of botanical metaphors for male sexual potency than either Pineau or Condé by questioning what constitutes "normal" or "natural" sexuality.[24] Initially, her novel follows the conventional gendering of the scientific exploration narrative in which the male scientist (Ambrose) pursues the feminized object of study (Mala/Mala's garden). Yet the novel also disrupts this narrative on several fronts. The narrator, Tyler, who is homosexual, attributes his departure from the island to his need to escape repressive sexual codes: "Over the years I pondered the gender and sex roles that seemed available to people, and the rules that went with them. After much reflection I have come to discern that my desire to leave the shores of Lantanacamara had much to do with wanting to study abroad, but far more with wanting to be somewhere where my 'perversion,' which I tried diligently as I could to shake, might be either invisible or of no consequence to people to whom my foreignness was what would be strange. I was preoccupied with trying to understand what was natural and what perverse, and who said so and why" (51). The community of Paradise that Mootoo's characters inhabit is a highly imperfect and in many ways exclusionary one, particularly for those who fall outside the normative sexual categories. Idyllic scenes of romantic fulfillment in a natural setting take place between Lavinia and Sarah and between Tyler and Otoh, and nature at times seems permissive of transgressive desire, but the novel suggests that such a vision is not sustainable for long. The mutability of the natural landscape echoes the fluidity of the sexual identities of her characters, who engage in a range of transgressive sexual behaviors and, in the case of Otoh, who switch genders. The cereus plant, which when it blooms transforms itself from an ugly and foul-smelling plant to an intoxicating aphrodisiac, is emblematic of this instability. The cereus plant's magical powers of transformation—and the novel's marvelous framework more broadly—create a space for formerly excluded presences that defy conventional categorization.

The fluidity of the sexual identities of Mootoo's protagonists and the transgressive character of their sexual relationships profoundly disrupt the foundationalist narrative that is associated with the garden. Instead of bringing about renewal, in Mootoo the garden is the site of father-daughter incest and the obstruction of a healthy sexual relationship between Mala and Ambrose. In addition, Mala's mother's abrupt departure from the island with her lesbian lover undermines not only the project of regenerating Caribbean identity but also the attachment of that regeneration to a fixed territorial location. While in *Spirits* the Edenic union of Léonce and Myrtha produces children plagued by maladies ranging from speech impediments to criminal tendencies, and while in *Mangrove* Francis Sancher attempts to abort Mira's pregnancy to prevent the continuation of the curse, in *Cereus* there are no offspring at all. The genealogical imperative of the garden narrative is frustrated by the loss of fertility in Pineau, by the curse placed on Sancher in Condé, and by homosexuality and incest in Mootoo.

Landscape and Emplacement

The mutual interdependence of place and displacement is signaled in the novels of Pineau, Mootoo, and Condé by their Caribbean—rather than diasporic—settings. The choice of a rural Caribbean setting bespeaks Pineau's, Mootoo's, and Condé's desire to retain a sense of place as meaningful. However, while their novels take place in the rural Caribbean, this locale is situated within a diasporic, globalized context; the inhabitants of their novels continually travel abroad or watch others depart and return. In *Mangrove,* the multiethnic and multilingual character of the rural community serves as a constant reminder of the migrations—past and present—that have sustained it. The presence of individuals of Haitian, Indian, Chinese, and European as well as African descent in the community of Rivière au Sel overturns any notion of the rural as static or homogeneous. In *Cereus,* Mootoo's Indo-Caribbean characters have a strong sense of uprootedness because the experience of arrival is relatively fresh. Over the course of the novel, Tyler and Ambrose travel abroad to study while Mala's mother escapes to the Wetlands with Lavinia, and Mala's sister immigrates to the Wetlands and later to Canada.[25] Similarly, in *Spirits,* the narrator and various of her characters move between the Guadeloupean countryside, the city, and the major European capitals. Initially, Pineau's narrator is mobile while her subjects are fixed in an isolated rural space, but as the novel progresses the rural and the urban increasingly interlock as Léonce's granddaughter becomes a successful fashion model, sending postcards from New York, Tokyo, and London and telephoning from "noisy airport lounges" (221).

Earlier Caribbean novels such as Roumain's *Masters of the Dew* and Schwarz-Bart's *The Bridge of Beyond* juxtapose natural landscapes and exile but understand them as firmly opposed terms: the garden is the place where exile comes to an end. By retreating into the interior of the island, Roumain's and Schwarz-Bart's protagonists are able to reconnect with an authentic Caribbean identity. Condé, Pineau, and Mootoo, on the other hand, highlight the impact of history and modernity on the "natural" landscape by foregrounding its relationship to colonial rule, the plantation system, and the circulation of plants and people. In their reading, natural landscapes and exile are no longer diametrically opposed.[26] Rather than serving as the antidote to exile, the Caribbean landscape itself becomes the signifier of displacement. In accordance with this entangled reading of Caribbean nature, plant imagery primarily serves to convey feelings of instability and uprootedness rather than plenitude. In *Mangrove*, Aristide contemplates leaving Guadeloupe and his job at his father's plant nursery, commenting that "flowers have no motherland. They'll perfume any land" (58). In *Spirits,* Guadeloupeans who are subject to the vagaries of seasonal and contract labor are compared to "tree[s] without roots" who lack enough "weight to resist a fierce blow from the wind" (124). In *Cereus,* the arrivals and departures of the characters tend to be accompanied by the transfer of plant cuttings, and plants and trees are often depicted with "protruding" or "exposed" roots (77, 132).[27]

Running through *Cereus* are botanical images of transplantation and hybridization. The opening sentences of the novel draw an analogy between the transplantation of plants and of people: "The cereus in the yard will bloom soon. We planted a slip from the original cutting at least a year ago. That is how long it has been since I left my village on the other side of the island and moved to Paradise" (5). Throughout Mootoo's novel, the journeys within the island as well as between the Caribbean, India, and the Wetlands that punctuate the novel are linked to botanical images. Mala's mother Sarah is brought cuttings from her lover Lavinia's orderly European garden: "Lavinia loved the freedom and wildness in Sarah's garden, so unlike her mother's well-ordered, colour-coordinated beds. She brought clippings and whole plants ripped from Mrs. Thoroughly's garden, the fresh, rich dirt still under her fingernails. She brought flame ixoras for Sarah, and one memorable day she arrived with cactus plants, one each for Pohpoh and Asha. Cereus, she called them, pronounced like the bright, fuzzy star, a climbing succulent whose leaves and trunk were ragged and unsightly until they bloomed" (57–58). This hybridization of the two gardens—the European and the Caribbean—anticipates the sexual union of Lavinia and Sarah and their own "transplantation" to the Wetlands. Over the course of the novel, the cereus plant travels from

Lavinia's garden, to Sarah's garden, to the garden of the almshouse, paralleling the movements of the novel's characters.

If botanical imagery serves to amplify human displacements in the three novels, it also supports their shared emphasis on mutability and transformation, in particular on the instability of identity and its connection to place. In *Mangrove,* Condé's Guadeloupean forest is a dynamic and dense space that points toward the unexpected and unknowable dimensions of human experience. Like the mangrove, the forest is characterized by its knotted indirection and lack of transparency. The forest obscures more than it reveals: Mira searches for her mother, "convinced she was hiding in the mountains . . . guarded by the giants of the dense forest and sleeping between the huge toes of their roots," only to fall into "the bottom of a gully, hidden under the mass of vegetation" (34). Condé's mysterious and elusive forest underlines, rather than resolves, the enigmas and uncertainties of modern life.

Similarly, while conventionally the garden is the repository of a fixed and essential identity that one can recover, for Pineau and Mootoo identity is forever being transformed, a process that is reflected in the changes that take place in the garden. Mootoo's eponymous cereus plant originates in a European garden already hybridized by virtue of its Caribbean location, suggesting the impossibility of tracing roots back to a pure and stable point of origin. Pineau's extraordinarily dynamic garden is subject to continual change, its relative state of fertility or infertility mirroring its human inhabitants' constantly shifting fortunes.

Mootoo's central image of the cereus plant also emphasizes mutability. The cereus plant is distinguished by its powers of metamorphosis: when it blooms, the normally unremarkable plant becomes suddenly impossible to ignore, emitting an intoxicating odor that functions as an aphrodisiac. It blooms only briefly, however, after which time its blossoms swiftly shrivel and hang limply from the stems. Even its scent has "two edges—one a vanilla-like sweetness, the other a curdling" (163–64). But if the cereus plant is emblematic of mobility and instability—its appearance continually altering and its cuttings constantly circulating—it is also described as having roots "like desperate grasping fingers" that bore their way through a wall of Mala's house (124). The cereus plant is no rhizome, spreading out laterally to create a loosely dispersed network, but instead is firmly rooted in the specific Caribbean spaces in which Mala and Tyler make their homes.

In the final scene of Mootoo's novel, Otoh tends to the cereus plant in the Alms House garden, patting the soil at its base in a gesture that "honour[s] its place" in Mala's life and at the same time reaffirms her connection to that soil (268). As a metaphor for identity, the cereus plant simultaneously points to mutability and mobility on the one hand, and to attachment to place on the other. The double valency of the cereus plant, its ability to connote both mobility and attachment, illuminates the function of botanical imagery more broadly in the novels of Condé, Pineau, and Mootoo. While all three authors reject notions of a stable identity and a fixed relationship to place, they do not celebrate placelessness. Instead, their novels indicate that, rather than exchanging old narratives of identity for new ones, or rural settings for urban cityscapes, territorialized and deterritorialized narratives of identity are most productively read in tension with one another.

6 Landscape and Indigeneity in the Installation Art of Isaac Julien and Jin-me Yoon

I see my film as cartography, mapping out different spaces.
—Isaac Julien, "Isaac Julien in Conversation"

I am wary of the risk of a new colonising and exoticisation of this land by those of us who are fairly new immigrants—even if we are immigrants of colour—to the country seeking refuge in land, in one form or the other.
—Shani Mootoo, "Dear Shani, Hiya Richard . . ."

THIS CHAPTER moves beyond the literary to consider works by two visual artists that extend the insights into New World belonging offered by the novels, poetry, and garden writing discussed in previous chapters. As this chapter attests, not only writers but also contemporary visual artists prove to be preoccupied by landscape and its relationship to diasporic identity. In particular, Isaac Julien's film installations and Jin-me Yoon's photography engage in critical rereadings of New World landscape that both parallel and deepen the literary interventions that I have been tracing in this study. While pastoral returns as a significant vehicle of critique in their work, Julien and Yoon also allude to notions of the sublime. Whichever landscape ideas they reference, in reimagining the spaces of New World exploration and settlement, Julien and Yoon remain mindful of the prior presence of indigenous peoples on the land.

Broadening our discussion of landscape representation to include visual art of the Americas acknowledges the inherently visual character of landscape. At the same time, such a move reveals the unique possibilities for reimagining landscape that expressive media such as video, installation, and photography afford. In the work of British Caribbean filmmaker Isaac Julien and Korean Canadian photographer Jin-me Yoon, the use of such dynamic formats as triple-screen projection and double-sided lightboxes enables the fragmentation of narrative perspective and the reorganization of both time and space. While Julien's film installations *Paradise Omeros* (2002) and *True North* (2004) transport the viewer to a paradisal St. Lucia and a sublime Arctic, respectively, Yoon's photographic series *Touring Home from Away* (1998–99) presents the pastoral setting of Prince Edward Island. Each of these works recasts an iconic landscape through strategies of juxtaposition and simultaneity that unsettle the linear, sequential plotting of travel discourses and the categories of belonging that these discourses inscribe. Julien and Yoon exploit the dynamic viewing space created by installation art to encourage the viewer to enter into a more active and critical engagement with landscape representation and to question its exclusionary power. Thus, they demonstrate the particular capacity of installation art to unsettle entrenched iconographies of the New World nation.

The interdisciplinary direction of my discussion of landscape representation is anticipated by the strongly visual sensibility of several of the literary texts examined in previous chapters, especially the writing of Derek Walcott and Shani Mootoo, both of whom are themselves also visual artists. Painting and painterly effects have long been themes of Walcott's writing, and *Tiepolo's Hound* is no exception. Indeed, in *Tiepolo's Hound,* Walcott includes his paintings in between the covers for the first time, and landscape emerges as a central subject of these paintings. It is not by chance that Walcott chooses to foreground his alternate vocation as a painter in *Tiepolo's Hound,* a work that is deeply preoccupied with rural landscape and its representations, and whose plot revolves around Italian and French painting traditions. Nor is it an accident that another of Walcott's works, *Omeros,* has inspired a visual interpretation: Julien's film installation *Paradise Omeros.*

For her part, as we will see below, Mootoo, who works across literary, visual, and video formats, brings an even more thoroughly interdisciplinary perspective to bear on the subject of landscape. Mootoo's visual art corpus comprises paintings and xerox-based montages as well as a number of works of video art. Like her writing, these works frequently privilege natural settings such as lakes, woods, mountains, and gardens. Mootoo's multimedia approach serves to deepen her critique of the systems of classification that are imposed on the natural world. As Monika Kin Gagnon observes, "The writerly quality of Mootoo's visual and video work" and "the highly visual dimension of her writing" signal her desire to challenge borders, both disciplinary and social ("Out in the Garden" 147). Mootoo's refusal to respect generic boundaries—what

Gagnon terms her "disciplinary irreverence"—is thus part and parcel of her larger critique of the boundaries that circumscribe sexual, gender, racial, and national identities.

The landscape ideas that are contested by the works discussed in this study historically have tended to be most forcefully inscribed in visual representations such as Albert Bierstadt's nineteenth-century paintings of the American West and the Group of Seven's early-twentieth-century post-Impressionist paintings of the Canadian wilderness, as well as cinematic genres such as the western. Before turning to Julien's and Yoon's interrogations of these kinds of settler visualizations, I will briefly consider several works of installation and video art that, on a somewhat smaller scale, similarly reconfigure the relationship between landscape and belonging in the Americas. The exhibit *"Nous venons en paix . . ."* and the video art of Shani Mootoo and Wendy Oberlander expose the racial and gender biases of exploration and settler colonial narratives of the land and call attention to indigenous presences with which, they suggest, any diasporic articulation of New World place ultimately must contend.

"Nous venons en paix . . .": Histoires des Amériques

The centrality of landscape to the expression of contemporary New World identities was compellingly demonstrated by *"Nous venons en paix . . .": Histoires des Amériques,* a 2004 exhibit at Montreal's Musée d'art contemporain. The exhibit brought together works by seventeen artists from North and South America, ostensibly on the basis of their joint preoccupation with two major themes: history and "America." In fact, a third theme emerged in the exhibition, for it was striking how many of the artworks related the vexed status of history and origins in the Americas to images of the land. *"Nous venons en paix . . . ,"* which contained works by Kara Walker, Stan Douglas, Kent Monkman, Adriana Varejão, Cynthia Girard, Roseângela Rennó, and Sergio Vega among others, pointed to the problematic legacies of colonial readings of New World landscapes. Accordingly, in her catalog essay Johanne Lamoureux identifies "a major subtext of this exhibition [as being] the contested occupation of a site" (143).[1]

Canadian artist Stan Douglas's video installation *Nu·tka·* (1996), for example, recreates the scene of New World contact while conspicuously omitting a First Nations presence. The viewer stands before a large screen onto which is projected a six-minute looping video that displays panoramic views of Nootka Sound, a key site in the British and Spanish contest for control over the Pacific Northwest in the late eighteenth century. Douglas blurs images of the sea and the coastline by interlacing two image tracks in a single video projection. The hazy video footage is coupled with a soundtrack of two colonial voices that, like the images, are interwoven, moving in and out of synchronicity. The audio voices represent those of the Spanish commander Estéban José Martínez and the English captain James Colnett, who in 1789 contested Martínez's claim to possession of Nootka Sound and declared it to be British territory. The sound recordings of the Spanish and British narratives of contact and exploration overlap, separating and then blending together, thereby destabilizing the authority of the colonial rhetoric of possession. By blurring both vision and sound, Douglas calls attention to the difficulty European explorers had in finding a vocabulary through which to describe—and claim possession of—the New World landscape.

Similarly, Brazilian artist Roseângela Rennó's video installation *Vera Cruz* (2000/2004) pairs colonial narratives of the landfall and discovery with visually obscured images of the landscape to suggest the gap that opens up between text and referent in a New World context. While indecipherable images are projected onto a freestanding screen, subtitles convey the dialogue of Portuguese sailors as they explore the coast of Brazil circa 1500. Unlike in Douglas's work, however, Rennó's subtitles track the Portuguese sailors' succession of responses to their encounter with indigenous peoples, which progress from fear, to censure, to missionary zeal. In Douglas's *Nu·tka·*, by contrast, an indigenous presence is eerily absent from the scene of discovery, but the camera's circling movement and perpetual scanning of the empty landscape draws attention to this absent presence.[2] The unrepresentable—in this case the First Nations point of view on the scene of colonial landfall—is a key concern of Douglas's work. In keeping with this concern, he associates *Nu·tka·* with the sublime as well as the gothic romance, inserting into the soundtrack an excerpt from Poe that contributes to the viewer's impression that the landscape is haunted by forgotten histories.[3]

African American artist Kara Walker's *Darkytown Rebellion* (2001) presents a gothic landscape of a different kind. In Walker's installation, cutout silhouettes of grotesque African American figures who are apparently engaged in a slave revolt are seen against a light-projected landscape. The superimposition of the cartoonishly colorful landscape onto the dark cutouts suggests the awkward and incomplete integration of these figures into their (post)slavery environment. Hanging opposite the projected landscape is a small, naïve rural scene painted in oil. The nightmarish quality of the slave revolt threatens to engulf the peaceful pastoral vision of the accompanying painting with its uncomplicated image of American belonging. *Darkytown Rebellion* thus contrasts gothic and pastoral visions to highlight the violent ruptures and disjunctures of slavery (and postslavery) landscapes.

As the viewer of Walker's *Darkytown Rebellion* stands in front of the projector, she casts a shadow that becomes part of the disturbing scene of slave rebellion and dissolution. Similarly, in Douglas's *Nu·tka·*, the viewer is incorporated into the space of contact by the act of vision itself and the effort required to apprehend the landscape through the uncomfortably blurry and inadequate perspective of the European colonists. The installation's large-screen format contributes to the viewer's sense of being inserted into the scene—of becoming a participant in the eighteenth-century drama of exploration and conquest. The embodied nature of the aural and visual confusion that the viewer experiences in relation to Douglas's work has no equivalent in literary texts such as *Burning Water*, George Bowering's rendering of the Nootka Sound Controversy.[4]

The paintings included in *"Nous venons en paix . . . ,"* such as Kent Monkman's parodies of the Hudson River School in his series *The Moral Landscape,* also call attention to the visual vocabulary of New World colonization.[5] Yet installation, in contrast to the more static medium of painting, has the capacity as a three-dimensional and time-based format to directly incorporate the viewer into the environment that it creates. Thus, if the relationship of contemporary New World belonging to established landscape ideas has been richly explored in the literary texts discussed in previous chapters, as well as in paintings such as Monkman's, installation art proves to be a particularly powerful vehicle through which to encourage a broader consideration of how *all* inhabitants of the Americas—historical and contemporary—participate in the production of New World place.

A Paddle and a Compass

In a dialogue on landscape with her fellow Trinidadian Canadian artist Richard Fung, Shani Mootoo writes: "My passion since youth for the outdoors is an instinctual recognition that here my desperate need for the freedom to self determine, to be, and to become can be most fulfilled" ("Dear Shani" 33). As her short stories and fiction testify, for Mootoo the natural world is a liberating space that has the potential to release the individual from oppressive, socially imposed categories of race and gender. Thus, for Mala in *Cereus Blooms at Night* (as we saw in chapter 5), the garden provides a refuge from her childhood trauma. Similarly, in

Mootoo's rather whimsical video *The Wild Woman in the Woods* (1993), a Hindu goddess on skis leads the heroine into the snowy mountains, where she finds freedom from her sexual and social inhibitions. In this enchanted wilderness, there are "no rules—you simply are as you are and you're perfect," the goddess tells her. In Mootoo's more stylized video *Her Sweetness Lingers* (1994), a lush, vibrant garden is an erotic space of female desire and sensuality. In both her writing and her visual art, Mootoo privileges "landscape as a significant haven and site of reinvention and imagining" ("Dear Shani" 33).

At the same time that landscape is a utopian space for Mootoo, her dialogue with Fung also points to more troubling aspects of the longing for place. Mootoo and Fung suggest that their status as Trinidadian immigrants to Canada of Indian and Chinese ancestry, respectively, attunes them to the politics of landscape representation. "As we launch our dialogue on landscape," Fung writes, "I think not only about our mutual interest in the land as the principal icon of Canadian national identity, but also of our actual journeys across geography. I'm truly convinced that our sensitivity to the political construction of landscape comes out of these displacements" ("Dear Shani" 26). In her contribution to the dialogue, however, Mootoo not only writes of her attraction to landscape as a transgressive space of escape but also recognizes it as a site of exclusion. She proves somewhat uneasy about her "desire to know and so to *own* this land [Canada]" and her "need for it to be that necessary place where I fortify myself, and am unconditionally welcome." Mootoo cautions Fung that she is "wary of the risk of a new colonising and exoticisation of this land by those of us who are fairly new immigrants—even if we are immigrants of colour—to the country seeking refuge in land" ("Dear Shani" 35).

Mootoo's complex understanding of landscape and its relationship to diasporic belonging is reflected in her collaboration with the Vancouver-based video and installation artist Wendy Oberlander. Wilderness as a site of dispossession is a recurring theme in the work of Oberlander, the daughter of German and Austrian Jewish refugees from Nazi Germany.[6] In her evocative forty-seven-minute documentary *Nothing to Be Written Here* (1996), Oberlander examines her father's experience during World War II when he was interned, together with German POWs and other "enemy aliens," in a camp in the Canadian wilderness.[7] The camp was located deep in the woods of New Brunswick, where the internees were made to perform that most "quintessential Canadian activity": felling trees in the snow. Throughout the video, the theme of displacement is linked to land- and seascapes. The restless sound of waves and images of the ocean suggest that for Oberlander herself, the sense of home is not yet secure. Through its use of the few photographs that survive of life in the camp, the video foregrounds how the internees, who pose holding their axes against a treed and snowy landscape, are ironically inserted into an iconic Canadian wilderness scene at the very height of their exclusion from the Canadian nation. While this episode of Canadian history has been largely forgotten (as were, Oberlander notes in the voice-over narration, Japanese Canadian internment and First Nations displacements), traces in the landscape remain. The perfectly straight rows of trees that the internees planted in the New Brunswick woods serve as a reminder of their internment and testify to the intimate relationship between nature and history.[8]

As in several of their independent efforts, Mootoo and Oberlander's coproduced video *A Paddle and a Compass* (1992) investigates the idea of wilderness and the potential for diasporic belonging that New World landscape affords. The video highlights the omission of immigrant presences —perceived as alien to the landscape—from representations of iconic New World settings such as the Rocky Mountains. Yet, at the same time, it problematizes those same immigrant presences in relation to competing and prior claims on the land. The double-edged question that *A Paddle and a Compass* poses—whose land is this really?—emerges in the video as fundamental to a diasporic sense of place in the Americas. Mootoo and Oberlander rely more heavily on voice-over narration than on visual language, but they nonetheless makes effective use of single-channel video to advance a critique of landscape representation from a diasporic perspective while also acknowledging the prior indigenous presence.

A Paddle and a Compass is set on Lake Louise in Banff National Park. While listening to the alternating voices of Mootoo and Oberlander, we watch canoeists traveling along the glacial lake with the snow-capped Rocky Mountains in the background. Throughout, the video strategically juxtaposes this iconic natural setting with minority and other eccentric presences. At the opening of the video, a South Asian family decked out in life jackets prepares to embark on a canoe trip. From behind the camera, Mootoo comments on the improbability of the scene she is witnessing: "Usually I don't see people from my background . . . doing this type of thing." This scene anticipates an episode in Mootoo's novel *He Drown She in the Sea* (2005) in which Harry St. George, a Caribbean immigrant living near Squamish, British Columbia, where he works as a landscape designer, is thrilled to be invited along on a canoe trip: "Ahead loomed range beyond range of ice-capped mountains. . . . Pride coursed through him; he had become an insider. By inviting him up, Kay was showing him something few people like him—he grinned at the thought—ever had the chance to glimpse. This was the Canada of postcards and tourism posters" (42).

In *A Paddle and a Compass,* the sight of the South Asian canoeists in the pristine wilderness landscape prompts Mootoo in her voice-over narration to recall commercial images of North American nature that were circulated during her Trinidadian childhood. The video reveals that the source of Mootoo's attraction to the North American wilderness is a Sears Roebuck catalog advertisement for camping equipment. As a child, Mootoo had longed to participate in the wilderness experience that she saw depicted in the catalog's photograph of dark green pine trees and canoes. She was given a tent with a Native American head stenciled on one side, confirming Fung's fear that many immigrants to Canada "arrive with ideas of First Nations and Inuit peoples drawn mainly from American popular culture, especially Hollywood" (Gagnon and Fung, "Imaginative Geographies" 86). If as a young girl Mootoo had "wanted to be in the picture" with the white family depicted in the catalog, now the video marks her formal entrance into the wilderness landscape.

Mootoo's reflections on the appeal of the North American wilderness are soon joined by those of Oberlander, who meditates in her voice-over narration on the themes of navigation and the North—in particular, the neglected history of female explorers. Late in the video, Mootoo and Oberlander read a list of statistics pertaining to the Canadian landscape, calling attention to the Western "obsession . . . with measuring, categorizing, and taming the natural environment." The video's treatment of this theme recalls Kincaid's insight that the obsessive need to isolate and categorize typifies both the botanist and the colonist. The critique of repressive systems of classification that the video pursues thus makes a critical link between representations of nature and systems of social organization. The desire to measure and categorize the natural world is, the video suggests, tied to the absence of female, diasporic, and indigenous presences from the iconography of Canadian nationhood.

The video concludes with a meditation on Woody Guthrie's song "This Land Is Your Land." "I wonder if Woody Guthrie ever saw the Canadian Rockies," Oberlander asks in the final lines of the video, "and I wonder whose land this really is." Like Mootoo's remark regarding the danger of "a new colonising and exoticisation of this land" in her dialogue with Fung, the video's conclusion points to tensions surrounding diasporic emplacement even as it critiques gendered and racialized configurations of the Canadian landscape. Standard representations of the Canadian wilderness tacitly exclude immigrant and diasporic presences such as that of the South Asian canoeists. At the same time, they notoriously empty the landscape of its First Nations inhabitants. Rendering immigrant and diasporic presences on the land more visible threatens a new colonization, Mootoo and Oberlander suggest, if one set of exclusions is redressed at the cost of the other.

Mapping a New Cartography in Isaac Julien's *Paradise Omeros* and *True North*

Isaac Julien, a founding member of the black British film collective Sankofa, adopts an experimental and antirealist approach to documentary films and installations. Best known for his queer critique of popular representations of the black male body, Julien resists identity politics and Afrocentric formulations, positioning his work against what he describes as "the rise of essentialist black thinking." According to Julien, the imperatives of identity politics problematically "overshadow questions of doubt, skepticism, or transgression. Identity politics in its positive-images variant is always purchased in the field of representation at the price of the repression of the other" ("Black Is, Black Ain't" 77).

Julien's artistic practice is characterized by a compelling combination of formal experimentation and theoretical sophistication. In keeping with his anti-essentialist stance, the dreamlike atmosphere and mannered performances in his highly innovative films and installations work to resist fixed meanings. The formalist strategy of Julien's films, a number of which are designed as triple-screen projections, tends to counteract the classificatory logic of identity politics. Instead of inscribing rigid racial and gendered categories, his films often evoke the uncanny and the enigmatic through their stark visual language and hypnotic soundtracks.

By the same token, narrative conventions and expectations relating to plot and character are consistently violated in Julien's films. While linear plot sequences are disarticulated by the triple-screen projection that he favors, "character" is reconceptualized in his films in a manner inspired by French director Robert Bresson. As Julien explains: "The characters or models . . . who are displayed in the film perform their own particular imaginary subversion of historical memory, which draws more from 'performance art' than theatrical acting. The figures do not have to be read as statements, however. It is important to see these characters sometimes performing independently of their indexical markers of ethnicity" ("Creolizing Vision" 152). Key to Julien's anti-essentialist poetics, then, is his approach to character as liberated from fixed categories of identity and belonging. As he put it in an interview, his aim is to challenge established and taken-for-granted categories of representation in order to encourage his audience "to learn how to look in a different way" ("States of Desire" 132).

Critical discussion of Julien's work has centered around his treatment of the taboo subjects of black male homosexuality and interracial desire in such films as *Looking for Langston* (1989). However, Julien's works also offer an increasingly rich consideration of the construction of space as it interrelates with categories of identity and belonging. Julien draws attention to this dimension of his work when he remarks that he sees his "film as cartography, mapping out different spaces" ("Isaac Julien" 84). In his essay "Creolizing Vision," Julien speaks of his attempt to "map a new cartography," one that reflects his double location as a resident of both England and the Americas. He frames this cartographic project within a practice that he terms "traveling cinema": "My practice has been an attempt at the visual archaeological expedition in transatlantic space and culture of diaspora, in effect a traveling cinema which moves against the tides of globalization" ("Creolizing Vision" 150). Julien's formulation echoes James Clifford's "traveling cultures," with its emphasis on "rethink[ing] cultures as sites of dwelling *and* travel" (*Routes* 31), but also ironically appropriates the language of exploration and travel narrative.

The settings of Julien's films and installations span the locations of the black diaspora, from the Britain of *Young Soul Rebels* (1991), to the Martinique and France of *Frantz Fanon* (1996), to the United States of *Baltimore* (2003). While urban capitals of the black diaspora such as London and Baltimore feature prominently in his oeuvre, installations such as *The Long Road to Mazatlán* (1999), *Paradise Omeros,* and *True North* interrogate standard representations of exurban spaces. If previous works such as *The Attendant* (1993), *Vagabondia* (2000), and *Baltimore* addressed the interior space of the museum as an institution of cultural memory, expansive outdoor landscapes typify *The Long Road to Mazatlán* (the American Southwest), *Paradise Omeros* (St. Lucia), and *True North* (the Arctic). In what follows, I will trace Julien's recharting of the territory of diasporic belonging in *Paradise Omeros* and *True North* and his dismantling of the spatial and temporal logic of travel narrative.

Paradise Omeros takes its title from the well-known work by Julien's compatriot Derek Walcott.[9] Loosely inspired by Walcott's epic poem

Omeros, Julien's installation juxtaposes the paradisal landscape of the Caribbean with a bleak London cityscape (fig. 1). The twenty-minute triple-channel film, which is projected onto three large screens, traces a young man's journey from St. Lucia to England, where he immigrates as a teenager with his parents. In Julien's installation, oversaturated colors, exquisite flowers, and flowing waterfalls characterize the impossibly paradisal landscape of St. Lucia, while the London that the film evokes—in part through documentary footage of riots—is concrete, sterile, at times nightmarish. The open space of the island's beach and seascape contrasts with the confined interior of a London flat. The paradisal island also contrasts sharply with what appears to be the underground arcade of a housing project through which the protagonist is pursued by a white youth, generating homoerotic tension. Juxtaposition is thus a key strategy that Julien employs in *Paradise Omeros* to generate a contrastive structure, one that aligns the work with a critical pastoral mode.

Toward the conclusion of *Paradise Omeros,* in a complex set of pastoral juxtapositions, a paradisal image occupies the center screen, flanked on either side by dystopian images of the concrete urban landscape. The triptych structure of the installation encompasses the two poles of home and away that conventionally organize the Caribbean migration narrative, but presents them as simultaneous rather than sequential. Instead of charting a linear trajectory from St. Lucia to London, the protagonist inhabits these two spaces simultaneously. In between lies the sea, in which the protagonist immerses himself before journeying to England. The unstable and transformative space of the sea further destabilizes the poles of home and away, confounding the conventional patterning of the migration narrative around fixed points of departure and arrival.

Chris Darke observes that in Julien's installations, the triple-screen format disperses and splinters the gaze in a "kaleidoscopic" manner: "In the relative absence of cinematic 'depth' to the image, the installation flattens, fragments and multiplies both the image and, in the process, the spectator's act of looking which . . . is made to move across, to scan laterally, to ricochet between images" (Mercer and Darke 79–80). The kaleidoscopic character of Julien's installations compels the viewer to become actively engaged rather than settle into the more conventional role of the passive consumer of images. Julien has described the effect of the triple-screen format as "meta-cinematic" in that it invites the viewer to deconstruct the cinematic narrative. Comparing single-screen and triple-screen versions of *The Long Road to Mazatlán,* he observes that "in the single-screen version, what is prioritized is the narrative, the linear progression

Figure 1. Isaac Julien, *Before Paradise (Man with Ball)*, 2002. Pigment ink print. Printed at Hare & Hound Press, San Antonio, Texas. Edition of four. Three panels, each 100 x 100 cm. (Courtesy the artist and Victoria Miro Gallery)

from one scene to the other. You have to think of the way in which you are going to suture various scenes together to make transitions. So the notion of time and viewing are thought through very differently. . . . I think the demands of a single-screen piece of work lead to a slightly conservative way of viewing. There is something about the three-screen version that allows a certain choreography that emphasizes movement and flexibility in narrative progression" ("Long Road" 54). Similarly, compared, for example, to Mootoo's and Oberlander's single-channel video *A Paddle and a Compass*, the triple-screen format of *Paradise Omeros* exhibits considerable flexibility, fragmenting the gaze in a manner that obstructs the smooth articulation of linear narrative.

The triple screen format enables Julien in *Paradise Omeros* to rechart the Caribbean immigrant narrative of departure and arrival in the Mother Country. The temporal and geographical progression of the immigrant is confounded by what Julien describes as an "oscillation effect": "Memories, both personal and public, lead him to the metropolis, London, yet he returns to St. Lucia and back to London again through the 'loop' of the film itself projected in the gallery—the oscillation effect begins as he travels back and forth in time" ("Creolizing Vision" 155). The installation reorganizes the spatial and temporal logic of the migration narrative so that home and away, past and present become simultaneous and fluid. In this sense, triple-channel projection becomes a metaphor for the fragmented self of the modern-day immigrant, whose identity is dispersed across space and time.

At a critical moment in *Paradise Omeros*, the gaze is not only dispersed but also inverted. While underwater, the protagonist looks up through the sea at the tropical landscape, which is upside-down and blurred. Julien writes that he had wanted in *Paradise Omeros* to "return to the Caribbean as a site of mythic cultural fantasy" ("Creolizing Vision" 154). Accordingly, *Paradise Omeros* cites both the tourist's vision of the Caribbean as an Edenic island (the cruise ship makes an appearance at one point in the film) and the Caribbean immigrant's idealized image of home and fantasy of return. In inverting the paradisal image, however, Julien suggests that the island offers no stable point of return and reconnection for the protagonist. In a second scene of underwater inversion, the protagonist is depicted upside down in the center screen with images of rioting in London on either side of him, so that the space of the sea becomes an image for the disorientation caused by immigration. The Caribbean landscape's vivid and dreamlike features in *Paradise Omeros* initially correspond to the tourist's and immigrant's fantasies of belonging. Yet both of these fantasies are undermined by Julien's inversion of the paradisal image and by his juxtaposition of the tropics with the dystopian landscape of urban alienation.

While *Paradise Omeros* references tourist and immigrant journeys, a different kind of travel narrative is the subject of Julien's yet more deeply provocative installation *True North*. This fourteen-minute film installation is the first in a trilogy of films by Julien about historical expeditions. *True North* once again adopts a triple-channel and large-screen format to meditate on landscape aesthetics and their relationship to belonging, but here it is the visual vocabulary of the sublime rather than the paradisal that Julien cites. In *True North*, Julien also reaches beyond the immediate geography of the Black Atlantic and chooses to portray an arctic adventure. He comments that "the whole idea of *True North* is to do something that could be perceived as unexpected, perhaps not directly related to the Black Atlantic in terms of its impulse. It is related to the idea of setting out on a quest which is not predestined" ("Isaac Julien" 85–86). Julien's departure from the Black Atlantic paradigm in *True North* and the metaphor of the open-ended quest signal that with this installation, he is moving still further away from the essentialist models of black aesthetics that he has long resisted.

Like Mootoo and Oberlander's *A Paddle and a Compass* and Kincaid's plant-hunting writing, *True North* introduces an unlikely presence into the wilderness landscape and at the same time references exploration narratives. *True North* is inspired by the story of Matthew Henson (1866–1965), an African American arctic explorer who accompanied Robert E. Peary on a series of arctic expeditions between 1891 and 1909, including a 1909 expedition that is generally credited as the first successful attempt to reach the North Pole. Henson, who was born in Maryland and began his career as a cabin boy and sailor, published an autobiographical account of the expedition entitled *A Negro Explorer at the North Pole* (1912). Henson's heroic narrative of his exploits and his idealized characterization of his relations with the Inuit differ sharply in tone and perspective from Julien's cinematic reimagining of the scene of arctic exploration.

In Julien's *True North,* we initially see the figure of the explorer from the back, walking across a wide, empty arctic landscape. The race and gender of the subject, who is covered in a long coat and fur hat, are not immediately discernable. However, the image of the black coat and silhouette of the explorer against the vast, snowy landscape creates a play of black and white that signals the film's concern with blackness and anticipates the black face that will eventually be revealed when the figure turns dramatically toward the camera (fig. 2). Thus, Julien introduces a nonwhite presence into the arctic wilderness to test the viewer's assumptions regarding who "belongs" in this setting. Neither white nor indigenous, the explorer becomes a third term in the installation's meditation on identity. The introduction of the third term of blackness against the arctic backdrop destabilizes binary formulations and challenges the easy equation of blackness with the Other, instead presenting a fluid and relational set of interdependent identities.

Julien's interrogation of the arctic exploration narrative goes beyond merely substituting a black presence for a white one, however. Julien casts a black female actress, Vanessa Myrie, in the role of the explorer,

Figure 2. Isaac Julien, *True North Series,* 2004. Digital print on Epson Premium Photo Glossy. Edition of six. Image: 100 x 100 cm each; frame: 114 x 114 cm. (Courtesy the artist and Victoria Miro Gallery)

problematizing the gendering of the exploration narrative in a manner that recalls *A Paddle and a Compass*'s commentary on the marginal status of female explorers. Adding to the gender confusion in *True North,* brief excerpts from what appears to be Henson's travel narrative are read by a female voice: "I think I am the first man to sit on top of the world," she remarks. In this way, Julien exposes the exploration narrative's masculine bias as well as its racial encoding.

Significantly, while *True North* seeks to recover the historical memory of Henson's forgotten exploration narrative, it does not celebrate or romanticize Henson's exploits. In his introduction to Henson's *A Negro Explorer at the North Pole,* Booker T. Washington situates Henson in a long tradition of African Americans who traveled with their European masters on voyages of New World exploration to find "the fabulous seven cities" and to found colonies. "There are few great adventures in which the American white man has engaged where he has not been accompanied by a colored man" (xviii), Washington asserts, and he declares himself eager to preserve "the records of the members of the race who have been a part of any great and historic achievement" (xix). Bradley Robinson's *Dark Companion* continues this mode of hagiography, as does S. Allen Counter's *North Pole Legacy: Black, White & Eskimo,* which records Counter's efforts to trace Henson's descendants and to have Henson's remains reinterred in Arlington National Cemetery next to those of Peary. By contrast, in Julien's reworking of Henson's exploration narrative, the black explorer's desire to take possession of the landscape is called into question. At one point, the narrator proclaims: "To be entombed in ice, to freeze as you walk, or to drop from starvation, is all in the game. Death can come from a hundred directions at once in that frozen waste. But there's a glory locked in the heart of that icy hell, and my soul will never give me peace until it's mine." Later, we see black hands reaching out to the landscape, a gesture that suggests a desire for possession of the land. The film interrogates this rhetoric of "glorious" possession, as well as Henson's sublime vision of the arctic landscape.[10]

Initially, the image of the lone figure of the explorer trekking across the stark, empty landscape appears to reinscribe the tropes of virgin wilderness and heroic conquest. The sublime character of the landscape is enhanced by the large-screen format and the almost abstract images of waterfalls and rocky terrain. At the same time, however, the triple-screen format enables multiple perspectives on the scene of exploration to emerge. The three adjacent projected images are often unsynchronized, their relationships to one another neither sequential nor causal. In *True*

North, as in many of his works, Julien directs his actors to stare directly into the camera, thematizing the power of the gaze both to define and to challenge.

Kobena Mercer suggests that Julien's films work to induce a kind of reverie and then insert a jarring "moment of surprise" that shakes the viewer out of his habitual ways of seeing (Mercer and Darke 8). In *True North*, such a "moment of surprise" comes when the explorer stumbles on the ice and apparently falls, knocking herself unconscious. The three screens briefly go blank, and when the images are restored, they reveal a significantly different scene. A dogsled comes into view on the left-hand screen while a male Inuit face fills the screen on the right, so that suddenly the arctic landscape is no longer virgin nor empty. The face of the black explorer subsequently reappears to fill the middle screen, but this time she is flanked on either side by male Inuit faces (fig. 3). Now, she appears to be traveling with the group of Inuit, and she is later shown walking with Inuit companions on either side of her. As throat singing is heard in the background, the screens fill with scenes of dogs and Inuit dwellings.

Thus, all at once, the landscape has become much fuller: busier and noisier with both human and animal activity. The voice-over narration, with its heroic overtones, briefly returns. But now the explorer's ambition to take possession of the landscape is recast in light of the revelation that it is a populated space into which she has intruded. "I think I've overrun my mark," the narrator subsequently confesses. The "moment of surprise" in *True North* leads to a shift in perspective, to the introduction of an alternative way of seeing in which the landscape of exploration is inhabited rather than virgin, and in which Inuit and intruder coexist in a relationship of contact and interdependence.

Julien's juxtaposition of black and Inuit figures in *True North* recalls Mordecai Richler's comic novel *Solomon Gursky Was Here* (1990), in which a Russian Jew travels to the Canadian Arctic and inserts himself into an Inuit community, becoming the progenitor of a tribe of Inuit Jews who abide by the laws of *kashrut* and braid their parkas like *tallit*. Indeed, Counter's *North Pole Legacy*, which documents the presence of "dark-skinned Eskimos in Greenland" descended from Matthew Henson, reads like a real-life version of Richler's fantasy of the indigenization of the immigrant through miscegenation with the Inuit. In his book, Counter, a professor of neuroscience and a professional explorer, explains how he traveled to the Arctic to locate Henson's half-Inuit son and his grandchildren, whom he subsequently brought to the United States to meet

Figure 3. Isaac Julien, *True North Series*, 2004. Digital print on Epson Premium Photo Glossy. Edition of six. Image: 100 x 100 cm each; frame: 114 x 114 cm. (Courtesy the artist and Victoria Miro Gallery)

their African American relatives. For Counter, the Inuit descendants of Henson are biological evidence of Henson's sympathetic bond with the Inuit. Richler's novel, by contrast, finds great comic potential in the juxtaposition of immigrant and Native.

Julien's *True North* follows neither the sentimental nor the comic model. *True North* is eerie, futuristic, containing science fiction–like sequences as well as dramatic scenes of the vast arctic landscape, and the broader impact of the film is to unsettle, rather than divert, the viewer. The cool, stark aesthetic of the film could be characterized as sublime, a mode that Julien associates with the Other and with the problem of belonging ("Isaac Julien" 86). Like Stan Douglas, Julien privileges the sublime for its evocation of the limits of representation. Even as *True North* deploys the sublime, however, it problematizes it as a mode of perception that empties the landscape, revealing its complicity in the dispossession of the land's indigenous inhabitants.

True North does not support Henson's claim in his autobiography to an easy identification and solidarity between black and Inuit. In *A Negro Explorer,* Henson describes how he had "gone native" in the Arctic: "Many and many a time, for periods covering more than twelve months, I have been to all intents an Esquimo, with Esquimos for companions, speaking their language, dressing in the same kind of clothes, living in the same kind of dens, eating the same food, enjoying their pleasures, and frequently sharing their griefs. I have come to love these people. I know every man, woman, and child in their tribe. They are my friends and they regard me as theirs" (6–7). Counter's *North Pole Legacy* makes similar assertions about Henson's unique capacity to assimilate into Inuit society, noting that Henson was the only one of Peary's crew to learn the language of the Inuit: "Even the great Ootah said that while the other outsiders were like children in the ways of the Eskimo, Mahri-Pahluk ["Matthew the Kind One"] was a natural in their world. He was one of them" (7).[11] Julien challenges such claims through his visually jarring juxtapositions of black and Inuit figures in *True North,* which generate a sense of tension rather than solidarity. Instead of celebrating the heroic exploits of Matthew Henson, Julien chooses instead to raise questions regarding the implications for the contemporary diasporic artist of perpetuating narratives of colonial exploration, even when their subject is black rather than white. Diasporic appropriations of the exploration narrative are, Julien suggests, no less subject to critique and interrogation than are their Euro-American counterparts.

Critical Pastoralism in Jin-me Yoon's *Touring Home from Away*

One of the most provocative contemporary commentators on diasporic identity and its relationship to landscape is Korean Canadian photographer and video artist Jin-me Yoon. A striking feature of Yoon's work is that it frequently departs from the urban setting that we often associate with diasporic cultural production. Several of Yoon's photographic works juxtapose minority presences with iconic Canadian landscapes, exposing the dynamics of inclusion and exclusion that inform them. *Souvenirs of the Self* (1991), one of Yoon's best-known pieces, features a young Asian woman, perhaps a tourist, posing before majestic views of the Western

Figure 4. Jin-me Yoon, *Souvenirs of the Self* (postcard project), 1991. Six perforated postcards. 4" x 6" each. (Courtesy Catriona Jeffries Gallery, Vancouver)

landscape of Banff National Park (fig. 4). In this postcard series, the insertion of a "foreign" presence into an iconic Canadian landscape challenges the viewer to consider whether a nonwhite woman can be naturalized as Canadian in this heroic setting. Another well-known work of Yoon's, *A Group of Sixty-Seven* (1996), similarly exposes the ideological underpinnings of entrenched images of the Canadian landscape. Here, sixty-seven Korean Canadians pose in front of landscape paintings by well-known early-twentieth-century Canadian painters Lawren Harris and Emily Carr, generating a sense of discomfort and incongruity, and calling attention to the role of landscape representation in the construction of national belonging. The Group of Seven, to whom the title of Yoon's work alludes, have been criticized for the wilderness mythology that they promoted as well as their appropriation and effacement of First Nation cultures. Yoon's photographs extend such critiques, unsettling the images of the Canadian wilderness that were so central to the project of Canadian nation building in the early twentieth century.[12]

Yoon's photographic installation *Touring Home from Away,* while continuing to foreground landscape, departs from her earlier work by developing a critical pastoral mode that promotes new forms of emplacement. Previous chapters suggested that the pastoral mode in its complex form is employed by contemporary writers from the Caribbean and North

America who seek to articulate a sense of place and at the same time to register experiences of dislocation. Yet these discussions also indicated that while the pastoral mode enables the retention of place as a meaningful concept in contemporary diasporic writing, it runs certain risks. How are these risks negotiated in the context of visual art, however?

We have already seen how Julien's *Paradise Omeros* dramatically juxtaposes the paradisal island with a dystopian urban setting in a manner that corresponds to a pastoral contrast between the ideal and the real. The triple-channel format enables Julien to present a "both/and" rather than an "either/or" scenario of contemporary identity in which place and displacement supplement rather than supplant one another. *Touring* achieves a parallel effect through the use of double-sided lightboxes. The installation consists of eighteen photographic prints displayed on nine illuminated double-sided lightboxes suspended from the ceiling.[13] In the image pairs displayed on the lightboxes, Yoon continues the investigation of the ideological function of landscape and the figure of the tourist that she had begun in *Souvenirs of the Self* and *A Group of Sixty-Seven,* but she now turns her attention to the East Coast and to a markedly different landscape: that of Prince Edward Island. In her artist's statement for the show, Yoon notes that "the touristic imagery of PEI largely presents it as 'the birthplace of Canada' and as a happily insular island that revels in a seemingly pristine and pastoral environment sheltered from the damaging effects of modernity" (qtd. in Hurtig 9). PEI is thus a site rich in associations with Canadian belonging and heritage, while also carrying the conventional associations of island space with protective insularity and separation.

Touring works to uncover contradictions between notions of inclusivity and exclusivity in the popular and touristic discourses surrounding PEI and to expose the ambiguities that attend such terms as "native," "tourist," "home," and "belonging." Here, as in Yoon's earlier work, it is frequently difficult for the viewer to determine whether the subjects of the photographs are locals or visitors to the landscape.[14] One pair of images depicts a mother, father, and child standing in a potato field (fig. 5). In the first of two paired photographs, the family, dressed as farmers in denim and gingham, faces away from us toward a bucolic landscape of rolling green fields and blue sky. With their backs to us, the figures are unidentifiable except as a man, a woman, and a young child. In the second photograph, however, the family members face toward us and wear Anne of Green Gables T-shirts, seemingly marking them as "visitors."[15] Yet with their faces now visible, we are able to identify them as a mixed-race family, generating further ambiguity with regard to their status. The mother's Asian appearance references the Japanese enthusiasm for Anne of Green Gables and the tourism industry to which this enthusiasm has contributed, but the father's apparent whiteness suggests that he may in fact be a "true blue" Prince Edward Islander.[16] Moreover, in both images the family members, who stand in the field in furrows so deep that their feet are hidden, appear embedded in the land, as though planting themselves in the pastoral landscape.

Yoon's move to the gentler landscape of PEI signals a subtle shift in her landscape aesthetics from a critique of conventional models of rootedness and national belonging toward the formulation of new modes of belonging. While this emphasis on emplacement is evident to some extent in the rather defiant presence of the subject of *Souvenirs of the Self*,[17] it becomes more pronounced in *Touring*. The pastoral landscapes of *Touring* are more inviting of a human presence than the sublime Rockies or the depopulated Group of Seven landscapes featured in Yoon's earlier work. For while the sublime would tend to thematize and heighten the alienated condition of the diasporic subject, the pastoral invites the human subject into a harmonious relationship with the land, incorporating rather than expelling a human presence.

Figure 5. Jin-me Yoon, *Touring Home from Away,* 1999. Nine custom-fabricated black-anodized, double-sided lightboxes on black metal pedestals. 32" x 26" x 5" each. (Collection of Confederation Centre for the Arts, Charlottetown. Courtesy Catriona Jeffries Gallery, Vancouver.)

However, if Yoon draws on a pastoral register of imagery in *Touring*, she does so in a highly self-conscious and critical manner. Each image pair functions to produce a sense of tension and ambiguity, as the images play off of and contradict one another. An instructive example is a pair of images portraying Yoon's mother and baby daughter. While the first image inscribes the "natural" relationship of the human subjects to the land (underscored by the grandmother's traditional Korean baby-wrap), the second image foregrounds their "foreignness" as tourist/visitors (signaled by the grandmother's golfing outfit). And while the first image presents a "natural" agricultural landscape, the second highlights the artificial, Disneyesque landscape of consumption and tourism. Thus, the relatively static medium of photography is rendered much more dynamic through the use of the double-sided lightboxes that juxtapose pastoral and anti-pastoral images. As in *Paradise Omeros*, the simultaneity of these conflicting images defies linear, progressive narrative and destabilizes the opposition of home and away, creating an oscillation effect.

The continual movement in *Touring* between the two poles of native and foreign, pastoral and antipastoral, natural and artificial, lends Yoon's pastoralism a complex, double-edged quality. Yoon's PEI idylls do not constitute an escapist fantasy but instead are always framed by contact with modernity. The island space of PEI is not allowed to remain insular and cut off from history, but rather is thoroughly informed by the tourist economy and other markers of modernity. The lush appeal of the PEI landscape is qualified by the homogenizing world of tourism and consumption that borders it. *Touring* thus encompasses *both* the anguish of exile *and* the deep pleasures of emplacement.

While pastoral supports an exploration of displacement, it does not evacuate the category of place. Accordingly, in Yoon's photographs, geographically specific conceptions of home and belonging continue to have meaning and relevance. However, such meanings must continually be questioned. Instead of either indulging in an Edenic fantasy of uncomplicated rootedness on the one hand, or positing a free-floating rootlessness on the other, Yoon continually moves between natural and artificial landscapes in such a way as to embed her pastoral landscapes in time, history, and modernity. In the final image pair of *Touring*, a vision of pastoral plenitude and familial harmony is coupled with a desolate image of the family at a strip mall pushing an empty shopping cart (fig. 6). Together, the two images at once evoke and problematize the pastoral fantasy of escape. The placelessness and anonymity of the strip mall is not cause for postmodern celebration, but neither is it an aspect of contemporary life

Figure 6. Jin-me Yoon, *Touring Home from Away*, 1999. Nine custom-fabricated black-anodized, double-sided lightboxes on black metal pedestals. 32" x 26" x 5" each. (Collection of Confederation Centre for the Arts, Charlottetown. Courtesy Catriona Jeffries Gallery, Vancouver.)

that can be denied. The contentment of the bucolic scene, on the other hand, is deeply appealing and makes up a part of the family's experience, but it is incomplete and does not preclude the strip mall scene. Both sets of experience are fundamental to the story of contemporary identity that Yoon tells, and it is their dissonant coexistence that generates meaning in her work.

Together with Julien's *Paradise Omeros,* Yoon's recuperation of the pastoral in *Touring* suggests how this mode in its complex, critical version may be productively employed by artists who seek to present experiences of dislocation without sacrificing the meaningfulness of place. The appeal of the pastoral mode for both contemporary writers and artists lies in its capacity to register simultaneously the experience of place and displacement. Julien's and Yoon's installations elaborate a tensive, contrastive structure resembling that developed in the contemporary fiction and poetry discussed in the first half of this book. Yet released from the constraints of linear narrative, their installations lend new dimension to this juxtapositional structure. The oscillation effect generated by the spatial arrangement of Yoon's double-sided lightboxes and Julien's triple-screen projection expresses the simultaneity of place and displacement with greater immediacy and intensity than is possible in the novel form, which is necessarily more linear and sequential in structure.

Yoon remains vigilant in her formulation of new possibilities of belonging and geographical attachment on a number of levels. But perhaps one of her most significant gestures is her juxtaposition of diasporic and First Nations presences. In *A Group of Sixty-Seven,* she had photographed Korean Canadian subjects gazing into a painting by Emily Carr, an early-twentieth-century Canadian artist known for her depictions of First Nations villages and the west coast landscape. Yoon's subjects pose in front of Carr's *Old Time Coastal Village* (1929–30) in such a way as to obscure the village depicted in the painting, problematically effacing the First Nations presence. Relatedly, in *Touring,* Yoon photographs herself together with the Mi'kmaq activist John Joe Sark (fig. 7). In the first image, Yoon's back is turned, and with her dark hair and skin, she "passes" for Native. In the second image, however, her face becomes partially visible just as the landscape is revealed to be not wild, as it had at first appeared, but a golf course. In this second image, a tension emerges between the two figures, as Yoon looks at Sark with a questioning gaze, while he appears closed off, arms crossed across his chest. Like Mootoo and Julien, then, Yoon hints at the cost of new emplacements by asking who risks being displaced by them. In Yoon's work, diasporic and First

Figure 7. Jin-me Yoon, *Touring Home from Away,* 1999. Nine custom-fabricated black-anodized, double-sided lightboxes on black metal pedestals. 32" x 26" x 5" each. (Collection of Confederation Centre for the Arts, Charlottetown. Courtesy Catriona Jeffries Gallery, Vancouver.)

Nations peoples are as likely to be in competition with one another as they are to be in solidarity.

In exploring the possibilities of diasporic belonging, the artworks considered in this chapter suggest that ultimately, the most perplexing aspect of the project of New World emplacement may concern the indigenous presence. Accordingly, Julien's *True North* and Yoon's *Touring* heighten rather than resolve tensions between place and displacement, settlement and dispossession, indigenous and diasporic perspectives, by attending to the expropriation of indigenous peoples. Even as Julien and Yoon contest from a diasporic perspective the exclusionary force of established traditions of landscape representation, they acknowledge their own potential collusion in these traditions. In their works, the deep sense of ambiguity surrounding place and its relationship to conquest indicates that to construct a sense of place is always to run the risk of displacing someone else.[18]

Conclusion

MARC AUGÉ'S *Non-Places: Introduction to an Anthropology of Supermodernity* opens with an anecdote about a French businessman traveling through Charles de Gaulle Airport. While awaiting takeoff, the man becomes captivated by a car advertisement in the in-flight magazine that reads: "'One day, the need for space makes itself felt. . . . The irresistible wish for a space of our own. A mobile space which can take us anywhere'" (4). The peculiarly postmodern fascination with "mobile space" and with the airport as a site of deterritorialized belonging that this passage from Augé exemplifies (one that also finds expression in numerous other texts including Pico Iyer's *The Global Soul* [2000]) reflects the extent to which, in our contemporary moment, previously assumed links between geography and identity have become deeply suspect. The presupposition that there is a homologous relationship between territory and identity is by now widely refuted. From this perspective, place is rejected as inherently nostalgic, while airport lounges, hotels, and theme parks as well as border zones and refugee camps are privileged as spaces in which the cultural, political, and economic implications of globalization can be registered. Fearing that a geographically fixed conception of home will inevitably fall back on myths of origin, Augé and other contemporary cultural commentators embrace a vision of perpetual unbelonging, inbetweeness, and emptied, fluid space. They tell a story about time-space compression that foregrounds travel and other deterritorialized "flows" and that relies on metaphors of vacuity as well as open spatial metaphors such as "contact zones" and "borderlands."

In this book, I have asked whether such an emphasis represents the full range of experiences of current cultural geographies. Critiques of territorializing constructions of identity, while compelling, leave many questions unanswered, particularly for those such as art historian Miwon Kwon who suspect that traditional conceptions of rootedness are not so easily dispensed with. Kwon identifies a "persistent, perhaps secret adherence to the actuality of places" that "may not be a lack of theoretical sophistication but a means of survival" (165). Many critics are uneasy about the persistence of this attachment to place because of its negative associations with nationalism and nostalgia. Perhaps less encumbered by such anxieties than their colleagues in the academy, however, contemporary writers and artists of the Americas continue to explore the multiple meanings of place, which they attempt to reinvent in a mode that reflects their time and perspective.

If the deterritorialization of culture has produced an urgent need for new narratives of belonging, the authors and artists discussed in this book suggest one such possible narrative. They employ landscape and botanical imagery despite the problematic history of its usage because it enables them to challenge exclusionary constructions of the relationship between land and identity and yet at the same time ensures that their works retain a strong connection to place. For example, the garden's dual associations with rootedness and transplantation keep both terms—*place* and *displacement*—in play. Most saliently, such rereadings of New World landscapes suggest that rather than dislodging older, more rooted models of identity, new insights into the processual and dynamic character of place and identity supplement and coexist with these prior models. Thus, in contrast to the polarization of place and displacement that characterizes much diaspora criticism, the writing and artworks that I have surveyed are governed by a "both/and" logic that understands rooted and nomadic models of identity as coterminous rather than mutually exclusive. Instead of exchanging old narratives of identity for new ones, these works juxtapose territorialized and deterritorialized narratives of identity.

The continuing prominence of botanical and landscape imagery in contemporary writing and art of the Americas is indicative of the failure of deterritorialized models of identity to supersede more traditional, rooted models. For while these works reject stable identities and fixed relationships to place, they do not celebrate placelessness, nor do they subscribe to a postmodern vision of mobile, emptied space. Instead, their focus on landscape suggests that it is their very recognition that no absolute stability is possible that compels them to seek out new strategies for establishing a sense of place. Landscapes such as Jamaica Kincaid's Vermont and Jin-me Yoon's Prince Edward Island, as well as botanical motifs such as Shani Mootoo's cereus plant and Maryse Condé's mangrove, insist by virtue of their dynamism that the rootedness they represent is never secure but instead must be continually renegotiated. To insert oneself into a landscape or to plant a garden is to lay claim to a sense of place, but place is understood as an ongoing, laborious, and always provisional process.

Taken together, these works articulate a revised New World landscape poetics, one that is complex, self-reflexive, and entangled with history. They demonstrate that it is possible to retain territorialized narratives of identity without at the same time perpetuating nostalgic and essentialist fantasies of uncomplicated belonging. What makes this new vision possible is their deep awareness of the histories of dispossession and competing claims to the land that haunt New World societies. By vigilantly acknowledging tensions between the basic human desire for a sense of place and the historical reality of displacement—and between diasporic and indigenous claims to the land—these authors and artists mobilize landscape and botanical imagery to generate a new poetics of American belonging. They revisit and reinvent established landscape ideas through a series of second arrivals, both geographical and conceptual, in the New World.

Notes

Introduction

1. On the relative absence of place from current critical discussions, see the preface to Edward S. Casey's *The Fate of Place*. Casey traces how space (undelimited and infinite) comes to supersede place (delimited and having to do with location and habitation) as a central concern of modern theology, philosophy, and science.

2. Similarly, Vijay Mishra distinguishes between older, "exclusive" diasporas that "share many of the characteristics of the so-called ideal type of the Jewish diaspora," and more recent "border diasporas" that are typified by their mobility (427).

3. See James Clifford's critique of William Safran's account of diaspora (305). See also Daniel and Jonathan Boyarin, who argue that Jewish theology itself invites a deterritorialization of identity. In their reading, Jewish tradition exhibits an ambivalent relationship to land and contains an internal critique of myths of autochthonous claims on the land (715–16).

4. The renewed attention to space in the work of such critics as Henri Lefebvre and Edward Soja has valuably shown that, far from being "innocent," "*(social) space is a (social) product*" (Lefebvre 26) and is "filled with politics and ideology" (Soja 6). Yet, as Patricia Yaeger notes, the postmodern analyses of space elaborated by Baudrillard, Foucault, and Lefebvre make particular generic choices and choices of imagery that may limit their usefulness: "Why is the postmodern object world perpetually arrayed in metaphors of emptiness, vacuity, or amnesia?" Yaeger asks. "Is this an adequate response to the crisis in translocality, globalization, deterritorialization, and postcolonization that has changed the face of the earth?" (9). The devaluation of place implicit in such metaphors has not gone unchallenged, however, particularly by feminist critics who have argued that the question is not whether place is obsolete but rather, what are the ways in which place can be reformulated? See Caren Kaplan (ch. 4) on the importance of theories of location and emplacement in feminist criticism.

5. Susie O'Brien notes that postcolonial studies similarly has developed an "urban outlook": "Notwithstanding a strong strand of pastoralism in postcolonial

literatures, postcolonial *criticism* tends, by contrast with ecocriticism, to envision the world through urban eyes" ("Articulating" 142). Relatedly, in *Sowing Empire,* Jill H. Casid remarks that landscape "is still hardly a popular concept in post-colonial studies," which tends to privilege "space" and "place" rather than the ideologically tainted notion of landscape (192).

6. Thus, for example, Iain Chambers writes that "this transformation in our understanding of movement, marginality and modern life is inextricably tied to the metropolisation of the globe, where the model of the city becomes . . . the model of the contemporary world" (27).

7. Anthony Orum and Xiangming Chen (55) cite Peter Hall's *The World Cities* (1966) as an early instance of the application of global perspectives to the city, with Saskia Sassen's *The Global City* (1991) providing another benchmark. For more recent examples, see Peter J. Taylor, *World City Network: A Global Urban Analysis* (New York: Routledge, 2004); Michael Peter Smith, *Transnational Urbanism: Locating Globalization* (Oxford: Blackwell, 2001); and Peter Marcuse and Ronald van Kempen, eds., *Globalizing Cities: A New Spatial Order?* (Oxford: Blackwell, 2000).

8. David Lowenthal notes, "Countries commonly depict themselves in landscape terms; they hallow traits they fancy uniquely theirs. Every national anthem praises special scenic splendours or nature's unique bounties" (17). On the role of rural scenes in British national representation, see Kenneth Olwig, Elizabeth Helsinger, and Alun Howkins. While Helsinger's focus is on the early nineteenth century, and Howkins deals with the late nineteenth century on through to the interwar period, Olwig's study takes in a broader historical sweep and also includes a discussion of the United States. On rural and wilderness scenes in the U.S. national imaginary, see Lawrence Buell's *Environmental Imagination;* on Canada, see W. H. New's *Land Sliding;* and on the Caribbean, see J. Michael Dash's *Other America*. On the Swiss example, see Anthony D. Smith (150–53).

9. See Roger Waldinger and Jennifer Lee's study of urban immigration in the United States. Compare to Orum and Chen, however, who write that immigration since 1965 has in fact followed a different pattern, in which many new immigrants to the United States have taken up residence in the suburbs rather than passing through the city first (86–87).

10. I am inspired here by Caren Kaplan's and Chris Bongie's observations that contemporary models of identity may not so much substitute as supplement earlier models. Kaplan suggests that "modernity's stress on fragmentation and change is best read in tension with the grand narratives of holistic systems of explanation, of social cohesion, and of national and other forms of identity" (19). Relatedly, Bongie observes that "the connection between fixed and relational identities is not (simply) a matter of either/or but (also) of both/and" (66).

11. Denis E. Cosgrove explains the concept of a "landscape idea" as follows: "Landscape is a way of seeing that has its own history, but a history that can be understood only as part of a wider history of economy and society; that has its

own assumptions and consequences, but assumptions and consequences whose origins and implications extend well beyond the use and perception of land; that has its own techniques of expression, but techniques which it shares with other areas of cultural practice" (1).

12. The landscape of Bernardin de Saint-Pierre's colonial idyll features abundant vegetation (mangoes, oranges, bananas, pineapples, etc.) as well as two highly romanticized slaves, Domingue and Marie. As Bongie comments in his discussion of *Paul et Virginie,* Bernardin answers the question "Will a new Arcadia never reappear in some corner of the globe?" (Saint-Pierre, qtd. in Bongie 87) by providing a specific geographical location for Arcadia in the French colony of Mauritius (87).

13. Pastoral takes on a similarly domesticating function in nineteenth-century Australian literature and art. As Bernard Smith notes in *European Vision and the South Pacific,* "The emergence of pastoral imagery in colonial Australia made it possible to present a version of Australian nature more amenable to the European imagination" (269). Accordingly, a publisher's blurb for an 1821 book of engravings of the Australian landscape assured its readers, "They will serve to show and convince from what slender beginnings, and in how few years, the primeval forest . . . may be converted into plains covered with bleating flocks, lowing herds and waving corn" (qtd. in Bernard Smith 236). See also Paul Carter, who shows how the task of persuading the Australian public that areas were habitable and "imaginable" was achieved through the application of landscape imagery in works such as Sir Thomas Mitchell's *Journal of an Expedition into the Interior of Tropical Australia* (1848) and its accompanying illustrations.

14. See, for example, Brenda Lafleur's critique of the Group of Seven. For revisionary readings of the American West, see especially the essays contained in William H. Truettner's edited collection *The West as America,* which accompanied the controversial Smithsonian exhibition of the same name.

15. What often goes unremarked upon in such discussions is that Raymond Williams's critique has a specific rather than a general target: it is directed primarily against the seventeenth-century country house pastorals of poets such as Ben Jonson and Thomas Carew, which naturalized the prevailing social order and excised laborers from the rural landscape. By contrast, in Virgil's *Eclogues,* as Williams points out, there is an awareness of the actual conditions of rural life that "breaks through into the poetically distant Arcadia" (16). But beginning with the Renaissance adaptation of Virgilian pastoral, "these living tensions are excised, until there is nothing countervailing" (18). In Williams's account, then, pastoral is not a static mode but instead undergoes a series of historical transformations that reflect particular social and political contexts; yet his denunciation of the seventeenth- and eighteenth-century country house pastoral is so persuasive that it is often taken as though it were a pronouncement on pastoral's essential nature.

16. At the same time, the juxtaposition of the ideal and the real that is the hallmark of complex pastoral may be traced back to its classical origins. Preeminently

in Virgil's *Eclogues,* a vision of the fullness of place is set alongside the experience of exile and dispossession. Virgil's first eclogue quite strikingly opens with the theme of exile, juxtaposing the tranquil repose of Tityrus, who has secured his claim to a plot of land, with the tragic predicament of Meliboeus, who is being expelled from the land he has farmed. Throughout "Eclogue I," Meliboeus repeatedly attempts to make his rather oblivious friend Tityrus acknowledge his plight. Thus we become acutely aware of the fragility of the Arcadian world, of the threat of dispossession and exile that lies just outside its borders. Accordingly, the more sensitive critical accounts of pastoral emphasize not its escapism but its attention to human vulnerability: "Separation and loss are also central in pastoral representations of social injustice, like the dispossessed homesteaders of Virgil's first and ninth Eclogues," Paul Alpers observes. "The usual ideas of nostalgia and idyllic retreat wrongly construe the way pastoral deals with such themes, but there is no doubt that from its beginning, the form has been concerned with various human separations and their implications" (92).

17. Joan Dayan makes the compelling argument in *Haiti, History and the Gods* (ch. 4) that if African religious traditions contributed to the emergence of a Caribbean gothic, it was also the product of Enlightenment attempts to rationalize the dehumanization of slaves by attributing monstrous and supernatural qualities to them. Thus, the significance of Haitian voodoo is not reducible to the retention of African religion under the guise of a superficial adherence to Catholic ritual, but instead must be understood in the historical context of slavery.

18. Dash notes the "link between landscape and self-possession" in Edouard Glissant's thinking, and identifies this motif as "the hallmark of Glissant's own creative imagination" (*Glissant* 12–13). See also Dash's introduction to Glissant's *Caribbean Discourse,* which helpfully situates the status of landscape in Glissant's poetics (xxxv–xxxviii).

19. In "Montreal," Glissant also draw parallels between the Caribbean and Quebec: "What I wish to say again about these Quebecois writers is that, paradoxically, whatever the nature of their speech and whatever they might think of the relationship I have formulated, *they are on the same side as we are in dealing with writing.* Ruralization and *Joal* have had the same effect [in Quebec] that the plantation and Creole have had on us" (*Caribbean Discourse* 153). Notably, however, the essay "Quebec" ends with a reference to Quebec's colonizing ambitions with regard to the Caribbean that would seem to work against the rapprochement of these two regions.

20. The term "First Nations" is commonly used in Canada to refer to aboriginal peoples.

1. V. S. Naipaul's and Derek Walcott's Postcolonial Pastorals

1. In his study of Naipaul, Rob Nixon suggestively describes *The Enigma of Arrival* as a "postcolonial pastoral." "There is decidedly no other British writer of Caribbean or South Asian ancestry," Nixon writes, "who would have chosen

a tucked away Wiltshire perspective from which to reflect on the themes of immigration and postcolonial decay" (161). He further observes that Naipaul's unorthodox choice of setting serves to disturb the English pastoral: "He elects himself to the great pastoral tradition of English literature, but his racial presence there ensures that he both continues and disrupts the lineage" (162).

2. While earlier in his career Naipaul had been charged with an insensitivity to landscape, a number of critics have noted a growing attention to landscape in his later writing. Indeed, in contrast to the flat, comic pastoral of *A House for Mr. Biswas* (1961), in *Enigma* the Wiltshire landscape so dominates that Naipaul's narrator tends to see it first, and its inhabitants only second. Jack is "at first a figure in the landscape to me, no more," the narrator remarks (28).

3. Walcott's paintings had previously made their way only onto the covers of his books. Walcott has exhibited his paintings but considers himself merely a competent painter. On the role of painting in Walcott's poetry, see Robert Bensen; Edward Baugh; Clara Rosa de Lima; and Rei Terada (ch. 4).

4. Naipaul's notion of the familiarity of the metropolitan landscape to the newly arrived colonial subject is echoed throughout postcolonial writing. For instance, the Indian poet Dom Moraes describes arriving in England for the first time as follows: "Showers had fallen as the *Strathmore* docked, but the clouds had moved away and from the train window the landscape, rinsed by rain, looked newly washed. Though I had never seen it before, I recognised it from books. . . . London seemed familiar too, when we reached it. . . . I knew the streets by name" (84). See also Jamaica Kincaid's essay "On Seeing England for the First Time," in which she writes that "the landscape was almost as familiar as my own hand, but I had never been in this place before, so how could that be again. And the streets of Bath were familiar, too, but I had never walked on them before. It was all those years of reading, starting with Roman Britain" (217–18).

5. Paula Burnett identifies the tamed southern English landscape as a central component of "the rhetoric of 'home'" that was initiated by white colonists but was widely disseminated among Britain's colonial subjects (34).

6. In an unpublished version of *Another Life*, Walcott writes of "a book that I used as my imaginary museum and where I had learnt all I now knew about the old masters and the great painters" (qtd. in Baugh 240).

7. Helsinger notes, "By the end of the nineteenth century, Constable's paintings had become icons of Englishness" (41). See Helsinger (ch. 1) on Constable's role as a "national painter."

8. Similarly, Walcott speaks in an interview of the peculiar importance of anthologies to the recipient of a colonial education—what he terms the "anthology influence." Growing up with a scarcity of individually published volumes, he found that "the range of the influence was simultaneous. It didn't matter if it was Shakespeare or Dylan Thomas or anyone else" ("Thinking Poetry" 176).

9. See also the similar account of this process in the section of *Enigma* entitled "The Journey" (169–70).

10. My usage of the term "entangled" is partly inspired by Helen Tiffin's discussion of Caribbean representations of nature as evoking an *"entangled* history of colonizer and colonized" (59, emphasis hers).

11. For example, Timothy Weiss, Dennis Porter, and John Thieme tend to see a new vision emerging in *Enigma,* while Walcott and Selwyn Cudjoe complain of the failure of this new vision to materialize and focus instead on the persistence of old habits. In contrast to both positions, Sara Suleri argues that Naipaul has consistently "map[ped] the complicity between postcolonial history and its imperial past" (156) and that he has not been given due credit for his "highly sophisticated ironizing of imperial mythmaking" (154). She concludes that "Naipaul's writing is perhaps more revisionary than it at first appears" (158).

12. Naipaul later writes in *Enigma* regarding his research into Trinidad's colonial and precolonial history: "Now in Trinidad . . . to see the landscape I had created in my imagination for the last two years . . . I had to ignore almost everything that leapt out at the eye, and almost everything in the vegetation that I had been trained to see as tropical and local, part of our travel-poster beauty— coconut, sugarcane, bamboo, mango, bougainvillea, poinsettia—since all those plants and trees had been imported later with the settlement and the plantations. The landscape of the past existed only in fragments" (160). In *A Way in the World* (1995), Naipaul similarly identifies a close relationship between nature and history when he remarks that it is possible to "look at the [Trinidadian] vegetation and tell you what was there when Columbus came and what was imported later" (10).

13. On this point, see also Kincaid's discussion of the contrasting meanings of gardening for Henry James and the Zimbabwean writer Tsitsi Dangarembga in her essay "To Name Is to Possess" in *My Garden (Book):*.

14. In *Another Life,* there are several references to Gauguin and one passing reference to Pissarro, but in general the attention given to the Impressionists is not as sustained as in *Tiepolo's Hound.*

15. On the Impressionists' treatment of perception, Bernard Denvir writes: "For a conceptual approach, based on ideas about the nature of what we see, [Impressionism] substituted a perceptual one, based on actual visual experience. Rejecting the idea that there exists a canon of expression for indicating moods, sentiments and arrangements of objects, it gave primacy to the subjective attitude of the artist, emphasizing spontaneity and immediacy of vision and of reaction" (11).

16. In an insightful discussion of form in *Tiepolo's Hound,* Jim Hannan identifies Walcott's chosen verse form as a radical reworking of the couplet that encourages the reader "to reenvision the familiar as the occasion for a new insight" (574). Paul Breslin, by contrast, identifies Walcott's broken quatrains as Gray's elegiac stanzas split in half, an observation that connects *Tiepolo's Hound* to the pastoral on a formal as well as a thematic level.

17. The ceiling motif appears on pages 19, 42, 70, 83, 88, and 97.

18. Svetlana Alpers and Michael Baxandall discuss the role of dogs in Tiepolo's painting and in particular their tendency to "diver[t] us from human affairs" (31). They note that Tiepolo's dogs, who "invert social hierarchy" (32), were borrowed from Veronese, whose work greatly influenced that of Tiepolo.

19. In book 4 of *Tiepolo's Hound*, "an admiring African peers from the canvas's edge" while the narrator "watch[es] from the painting's side" (129).

20. For example, Richard Brettell's *Pissarro and Pontoise* makes hardly any reference to Pissarro's Caribbean background or his Jewishness. See Nicholas Mirzoeff for a revisionist reading that identifies both Pissarro's Jewishness and his Caribbean background as central to his aesthetics and politics.

21. Other examples of this reciprocity of the two landscapes in *Enigma* include the skeleton of a hare that reminds the narrator of that of a pelican in a channel between Trinidad and Venezuela (185) and a ruined boathouse on a creek that recalls a more tropical scene of ruin on the Orinoco, Amazon, or Congo rivers (207).

22. Nonetheless, Terada notes, "The pastoral wish that poetry may be simple, like carpentry or gardening, lies behind many of these poems. Although Walcott doesn't use the word 'pastoral' much—Caliban *would* view pastoral with a skeptical eye—his whole enterprise is pastoral, if we mean by that the transfer of peace to a phantasmal realm, or a verbal harmony so pure that in its hush no one can recall contention" (180–81). Terada also discusses Walcott's "pastoralization of epic" in *Omeros*, his privileging of the humble, the modest, and the peaceful over traditional epic values (186). Terada's definition of pastoral is, however, somewhat different from mine, focusing more on formal than on thematic concerns. Burnett (again defining pastoral differently) rejects the term altogether: Walcott's "representation of the island space cannot be contained as a species of pastoral, in which a 'locus amoenus' is held up in opposition to a metropolitan society as a means of interrogating the latter. Its primary motor is, rather, an assertion of its own particularity, for its own sake, and for its own community" (30). Burnett is using pastoral here in a simple or nostalgic sense rather than a complex one.

23. See, for instance, ch. 7 of *Another Life*. For a fuller discussion of Wordsworthian influences in *Another Life*, see my essay "Autobiography as Rewriting."

24. In *Omeros*, Caribbean fishermen take on the traditional role of shepherds in Virgilian pastoral, establishing a Caribbean pastoral that exists in tension both with Major Plunkett's Edenic vision of the Caribbean and with the "pastoral sites" of England. See Gregson Davis for a discussion of pastoral motifs in *Omeros*.

25. A. Alvarez comments that "*Tiepolo's Hound* is illustrated by a not particularly relevant selection of his watercolors," while John Kinsella complains that the inclusion of Walcott's "competent" but "dated and drab" paintings is "bewildering except in terms of the aims of a gift book." Breslin is more sympathetic toward Walcott's skills as a painter but draws no thematic connections between the paintings and the poem's content.

26. See *Another Life*, ch. 9, sec. 3, for another example of the pastoralism inspired by the legacy of his father. In the poem, the blond-haired Anna—"Anna of the wheatfield and the weir"—is also strongly associated with pastoral imagery, as for instance in ch. 15.

2. The Myth of the West in Bernard Malamud and Philip Roth

1. See, for instance, Murray Baumgarten's emphasis on the Jewish experience of urban life in his *City Scriptures*. For Baumgarten, the paradigmatic narrative of modern Jewish writing is that which traces the move from the *shtetl* to the city and modernity. In his study of Bellow, Malamud, and Roth, Robert Nadon also identifies the city as the site of authentic Jewish experience. According to Nadon, although these writers acknowledge a desire for a retreat into nature, each insists on the futility of this impulse and on the need to embrace the city as the place of modern Jewish American experience. Another example of this kind of reading is Charles Nash's discussion of Roth's engagement with pastoral in *Goodbye, Columbus*: "For an urban writer born in the Depression and nurtured on Kafka, as Roth was, the pastoral ideal, with its promise of boundless individual human possibility, could well seem irrelevant and wholly illusory, the product of an alluring but alien sensibility best relegated to the ash heap of history" (26). Nash argues that while in *The Great Gatsby* pastoral supplies a moral principle, in *Goodbye, Columbus* pastoral is morally bankrupt.

2. Buell favors the sociological and historical explanation that the Jewish American hostility to nature is a function of a lack of rural experience, while Andrew Furman points to the text-centered cultural traditions that have privileged text over land as the location of Jewish identity. In an Israeli literary context, however, land and nature become suitable literary material because a diasporic prohibition on an attachment to land no longer applies. In addition to this cultural emphasis on text/memory over land/space, other critics point to theological obstacles to a Jewish American engagement with nature, in particular the rationalist religious tradition that holds that the natural world threatens to distract the observant Jew from the Law and to lure him into a pantheistic worship of nature (see Jeremy Benstein and Norman Lamm). This Jewish rejection of the divinity of nature conflicts sharply with a Romantic or transcendentalist view of nature as inspiring faith and of landscape as conducive to religious feeling. In my view, theological objections to nature worship may be in the deep background of the novels considered in this chapter, but there is little evidence that they are driving the narratives.

3. "The key difference between [the Jewish American and African American] cases," Buell writes, "is that African American writers have felt able to draw on a cultural memory of a rural phase that intersected . . . with the likes of Mark Twain, Robert Frost, and Sherwood Anderson" (19). According to Buell, Jewish

writers, on the other hand, have lacked points of intersection with the canonical American tradition.

4. At the end of the eighteenth century, Eastern European Jews began to be transformed from a rural population into an urban population of merchants and artisans, and in general in the modern era, Jews have been disproportionately urban in relation to the populations of their host countries. Urbanization was encouraged by restrictions on Jewish life (on land ownership, occupation, and so on), as well as by the fact that urban environments facilitated religious observance. Urbanization was also intensified by migration patterns, as Jews who migrated within Europe and to the New World tended to move to big cities. Yet at the same time, Jews also participated in agricultural life in both the Old World and the New, either directly or as intermediaries—for example, as peddlers and merchants who moved between country and city. In an entry on "Agriculture," the *Encyclopedia Judaica* notes, "It is safe to generalize that the greater part of Eastern European Jewry was conditioned by [a] semirural environment until well into the 19th century" (403). Moreover, various New World settlement schemes over the last two centuries fostered Jewish agricultural activities. Jewish farming in the United States began in the early 1880s, and rural Jewish settlement was promoted by Western European Jews who had immigrated earlier and who feared repercussions and rising anti-immigrant sentiment if too many Jews flooded American cities.

5. For example, in his preface to his edited collection *Judaism and Ecology*, Aubrey Rose attributes his interest in the environment to his father's rural roots: "My parents were pre-1914 immigrants to Britain from East Europe where my father, like many Jews, grew up in the countryside. As a child I was fascinated to see how he turned a few square yards of earth in the so-called garden of an East End London slum into a home for flowers, vegetables, chickens, even a vine. The memory stayed with me so that gardens and flowers have since held pride of place among my interests" (4–5).

6. On ghetto pastoral, see Adam Meyer. In a somewhat different context, Michael Denning's *The Cultural Front* uses the term "ghetto pastoral" to designate a genre of proletarian city writing that constituted a "subaltern modernism." Denning draws heavily on Empson's understanding of pastoral as a form of proletarian literature.

7. Other examples of ghetto pastoral include Daniel Fuchs's *Homage to Blenholt* (1936) and *Summer in Williamsburg* (1934), as well as Abraham Cahan's *Yekl* (1896).

8. The interviewer reported that "Mr. Malamud, Brooklyn-raised, is amused that he continued to be thought of as the archetypal city writer after having lived in the country" (Malamud, "A Talk" 83).

9. Cynthia Ozick's "The Pagan Rabbi" offers a rather literal interpretation of the theological ban on communing with nature. Ozick's story, in which a

learned rabbi's obsession with nature ends with him hanging himself from a tree with his *tallis*, provides a graphic illustration of the maxim that for an observant Jew, an interest in nature is tantamount to abandoning one's faith. See Furman (120–21) for a more detailed discussion.

10. On connections between the American myth of the frontier and definitions of American identity, see William Cronon, who writes, "As [Frederick Jackson] Turner described the process, easterners and European immigrants, in moving to the wild unsettled lands of the frontier, shed the trappings of civilization, rediscovered their primitive racial energies, reinvented direct democratic institutions, and thereby reinfused themselves with a vigor, an independence, and a creativity that were the source of American democracy and national character. Seen in this way, wild country became a place not just of religious redemption but of national renewal, the quintessential location for experiencing what it meant to be an American" (76). On the Jewish reception of this myth, see Sam Girgus's *The New Covenant*.

11. The extent to which Levin's journey is based on Malamud's own experiences teaching in Oregon has been the subject of much speculation. In "Bernard Malamud in Oregon," Suzanne Clark carefully traces the parallels between Malamud's own experiences at Oregon State University and those of his fictional protagonist. See also Leslie Fiedler's recollections of this period in which western colleges opened their doors to Jewish academics from the East, precipitating "the most absurd and touching of all the waves of migration that have ever moved across this country from East to West" (155).

12. See Perry Miller's *Nature's Nation* on the identification of America with nature in nineteenth-century American literature. See also Henry Nash Smith, R. W. B. Lewis, Leo Marx, and Lawrence Buell on the deep preoccupation with nature in American literature.

13. See, for instance, Marcus Klein: "Nature is a large part of the reality which Levin is to engage, and he does learn to perform some chores of gardening and such. . . . But the intimate connection, the real engagement, despite Malamud's forcing of a couple of moments, just never takes place" (255).

14. Leo Marx observes in his discussion of *Walden* that while Thoreau's classic work initially seems to transform the pastoral into real, lived experience, in the end Thoreau removes the pastoral from history and restores it to the literary realm (265). Similarly, Buell points to the split that emerges in Thoreau between a pastoral and an agrarian sensibility, and notes that Thoreau's identification of pastoral with leisure rather than with a working landscape has a profound impact on the genre of writing he inspired: "In the tradition of Thoreau's unwillingness to write about social life at Walden, American literary naturists in general underrepresent community. The segmentation of 'nature' from 'civilization,' 'country' from 'town,' already endemic to pastoral becomes even more accentuated" (128).

15. See Lewis (ch. 5) on the spatial orientation of nineteenth-century American fiction. See also Bonnie Lyons, who argues that there is a basic conflict between

the Jewish and American worldviews in Jewish American writing: "While most American literature posits the United States as a new beginning, an Eden in which every man and every woman can see themselves as Adam and Eve, Jewish memory is long and profound. For the Jewish imagination Thoreau's ecstatic perpetual dawn is a terrifying amnesia, and the linked themes of time, history, and memory pervade American-Jewish fiction" (76).

16. Louis Harap maintains that Lonoff is "a transparent representation of Bernard Malamud, whom Zuckerman deeply admires" (146), while Baumgarten suggests that Lonoff is based in part on Malamud and in part on I. B. Singer (28).

17. Irving Howe notes that Jewish American fiction is characterized by "that deep rending struggle which marked those writers who had to make, rather than merely assume, America as their native ground" (11).

18. As George Handley maintains, "Considering American places within the larger context of New World colonialism means that we need to work carefully to unveil the hidden commonalities between the American West's legacy of Manifest Destiny with the larger expansion westward of European colonialism that stretches back to Columbus's arrival in the Caribbean" (8).

3. Joy Kogawa's Native Envy

1. Essay collections such as *Do the Americas Have a Common Literature?* (1990), edited by Gustavo Pérez Firmat, and *Poetics of the Americas* (1997), edited by Bainard Cowan and Jefferson Humphries, pay scant attention to Canadian authors, implicitly suggesting that if the Americas do have a common literature, it is one that largely excludes Canadian writing. For a more detailed discussion, see Adams's and Casteel's introduction to a special issue of *Comparative American Studies* entitled "Canada and the Americas."

2. Accordingly, in his book *Borderlands: How We Talk About Canada*, New complains that Chicano author Richard Rodriguez's call for a reorientation of American culture from the East-West axis to a North-South one effaces the symbolic importance of Canada's West. New worries that Rodriguez's model "enmeshes Canada in a grand continental (read 'US') design" that is simply another version of U.S. cultural imperialism (75).

3. See Arnold Davidson's *Writing Against the Silence*, which surveys the novel's reception and gives particular attention to the novel's role in securing a compensation package for Japanese Canadians.

4. For instance, Shirley Geok-Lin Lim reads *Obasan* under the heading of "Japanese American" women's writing, a homogenizing practice that is reinforced by her pairing of Kogawa's novel with Monica Sone's *Nisei Daughter*. In a 2002 keynote address to MESEA in Padua, Italy, Sau-ling Wong acknowledged that she herself in the past similarly had conflated Asian Canadian and Asian American writing.

5. For example, the editors of *Painting the Maple: Essays on Race, Gender, and the Construction of Canada* single out *Obasan* as evidence of the role a literary

text can play in the struggle to construct the Canadian nation (Strong-Boag et al. 14).

6. These same lines from Scott's poem feature in the first volume of Henry Roth's *Mercy of a Rude Stream* (1994). Roth's young protagonist, Ira, the child of Yiddish-speaking Jewish immigrant parents, recites the poem "eloquently" for his Harlem English teacher. Yet Ira disappoints his teacher when he is unable to repeat the performance in front of a larger audience: "The words which he had spoken with such feeling became stiff and mechanical in the assembly" (140). In Roth's novel, Ira's halting delivery of Scott's patriotic poem is suggestive of his incomplete assimilation into American life.

7. The abundant critical literature on *Obasan* has tended to focus either on questions of language and silence or on gender, sexuality, and the body. Considerably less attention has been given to Kogawa's treatment of landscape and nature. The most sustained discussion of Kogawa's landscape imagery is provided by Karin Quimby, who points out that "the landscape functions, in *Obasan*, to signify the problems of national and personal identity" and in particular the central problematic of internal exile, of the displacement of thousands of Japanese Canadians from the province in which they were born (258). However, Quimby's discussion is limited on the one hand by the exclusively U.S. critical framework that she adopts (drawing on the feminist critiques of landscape representation of Annette Kolodny, Nina Baym, and Gloria Anzaldúa), and on the other by her heavy reliance on the category of "wilderness," which tends to obscure the highly varied character of *Obasan*'s landscapes.

8. On the history of the Japanese Canadian experience during World War II, see Tomoko Makabe (22–24); Patricia Roy, J. L. Granatstein, Masako Iino, and Hiroko Takamura (ch. 6); Davidson (9–10); and Cheng Lok Chua (97–98). Makabe suggests that the Canadian policy was more punitive than the American one: "Internment began earlier and ended later in Canada. The Canadian government's post-war strategy of mass deportation had no counterpart in the United States. As the war against Japan drew to an end, the United States permitted Japanese Americans to return to their homes in the coastal area; in Canada, Japanese Canadians were not allowed to return to the coast until 1949. And the Canadian government rejected Nisei for military service until near the very end of the war, while in the United States, from early 1943 Nisei could enlist" (24–25).

9. In Japanese literature, "harmonious relations between humans and nature have historically been taken as a self-evident truth" (Ikuta 277). Shogo Ikuta writes, "It will not be possible to fully understand the various Japanese discourses on nature unless we recognize the fact that pastoralism has been the underlying basis of Japanese literature" (277). Takashi Kinoshita and Masataka Ota concur that "since early times the Japanese have always felt close to nature" (286). They attribute this sense of intimacy with nature to an animistic worldview that did not differentiate between outer and inner nature. Both studies also point to Japanese writers' attraction to the Romantic motif of the communion with nature,

which coincided with traditional Japanese pastoralism and its basic belief in the unity of the human and the nonhuman.

10. Gaile McGregor's *The Wacousta Syndrome* pursues the arguments outlined by Frye and Atwood and gives them an even stronger exceptionalist tone. McGregor's central claim is that in contrast to the American view of nature as potentially both threatening and redemptive, the Canadian response to nature—which she characterizes as "persistent and surprisingly homogeneous" (26)—is "one-sided" and wholly negative. She illustrates this national difference by contrasting the American wilderness romance of James Fenimore Cooper's Leatherstocking novels to the Canadian-born Major John Richardson's *Wacousta* (1832), a gothic wilderness novel set in Fort Detroit in 1763. McGregor then extrapolates from this reading of Richardson a theory of Canadian responses to nature that encompasses Canadian cultural production as a whole: "The fact is, leaving Richardson aside for the moment, there is plenty of evidence in the Canadian corpus to suggest that our national response to the environment has been almost completely negative" (10).

11. Mary Lu MacDonald also points to a broad range of literary responses to Canadian nature. In her survey of nineteenth-century Canadian nature writing by both native-born and immigrant anglophone and francophone writers, MacDonald finds that "regardless of the writer's language or place of birth, nature was not described as cold and indifferent or 'red in tooth and claw'" (217). Overall, MacDonald concludes, nineteenth-century Canadian descriptions of the Canadian landscape "bear no relation to Northrop Frye's famous statement" (192).

12. One example of this popular argument can be found in eminent Canadian literary critic George Woodcock's reading of *The Rising Village* in his 1977 essay "Possessing the Land: Notes on Canadian Fiction." Woodcock's somewhat dismissive reading may be contrasted with Glickman's suggestion that works such as Thomas Cary's *Abram's Plains* (1789), J. Mackay's *Quebec Hill: or, Canadian Scenery* (1797), and Charles G. D. Roberts's *Ave* (1892), which appropriate pastoral, sublime, and Wordsworthian motifs in their renderings of the Canadian landscape, are examples of how European literary conventions enabled rather than constrained the expression of a New World culture.

13. The texture of Susan Glickman's argument is much richer than I have space to do justice to here. She argues that the turn in European aesthetic culture toward nature as the standard of aesthetics, which coincided with the beginnings of literary culture in Canada, was fortuitous because the sublime proved particularly apt for expressing the Otherness of the colonial landscape and culture. In light of the suitability and persistence of these European aesthetic models, the separation of Canadian literature into colonial and postcolonial, which implies a liberation from earlier imitative forms, is "problematic, and perhaps simplistic" (Glickman viii).

14. See, for example, the collection *Landmarks: An Anthology of New Atlantic Canadian Poetry of the Land,* which testifies to the continuing relevance

of pastoral to Canadian writing. Brent MacLaine notes in his introduction to *Landmarks* that "it becomes clear after reading such a collection as this that the literary pastoral tradition remains a fertile one for the poetic imagination and continues to find a contemporary voice" (13).

15. This pattern of imagery continues in *Itsuka*: "I'm a transplant. Not a genuine prairie rose" (43); "a potted plant marks the place where I live" (170); "we must dig up determined fistfuls of roots and tamp them into the eroding soil" (258).

16. "Again and again," notes Erika Gottlieb, "it is less through the people than through the landscape that [Naomi] approaches the troubled question of her Canadian identity" (42).

17. Similarly, in *Itsuka* the wilderness (this time of the southern Alberta beet farm) is the site of unwanted and disturbing sexual advances (25–26). The strong biblical overtones of *Obasan* and the blending of biblical, Japanese, and pantheistic motifs that it contains have been discussed by Lok Chua (101–4) and Gottlieb.

18. In his discussion of *Obasan*, Frank Davey observes that the landscape functions as "the Wordsworthian refuge that compensates for social cruelties" (105). Davey identifies "a persistent pattern in [Naomi's] life of retreat from the social to the natural" (106).

19. Deloria uses the phrase "natural Indians" in his *Playing Indian* to refer to U.S. constructions of Indianness as outside of modernity and as embodying "authenticity and natural purity" (103). According to Deloria, in the United States in the late nineteenth and early twentieth century, contact with the primitive natural Indian was thought to assuage "the anxious displacements of modernity" and to offset the negative impact of the closing of the frontier on American national identity (101). For a Canadian discussion of the motif of the natural Indian, see Goldie (ch. 2).

20. While not all critics have read the woman as indigenous, in my view her indigeneity is strongly suggested by such features as the "golden brown" color of her face.

21. In an article entitled "Literature and Ethnicity," Werner Sollors cites instances of this kind of identification ranging from Abraham Cahan's 1896 novel *Yekl*, in which the Jewish wife recently arrived from Europe is negatively labeled a "squaw," to Mel Brooks's *Blazing Saddles* (1974), with its Yiddish-speaking Indian chief (played by the Jewish American Brooks). Canadian examples cited by Fee and Mandel include Rudy Wiebe's *The Temptations of Big Bear* (1973) and Mordecai Richler's *The Incomparable Atuk* (1963).

22. I am grateful to Jigna Desai for drawing to my attention *Masala*'s reliance on the myth of the West.

23. In a unique blending of Hollywood Western dialogue and Japanese Canadian themes, Goto's heroine's grandmother sets out on a journey across Alberta and is picked up by a cowboy who has recently returned from Japan. The Japanese-speaking cowboy has done "a comparativ study on the origins 'n developminta Japanese *enka* 'n if ther any parallels with the developminta country 'n western

in North America" (111). In the final scene of the novel the grandmother dons a cowboy outfit, becomes "The Purple Mask," and takes part in the Calgary Stampede.

24. See Yezierska's *Bread Givers*, Roth's *American Pastoral*, Jen's *Mona in the Promised Land*, and Rodriguez's *Brown*.

25. The critical literature on *Obasan* reads Kogawa's identification of First Nations and diasporic experiences as straightforward. Matthew Beedham maintains that *Obasan* helps to overcome "the false dichotomies of 'indigenous' and 'immigrant' defined in the past" (148). Similarly, Quimby obscures the distinction between the diasporic and the indigenous when she writes that, in *Obasan*, "Naomi claims a position on a landscape to which she belongs as much as the native peoples before her" (262). Such interpretations of the novel tacitly endorse Kogawa's conflation of historically distinct experiences.

26. See Margery Fee's discussion of "totem transfer," in which the transfer of an object from Native to newcomer symbolically validates the land claim of the new arrival (21).

27. Deloria's cultural history of the U.S. tradition of "playing Indian" links this practice to the desire for a sense of American belonging. Although Deloria is primarily concerned with mainstream U.S. appropriations of Indianness, his model also seems to me to have application to Canadian and diasporic instances of "playing Indian" such as those contained in Kogawa's novels.

4. Jamaica Kincaid's and Michael Pollan's New World Garden Writing

1. The borderland draws our attention to the permeable and dynamic boundaries of national space (see Anzaldúa; New, *Borderlands*). On the metaphor of the circuit, see Nikos Papastergiadis (113–15). See Christopher Miller (171–209) and Kaplan (ch. 2) for important critiques of Deleuze and Guattari's theory of nomadism.

2. Culture and colonization both derive from the Latin *colere*: to cultivate, to inhabit, to take care of a place (Young 30–31). In addition, the term *diaspora* also has etymological ties to cultivation, referring to the dispersal of seeds. See Robert Young on the biological and botanical origins of contemporary theories of hybridity. See also Papastergiadis (171) on the influence of botany on American ethnologist George Morton's theories of racial hybridity; see Michael Osborne on the theories of acclimatization developed by the nineteenth-century French zoologist Isidore Geoffrey Saint-Hilaire and the shift to anthropological and human themes in the science of acclimatization (62–97).

3. Exceptions include O'Brien's article on Kincaid's garden writing, which I discuss below, as well as Soto-Crespo and Tiffin.

4. Pollan's remark contrasts with the reverential attitude that Roth's and especially Malamud's protagonists adopt with regard to the U.S. nature-writing tradition.

5. The historian Richard Drayton offers an illuminating and detailed analysis of colonial botanical gardens: "In these colonial gardens we may discern a complex agenda. They were, of course, at the simplest level, places through which desirable foods and flowers might be disseminated. They were, like public gardens at home, symbols of wise government. But we may also see in them spaces to which Europeans might retreat from the strangeness of alien environments. They often encompassed areas of wilderness, making islands of the same forest plants which encircled the boundaries of civility. They were theatres in which exotic nature was, literally, put in its place in a European system. This spectacle of the inclusion of the strange within the familiar comforted the expatriates and impressed the locals" (183). See also Donal McCracken on British colonial gardens.

6. Pratt writes that "natural history asserted an urban, lettered, male authority over the whole of the planet; it elaborated a rationalizing, extractive, dissociative understanding which overlaid functional, experiential relations among people, plants, and animals. In these respects, it figures a certain kind of global hegemony, notably one based on possession of land and resources rather than control over routes. At the same time, in and of itself, the system of nature as a descriptive paradigm was an utterly benign and abstract appropriation of the planted. Claiming no transformative potential whatsoever, it differed sharply from overtly imperial articulations of conquest, conversion, territorial appropriation, and enslavement" (39).

7. According to Drayton, science and colonial power were allied in a number of ways: "The natural sciences in general, and botany in particular . . . provided information on geography and population which had military and strategic significance. As savants plotted the oceans, and discovered the use and culture of new plants and animals, knowledge also found economic application. Equally, the sciences might help to show British government as efficient and wise" (107–8).

8. Robinson writes in his preface to *The Wild Garden* that in contrast to the contemporary vogue for formal arrangements of exotic flowers which require high levels of maintenance, he "was led to think of the vast numbers of beautifully hardy plants from other countries which might be naturalized, with a very slight amount of trouble, in many situations in our plantations, fields, and woods" (xiv).

9. Anglophone Caribbean children of Kincaid's generation were made to recite Wordsworth's poem "The Daffodils," and as a result, derisive references to the foreign flower appear in a number of contemporary Caribbean texts. See Tiffin for a detailed discussion of this floral motif in relation to Kincaid's *Lucy* and other works.

10. Bonnie Marranca, the editor of the anthology, observes that "somewhere in this age of glamour and empire and tourism, there is a story to be written

about the politics of horticulture" (209), but she leaves this story largely unexplored in the biographical notes that accompany the excerpts.

11. These kinds of ambiguities are also highlighted in Kincaid's essay "To Name Is to Possess" in *My Garden (Book):* and in her memoir *My Brother* (1997).

12. In "Plant Hunting in China," Kincaid similarly writes that her journey begins in books and provides a list of relevant botanical exploration narratives (190).

13. The unsettling impact of these photographs may be compared to that generated by Isaac Julien's presentation of the figure of the black explorer in his film installation *True North*. (See chapter 6.)

14. Kincaid makes oblique reference to the expropriation of Native Americans in a passage in which she notes that Thomas Jefferson "owned slaves and supported the idea of an expanded American Territory, which meant the demise of the people who owned and lived on this land" (*My Garden* 134).

15. Pollan's discussion of ecological imperialism is indebted to Alfred Crosby's conceptualization of European conquest as made possible by a symbiosis of human, animal, and plant migratory patterns. According to Crosby, "The demographic triumph of Europeans in the temperate colonies is one part of a biological and ecological takeover that could not have been accomplished by human beings alone, gunpowder notwithstanding" (65).

16. See Cheryll Glotfelty's introduction to *The Ecocriticism Reader* and Laurence Coupe's introduction to *The Green Studies Reader* for two major attempts to consolidate the field of ecocriticism and to articulate its fundamental principles.

17. According to Dominic Head, an alliance between the novel and ecocriticism becomes more plausible if, rather than positing anthropocentrism and ecocentrism as polar opposites, we "imagine a novel which incorporates contemporary environmental concerns; which traces the intersection of time and space; which shows how personal time and personal identity are implicated in both social and environmental history; and does all of this—not *despite*—but *because* of its self-consciousness about textuality" (239).

18. See also O'Brien's "Articulating a World of Difference."

19. A sense of competition is implicit in *The Green Studies Reader*'s definition of green studies as "an emerging academic movement which seeks to ensure that nature is given as much attention within the humanities as is currently given to gender, class and race" (Coupe 302–3).

20. One of the few exceptions is a passage in which Kincaid recalls a couple who supplied her family in Antigua with charcoal from trees they had cut down. Kincaid writes: "I do not believe that they, Mr. and Mrs. Roberts, worried about the management of woods and their effect on the general arrangement of things in the small world in which we lived" (*My Garden* 44).

21. See O'Brien, "The Garden and the World," on Kincaid's violation of the ecological principle that gardens should be planted for sustenance only (175). O'Brien further observes that, given New England's strong ties to American

environmentalist traditions, the New England location of Kincaid's garden fore-grounds her tense relationship with environmentalism (171).

5. Marvelous and Gothic Gardens in Shani Mootoo, Gisèle Pineau, and Maryse Condé

1. See also the concluding pages of *Faulkner, Mississippi* (1996), in which Glissant meditates on the variety of flowers "other than the flowers of the great Mansions" that have grown in Faulkner's landscape (255).

2. Recent Caribbean criticism, however, has tended to celebrate a turn away from pastoral settings in favor of more urban ones. For example, the editors of *Créolité and Creolization* assert that "cities are today's sites of creolization" and are therefore where Caribbeanists should focus their attention (Enwezor et al. 16). Relatedly, Dash writes that "increasingly, urban vitality, street performance, and the maelstrom of the crowd will enter Caribbean writing. A new, antipastoral modernism will attempt to create an art form from the dissonance, incongruity, and chaos of modernity" (*Other America* 106). Benitez-Rojo's *The Repeating Island* contains an analysis of what he calls "the 'other' Caribbean city," while the final chapter of Rodríguez's *House/Garden/Nation* shifts the book's focus from rural spaces to urban ones, which are deemed more adequate to the cre-olized realities and postcolonial ambiguities of modern Caribbean society.

3. The Caribbean Islands proved particularly susceptible to an Edenic reading of the New World due to the character of island space, which is easily demarcated, empty and cut off from history, and therefore appears readily avail-able to the imposition of an external vision. Dash notes, "Island space offers itself as easily mastered terrain that invites experiments in radical transformation. . . . The tropical island could have no essential meaning but, from the outset, to be a kind of tabula rasa on which various projects, experiments, and utopias could be conceived" (*Other America* 13–14).

4. See Sheller (ch. 2) for a valuable discussion of this series of shifts in what she terms the "visual regimes" that have been brought to bear on the Caribbean landscape, as well as Rodríguez's *Transatlantic Topographies* (ch. 2) on the dra-matic change in the colonial vision of the Caribbean from paradise to inferno that accompanied the end of slavery in the nineteenth century. The extent to which the Caribbean has been read—and continues to be read—through such discourses accounts for the prominence of discussions of nature and landscape in Caribbean literature and criticism (see Dash, *Other America* 28–36).

5. See Casid's discussion of the slave garden both as an instrument of con-trol through which the planters attempted to ensure the slaves' obedience and attachment to the land, and as a threat to the plantation by virtue of its associa-tions with obeah and other forms of resistance (193–212). See also Beth Fowkes Tobin for a detailed discussion of the eighteenth-century kitchen and provision gardens and their relationship to the emergence of an independent cultural iden-tity under slavery. Tobin suggests that slaves' experiences tending the provision

gardens not only helped them survive slavery but also facilitated their transition to farming after emancipation. Lydia Mihelic Pulsipher draws on ethnographic and geographical research conducted in Montserrat to distinguish between three types of slave gardens: common grounds, ravine and mountain grounds, and houseyard gardens. Finally, Ramón Soto-Crespo discusses the slave garden with regard to Jamaica Kincaid's garden writing, emphasizing its relationship to acts of resistance (356–58).

6. Roberto González Echevarría identifies this narrative of the retreat into nature, which is exemplified by the nineteenth-century scientific exploration literature of Humboldt, Schomburgk, Conan Doyle, and others, and which finds its modern incarnation in the ethnographic account, as the "masterstory" of Latin American literature (106).

7. As Buell suggests, "Negritude can be thought of as a pastoral mode because it evokes a traditional, holistic, nonmetropolitan, nature-attuned myth of Africanity in reaction to and critique of a more urbanized, 'artificial' European order—and evokes it, furthermore, from the standpoint of one who has experienced exile and wishes to return" (64). See also Dash (*Other America,* ch. 3) and Bongie (87–88) on the pastoral impulse among Negritude writers.

The narrative of the retreat into nature is taken up in various forms in Aimé Césaire's *Notebook of a Return to a Native Land* (1939), Jacques Roumain's *Masters of the Dew* (1944), Alejo Carpentier's *The Lost Steps* (1953), Wilson Harris's *Palace of the Peacock* (1960), Michelle Cliff's *No Telephone to Heaven* (1987), and Marlene Nourbese Philip's *Looking for Livingstone* (1991) among many other Caribbean texts.

8. My account of the garden narrative is indebted to Dash's reading of *Masters of the Dew* and other New World texts in *The Other America* as well as to González Echevarría's discussion of Latin American narrative. Here I echo them in identifying New World literature's preoccupation with nature, origins, the escape from history, and ethnography.

9. Jean Jonassaint notes that the intertextual links between Condé's and Roumain's novels have been largely neglected, but he does not address in any detail Condé's critique and revision of Roumain's landscape poetics.

10. All quotations from *Crossing the Mangrove* are taken from Richard Philcox's translation. Page references are to the Philcox translation.

11. See Françoise Lionnet (76) on Condé's relationship to the peasant literature tradition exemplified by such authors as Roumain.

12. "Anthropology," González Echevarría writes, "offered those countries the possibility of claiming an origin different from that of the West; a fresh beginning that could lead away from the debacle of Western civilization. Anthropological knowledge could correct the errors of the conquest, atone for the crimes of the past, and make for a new history" (150).

13. This strategy parallels the reflexive critiques associated with postmodern anthropology.

14. All quotations from *The Drifting of Spirits* are taken from Dash's translation. Page references are to the Dash translation.

15. See, for example, Pineau's interview with Nadège Veldwachter (184).

16. After her separation from Jeremiah and her retreat to the remote village of La Folie, Schwarz-Bart's heroine, Télumée, is joined by Amboise, whose appreciation for his new surroundings is heightened by his prolonged experience of exile in France. The pair live in perfect harmony, sharing the labor of the garden, which, as in Roumain, is a highly sexualized space: "Every year this out-of-the-way place appealed to and attracted us more. As our sweat seeped into the soil, it became more and more ours, one with the odor of our bodies. . . . The garden improved every year, and we spent most of our time there" (146–47). It is in reclaiming land from the forest to make her garden that Télumée finds the sense of place and security that had eluded her for so long. There is rather more emphasis in Schwarz-Bart than in Roumain, however, on the labor involved in this reclamation of Edenic space from the wild. Once found, Manuel's spring appears to be inexhaustible and readily available; Télumée's garden, on the other hand, requires constant attention and comes into being only after a long period of labor.

17. For example, Lois Parkinson Zamora has argued that magical realism is a mode that highlights narrative form, inviting the reader to consider his or her role in the creation of "reality" and "truth." Magical realism signals the self-reflexivity of New World literature, which "obliges us to recognize our responsibility for the constitution of all meanings in the world, to recall our fundamental and necessary implication in the definition of reality as such" (79).

18. *The Handbook to Gothic Literature*, edited by Marie Mulvey-Roberts, suggests that the two modes are closely affiliated by including an entry on magical realism under the heading of "Gothic Specialisms." Amaryll Chanady notes in the entry that, like the gothic, marvelous or magical realism incorporates supernatural elements, but it does so "not as a threat to the individual or to the laws of nature, but as a normal part of experience" (Chanady 278).

19. As Casid notes in her subtle reading of the novel, Mala is, paradoxically, a "gardener who does not attempt to domesticate or tame nature's uncanny power to decompose" (xx).

20. In Walcott's "Ruins of a Great House," vegetation encroaches on an old colonial estate that is disintegrating into the Caribbean landscape. See Carol Margaret Davison for an extended discussion of the architectural trope of the Great House as a site of the return of repressed memories and of the meeting of present and past.

21. This reading of landscape resonates with the notion that nature "remembers the past" that circulates in Mootoo's novel. One of Mootoo's characters remarks that "snails, like most things in nature, have long memories" (58), and the young Mala becomes convinced that plants experience pain when her teacher tells her that "plants could show signs of trauma" (97).

22. Hugo's novels, including his novel about the Haitian Revolution, *Bug-Jargal* (1826), are also referred to in Condé's *Windward Heights.*

23. See Dayan's illuminating discussion of this motif (124–39), which is exemplified by René Dépestre's *Hallélujah pour une femme jardin* (1973) and is significantly challenged, as Dayan demonstrates, by the Haitian author Marie Chauvet. As Dayan notes, the motif of the *femme-jardin* also has connections to Roumain's *Masters of the Dew,* which exploits associations between women and land.

24. Throughout the novel, as Heather Smyth notes, Mootoo "plays with the designations of 'perverse' and 'natural' in relation to the 'natural' world of plants and insects that surrounds Mala's house" (149).

25. In Mootoo's second novel, *He Drown She in the Sea* (2005), we learn that Mala's sister Asha is now living in British Columbia, where she is the owner of Asha's Garden Supply. Asha's store is frequented by Harry St. George, a Caribbean immigrant and landscape designer who is the primary protagonist of the novel.

26. Mootoo had first begun to revise the garden's relationship to exile in her story "A Garden of Her Own" (included in her collection *Out on Main Street,* 1993). Initially, "A Garden of Her Own" presents a conventional opposition of home and away, the garden and exile. In Mootoo's story, a recently arrived Indo-Caribbean immigrant to Canada longs for her home, which is figured in her memory as her mother's Caribbean garden. At first, the garden is powerfully identified with a strictly delimited reading of home and an attendant sense of plenitude. However, at the conclusion of the story, the opposition of home (the Caribbean garden) and exile (the North American city) is destabilized when the protagonist purchases seeds and gardening tools so that she can plant a "garden-in-the-making" on the balcony of her new home in Canada. By the end of the story, the garden is no longer exclusively identified with home but can also be created in exile.

27. This reading of the Caribbean landscape as the signifier of displacement is supported by the historical fact that so many of the plants that now populate this landscape were imported into the Caribbean by its colonizers. Kincaid's catalog of Antiguan plants includes bougainvillea from South America, plumbago from Africa, croton from Malaysia, hibiscus from Asia and East Africa, allamanda from Brazil, poinsettia from Mexico, Bermuda lily from Japan, mango from Asia, and breadfruit from the East Indies (*My Garden* 135).

6. Landscape and Indigeneity in the Installation Art of Isaac Julien and Jin-me Yoon

1. Also striking was the exhibit's contextualization of contemporary Canadian art—particularly Quebec and First Nations art—within a hemispheric framework. In contrast to the hesitancy and suspicion with which Canadian literary studies has tended to greet hemispheric initiatives (see chapter 3 and Adams and Casteel), the exhibit made a compelling case for the relevance of such a

framework to contemporary Canadian art by including a number of Canadian works alongside U.S., Caribbean, and Latin American pieces.

2. Daina Augaitis observes that in *Nu·tka·*, "as the camera makes a panoramic study, it symbolically encircles a voice that is absent from the piece: that of the First Nations who have populated these lands for thousands of years. These inhabitants become present through their very absence, indicative of their under-representation in most forms of ensuing colonial power structures" (36). Indeed, Douglas explains in an interview that "absence is often the focus of my work. Even if I am resurrecting these obsolete forms of representation, I'm always indicating their inability to represent the real subject of the work. It's always something that is outside the system." He continues: "The hugest absence in *Nu·tka·* is the natives. They were the trading partners, they were the people who were residing on the land before the Europeans got there, but they are completely out of the discussion that goes on between the two characters" ("Interview" 15–16).

3. In his commentary on the piece, Douglas writes that *Nu·tka·* "is set in one of the most sublime moments of the romantic period—that of first contact between Aboriginals and Europeans on the west coast of Vancouver Island at Nootka Sound" ("*Nu·tka·*: Historical Background" 165). He also describes the work as "a Canadian Gothic," noting the gothic's popularity during "the era of high imperialism, when remote and exotic areas of the world were being drawn into the European orbit and providing, if not the *mise en scène*, then at least the sublimated object of Gothic anxiety" (165).

4. *Burning Water* parodically recreates George Vancouver's eighteenth-century voyages of exploration in the Pacific Northwest and his interactions with the Spanish, thereby making for an interesting comparison with Douglas's work.

5. For instance, Kent Monkman's *The Fourth of March* (2004) skillfully mimics the sublimity of Hudson River School landscape paintings, at first deceiving the viewer into believing that he is standing before an authentic nineteenth-century work. Closer examination reveals, however, that Monkman has inserted homoerotic scenes of cowboys and Indians into the wilderness landscape to unsettle traditional readings of relations between these two groups.

6. In his discussion of *A Paddle and a Compass*, Fung identifies Oberlander as "the white Canadian," eliding Oberlander's own background of displacement as the daughter of European Jewish refugees ("Bodies Out of Place" 167).

7. In the video, Oberlander attempts to recover the largely forgotten story of 5,700 British internees, many of them Jews, who were interned in six camps in Quebec, Ontario, and New Brunswick between 1940 and 1945.

8. Here, as in Glissant's work, nature "remembers" what history forgets. Oberlander's interest in the trees planted by the internees resonates with Glissant's observations in *Faulkner, Mississippi* about a cluster of trees that serves as the only marker of the site of a slave graveyard (12).

9. Julien's parents are St. Lucian and immigrated to England before Julien's birth. Although he was born in London, Julien describes himself as "liv[ing] in two

places at once (London and the Americas)" ("Creolizing Vision" 150). Walcott appears briefly in one of the Caribbean scenes of Julien's installation, and lines from *Omeros* are read out in the voice-over narration. The Omeros figure and the scenes of the young protagonist working as a waiter on the beach also recall passages from the poem.

10. Henson employs the language of the sublime in *A Negro Explorer,* in which he describes the "gorgeous bleakness, beautiful blankness" of the arctic landscape (66).

11. The 1998 television movie *Glory and Honor* (dir. Kevin Hooks) also presents Henson as unique among the members of the expedition in sympathizing and communicating with the Inuit.

12. Charles Hill summarizes these complaints in his 1995 exhibition catalog for *The Group of Seven: Art for a Nation* (15–16). See Lafleur for a discussion both of the Group of Seven's contribution to Canadian nationalism and of Yoon's critique of the Group's formulation of Canadian national identity in *Souvenirs of the Self.*

13. Curator Annette Hurtig describes the installation as follows: "The double-sided lightboxes in the exhibition immediately suggest the proverbial 'two sides to a story' and also the contradictory ideas or antitheses of a dialectical concept. The electrical cords that descend from and are coiled beneath the lightboxes, visually and electrically connecting them, resemble root systems, connective threads and linked chains, recalling the various threads of a complex story and also bringing to mind the chain of events within a narrative structure" (9).

14. Notably, however, in *Touring,* Yoon focuses on the family grouping rather than on the solitary, heroic figure featured in *Souvenirs of the Self,* again suggesting a shift in this work toward an emphasis on emplacement rather than displacement.

15. This moment parallels that in Julien's *True North* in which the explorer reveals her race by turning toward the camera.

16. In a subsequent image, the addition of a blond child to the family group-ing intensifies this ambiguity.

17. Hurtig comments on the "quiet insistence" of the central figure's presence in *Souvenirs of the Self* (7).

18. Relevant here are Caribbean Canadian writer Dionne Brand's observa-tions about the risks of belonging in an interview with Eleanor Wachtel. When asked by Wachtel, "Where is home, where is belonging?" Brand responds this way: "Home is of course here, where I live. Belonging is another thing altogether. Because I'm not even sure that I want to . . . belong. What would that mean, you see. Would it mean the end of thinking? That I'm satisfied with how the world is? . . . I'll never be." Brand's comments suggest that while the desire for belonging may be a dominant theme of diasporic writing and visual art, it is paradoxically one that the author or artist may not want to satisfy, because to do so would be to risk succumbing to a dangerous form of complacency.

Bibliography

Adams, Rachel, and Sarah Phillips Casteel. Introduction. "Canada and the Americas." Ed. Rachel Adams and Sarah Phillips Casteel. Spec. issue of *Comparative American Studies* 3.1 (Mar. 2005): 5–13.

"Agriculture." *Encyclopedia Judaica*. Vol. 2. New York: Macmillan, 1972. 382–415.

Alpers, Paul. *What Is Pastoral?* Chicago: Chicago UP, 1996.

Alpers, Svetlana, and Michael Baxandall. *Tiepolo and the Pictorial Intelligence*. New Haven: Yale UP, 1994.

Alvarez, A. "Visions of Light." Rev. of *Tiepolo's Hound*, by Derek Walcott. *New York Review of Books* 47.8 (11 May 2000): 27–28.

Andrews, Malcolm. *Landscape and Western Art*. Oxford: Oxford UP, 1999.

Anzaldúa, Gloria. *Borderlands / La Frontera: The New Mestiza*. San Francisco: Aunt Lute, 1999.

Armbruster, Karla, and Kathleen R. Wallace. "Introduction: Why Go Beyond Nature Writing, and Where To?" *Beyond Nature Writing: Expanding the Boundaries of Ecocriticism*. Ed. Karla Armbruster and Kathleen R. Wallace. Charlottesville: U of Virginia P, 2001. 1–25.

Armstrong, Jeannette. *Whispering in Shadows*. Penticton, BC: Theytus, 2000.

Atwood, Margaret. "Death by Landscape." *Wilderness Tips*. New York: Doubleday, 1991. 99–122.

———. *The Journals of Susanna Moodie*. Toronto: Oxford UP, 1970.

———. *Survival: A Thematic Guide to Canadian Literature*. 1972. Toronto: McClelland & Stewart, 1996.

Augaitis, Daina. "Casting Doubt: The Narratives of Stan Douglas." *Stan Douglas*. Vancouver: Vancouver Art Gallery, 1999. 33–38.

Augé, Marc. *Non-Places: Introduction to an Anthropology of Supermodernity*. Trans. John Howe. London: Verso, 1995.

Badami, Anita Rau. *Tamarind Mem*. Toronto: Viking, 1996.

Baugh, Edward. "Painters and Painting in *Another Life*." Hamner 239–50.

Baumgarten, Murray. *City Scriptures: Modern Jewish Writing.* Cambridge: Harvard UP, 1982.

Beedham, Matthew. "*Obasan* and Hybridity: Necessary Cultural Strategies." *The Immigrant Experience in North American Literature.* Ed. Katherine B. Payant and Toby Rose. Westport, CT: Greenwood, 1999. 139–149.

Bellow, Saul. *Herzog.* 1961. New York: Penguin, 2001.

Benitez-Rojo, Antonio. *The Repeating Island: The Caribbean and the Postmodern Perspective.* Trans. James Maraniss. Durham: Duke UP, 1992.

Bensen, Robert. "The Painter as Poet: Derek Walcott's *Midsummer.*" *Literary Review* 29.3 (Spring 1986): 259–68.

Benstein, Jeremy. "Nature vs. Torah." *Torah of the Earth: Exploring 4,000 Years of Ecology in Jewish Thought.* Ed. Arthur Waskow. Vol. 1. Woodstock, VT: Jewish Lights, 2000. 180–207.

Berkhofer, Robert F., Jr. *The White Man's Indian: Images of the American Indian from Columbus to the Present.* New York: Knopf, 1978.

Bongie, Chris. *Islands and Exiles: The Creole Identities of Post/colonial Literature.* Stanford: Stanford UP, 1998.

Bowering, George. *Burning Water.* Don Mills, ON: Musson, 1980.

Boyarin, Daniel, and Jonathan Boyarin. "Diaspora: Generation and the Ground of Jewish Identity." *Critical Inquiry* 19 (Summer 1993): 693–725.

Brand, Dionne. Interview with Eleanor Wachtel. *Writers and Company.* Ottawa: CBC. 19 Dec. 2004.

———. "Islands Vanish." *Land to Light On.* Toronto: McLelland & Stewart, 1997. 73–77.

———. *A Map to the Door of No Return: Notes to Belonging.* Toronto: Doubleday Canada, 2001.

Brantlinger, Patrick. *Rule of Darkness: British Literature and Imperialism, 1830–1914.* Ithaca: Cornell UP, 1988.

Breslin, Paul. "Tracking Tiepolo's Hound." *Poetry* 178.1 (April 2001): 38–40.

Brettell, Richard R. *Pissarro and Pointoise: The Painter and the Landscape.* New Haven: Yale UP, 1990.

Buell, Lawrence. *The Environmental Imagination: Thoreau, Nature Writing, and the Formation of American Culture.* Cambridge: Harvard UP, 1995.

Burnett, Paula. *Derek Walcott: Politics and Poetics.* Gainesville: UP of Florida, 2000.

Carpentier, Alejo. "The Baroque and the Marvelous Real." Zamora and Faris 75–88.

———. *The Lost Steps.* 1953. Trans. Harriet de Onís. Minneapolis: U of Minnesota P, 2001.

———. "On the Marvelous Real in America." Zamora and Faris 89–108.

Carter, Paul. *The Road to Botany Bay: An Essay in Spatial History.* London: Faber & Faber, 1987.

Casey, Edward S. *The Fate of Place: A Philosophical History.* Berkeley: U of California P, 1998.

Casid, Jill H. *Sowing Empire: Landscape and Colonization.* Minneapolis: U of Minnesota P, 2005.

Casteel, Sarah Phillips. "Autobiography as Rewriting: Derek Walcott's *Another Life* and *Omeros.*" *Journal of Commonwealth Literature* 34.2 (Sept. 1999): 9–32.

Césaire, Aimé. *Notebook of the Return to the Native Land.* 1939. Trans. Clayton Eshleman and Annette Smith. Middletown, CT: Wesleyan, 2001.

Chambers, Iain. *Migrancy, Culture, Identity.* London: Routledge, 1994.

Chanady, Amaryll Beatrice. "Magical Realism." *The Handbook to Gothic Literature.* Ed. Marie Mulvey-Roberts. New York: NYU P, 1998. 277–78.

Chateaubriand, François-René, Vicomte de. *Atala and René.* 1801. Trans. Irving Putter. Berkeley: U of California P, 1980.

Clark, Suzanne. "Bernard Malamud in Oregon." *American Scholar* 59 (Winter 1990): 67–79.

Clarke, Austin. "In the Semi-Colon of the North." *Canadian Literature* 95 (Winter 1982): 30–37.

Cliff, Michelle. *No Telephone to Heaven.* 1987. New York: Plume, 1996.

Clifford, James. "Diasporas." *Cultural Anthropology* 9.3 (August 1994): 302–44.

———. *Routes: Travel and Translation in the Late Twentieth Century.* Cambridge: Harvard UP, 1997.

Cohen, Robin. *Global Diasporas: An Introduction.* Seattle: U of Washington P, 1997.

Columbus, Christopher. *The Voyage of Christopher Columbus.* Trans. John Cummins. New York: St. Martin's, 1992.

Condé, Maryse. *Crossing the Mangrove.* Trans. Richard Philcox. New York: Anchor, 1995.

———. *Traversée de la Mangrove.* Paris: Mercure de France, 1989.

———. *Windward Heights.* Trans. Richard Philcox. New York: Soho, 1998.

Cosgrove, Denis E. *Social Formation and Symbolic Landscape.* Madison: U of Wisconsin P, 1998.

Counter, S. Allen. *North Pole Legacy: Black, White & Eskimo.* Amherst: U of Massachussetts P, 1991.

Coupe, Laurence. General Introduction. *The Green Studies Reader: From Romanticism to Ecocriticism.* Ed. Laurence Coupe. New York: Routledge, 2000. 1–8.

Cronon, William. "The Trouble with Wilderness." *Uncommon Ground: Rethinking the Human Place in Nature.* Ed. William Cronon. New York: Norton, 1996. 69–90.

Crosby, Alfred W. "Ecological Imperialism: The Overseas Migration of Western Europeans as a Biological Phenomenon." *American Encounters: Natives and*

Newcomers from European Contact to Indian Removal—1500–1850. Ed. Peter C. Mancall and James H. Merrell. New York: Routledge, 2000. 55–67.

Crozier, Michael. Introduction. *After the Garden?* Spec. issue of *South Atlantic Quarterly* 98.4 (Fall 1999): 625–31.

Cudjoe, Selwyn. *V. S. Naipaul: A Materialist Reading*. Amherst: U of Massachusetts P, 1988.

Dash, J. Michael. *Edouard Glissant*. New York: Cambridge UP, 1995.

———. *The Other America: Caribbean Literature in a New World Context*. Charlottesville: U of Virginia P, 1998.

Davey, Frank. *Post-National Arguments: The Politics of the Anglophone-Canadian Novel since 1967*. Toronto: U of Toronto P, 1993.

Davidson, Arnold. *Writing Against the Silence: Joy Kogawa's* Obasan. Toronto: ECW, 1993.

Davis, Gregson. "'Pastoral Sites': Aspects of Bucolic Transformation in Derek Walcott's *Omeros*." *From Homer to Omeros*. Spec. issue of *Classical World* 93.1 (Sept./Oct. 1999): 43–50.

Davison, Carol Margaret. "Burning Down the Master's (Prison)-House: Revolution and Revelation in Colonial and Postcolonial Female Gothic." *Empire and the Gothic: The Politics of Genre*. Ed. Andrew Smith and William Hughes. Houndmills, Basingstoke: Palgrave MacMillan, 2003. 136–54.

Dayan, Joan. *History, Haiti and the Gods*. Berkeley: U of California P, 1998.

de Lima, Clara Rosa. "Walcott, Painting and the Shadow of Van Gogh." *The Art of Derek Walcott*. Ed. Stewart Brown. Chester Springs, PA: Dufour, 1991. 171–90.

Deloria, Philip J. *Playing Indian*. New Haven: Yale UP, 1998.

Denning, Michael. *The Cultural Front: The Laboring of American Culture in the Twentieth Century*. London: Verso, 1997.

Denvir, Bernard. "Impressionism." *Impressionism to Post-modernism*. Ed. David Britt. London: Thames & Hudson, 1989. 11–58.

Douglas, Stan. "Interview: Diana Thater in Conversation with Stan Douglas." *Stan Douglas*. By Scott Watson, Diana Thater, and Carol J. Clover. London: Phaidon, 1998. 8–29.

———. *Nu·tka·*. 1996. Landry 53–55.

———. "*Nu·tka·*: Historical Background." Landry 165–67.

Drayton, Richard. *Nature's Government: Science, Imperial Britain, and the "Improvement" of the World*. New Haven: Yale UP, 2000.

Enwezor, Okwui, et al. Introduction. *Créolité and Creolization: Dokumenta 11 Platform 3*. Ed. Okwui Enwezor et al. Ostfildern-Ruit, Ger.: Hatje Cantz, 2003. 13–16.

Faris, Wendy B. *Ordinary Enchantments: Magical Realism and the Remystification of Narrative*. Nashville: Vanderbilt UP, 2004.

Fee, Margery. "Romantic Nationalism and the Image of Native People in Contemporary English-Canadian Literature." *The Native in Literature*. Ed. Thomas King, Cheryl Calver, and Helen Hoy. Toronto: ECW, 1987. 15–33.

Fiedler, Leslie. "The Many Names of S. Levin: An Essay in Genre Criticism." *The Fiction of Bernard Malamud.* Ed. Richard Astro and Jackson J. Benson. Corvallis: Oregon State UP, 1977. 149–61.

Frost, Robert. "The Gift Outright." *The Norton Anthology of Poetry.* 1st ed. New York: Norton, 1970. 952.

Frye, Northrop. *The Bush Garden: Essays on the Canadian Imagination.* Toronto: Anansi, 1971.

———. "Conclusion." *Literary History of Canada: Canadian Literature in English.* Ed. Carl F. Klinck. 2nd ed. Vol. 2. Toronto: U of Toronto P, 1976. 333–61.

Fung, Richard. "Bodies out of Place: The Videotapes of Shani Mootoo." *Women and Performance: A Journal of Feminist Theory* 8.2 (1996): 160–73.

Furman, Andrew. "No Trees Please, We're Jewish." *ISLE* 7.2 (Summer 2000): 115–36.

Gagnon, Monika Kin. "Out in the Garden: Shani Mootoo's Xerox Works." *Other Conundrums: Race, Culture, and Canadian Art.* Vancouver: Arsenal Pulp, 2000. 146–55.

———, and Richard Fung. "Imaginative Geographies." *13 Conversations about Art and Cultural Race Politics.* Montreal: Artextes, 2002. 77–87.

Gessell, Paul. "Mootoo, Book Two." *Ottawa Citizen* 1 May 2005: B8.

Gifford, Terry. "Towards a Post-Pastoral View of British Poetry." *The Environmental Tradition in English Literature.* Ed. John Parham. Aldershot, Hampshire: Ashgate, 2002. 51–63.

Girgus, Sam B. *The New Covenant: Jewish Writers and the American Idea.* Chapel Hill: U of North Carolina P, 1984.

Glickman, Susan. *The Picturesque and the Sublime: A Poetics of the Canadian Landscape.* Montreal: McGill-Queen's UP, 1998.

Glissant, Edouard. *Caribbean Discourse.* Trans. J. Michael Dash. Charlottesville: U of Virginia P, 1989.

———. *Faulkner, Mississippi.* Trans. Barbara Lewis and Thomas C. Spear. 1996. New York: Farrar, Straus & Giroux, 1999.

———. *Soleil de la conscience.* Paris: Gallimard, 1997.

———. *Traité du tout-monde.* Paris: Gallimard, 1997.

Glotfelty, Cheryll. "Introduction: Literary Studies in an Age of Environmental Crisis." *The Ecocriticism Reader: Landmarks in Literary Ecology.* Ed. Cheryll Glotfelty and Harold Fromm. Athens: U of Georgia P, 1996. xv–xxxvii.

Gold, Michael. *Jews without Money.* 1930. New York: International, 1935.

Goldie, Terry. *Fear and Temptation: The Image of the Indigene in Canadian, Australian, and New Zealand Literatures.* Kingston: McGill-Queen's UP, 1989.

Goldsmith, Oliver. "The Deserted Village." *The Norton Anthology of Poetry.* 1st ed. New York: Norton, 1970. 500–507.

———. *The Rising Village.* 1825 and 1834. Ed. Gerald Lynch. London, ON: Canadian Poetry, 1989.

González Echevarría, Roberto. *Myth and Archive: A Theory of Latin American Narrative*. Cambridge: Cambridge UP, 1990.

Goto, Hiromi. *Chorus of Mushrooms*. 1994. Edmonton: NeWest, 1997.

Gottlieb, Erika. "The Riddle of Concentric Worlds in 'Obasan.'" *Canadian Literature* 109 (1986): 34–53.

Greenblatt, Stephen. *Marvelous Possessions: The Wonder of the New World*. Chicago: U of Chicago P, 1991.

Gupta, Akhil, and James Ferguson. "Beyond 'Culture': Space, Identity, and the Politics of Difference." *Cultural Anthropology* 7.1 (1992): 6–23.

Hall, Stuart. "Cultural Identity and Diaspora." *Identity: Community, Culture, Difference*. London: Lawrence & Wishart, 1990. 222–37.

Hamlin, William M. *The Image of America in Montaigne, Spenser, and Shakespeare: Renaissance Ethnography and Literary Reflection*. New York: St. Martin's, 1995.

Hamner, Robert, ed. *Critical Perspectives on Derek Walcott*. Washington: Three Continents, 1993.

Handley, George. "A Postcolonial Sense of Place and the Work of Derek Walcott." *ISLE* 7.2 (Summer 2000): 1–23.

Hannan, Jim. "Crossing Couplets: Making Form the Matter of Walcott's *Tiepolo's Hound*." *New Literary History* 33 (Summer 2002): 559–79.

Harap, Louis. *In the Mainstream: The Jewish Presence in Twentieth-Century American Literature, 1950s–1980s*. New York: Greenwood, 1987.

Harris, Wilson. "The Music of Living Landscapes." *Selected Essays of Wilson Harris*. Ed. Andrew Bundy. New York: Routledge, 1999. 40–46.

Head, Dominic. "Ecocriticism and the Novel." Coupe 235–41.

Helsinger, Elizabeth K. *Rural Scenes and National Representation: Britain, 1815–1850*. Princeton: Princeton UP, 1997.

Henson, Matthew A. *A Negro Explorer at the North Pole*. 1912. New York: Arno, 1969.

Highway, Thomson. *Kiss of the Fur Queen*. Toronto: Doubleday Canada, 1999.

Hill, Charles C. *The Group of Seven: Art for a Nation*. Ottawa: National Gallery of Canada, 1995.

Hodge, Merle. *Crick Crack Monkey*. 1970. Oxford: Heinemann, 1981.

Hollander, John. "To Find the Westward Path." Rev. of *A New Life*, by Bernard Malamud. *Partisan Review* 29 (Winter 1962). Rpt. in *Modern Critical Views: Bernard Malamud*. Ed. Harold Bloom. New York: Chelsea House, 1986. 11–14.

Honour, Hugh. *The New Golden Land: European Images of America from the Discoveries to the Present Time*. New York: Pantheon, 1975.

Howe, Irving. "Strangers." *Celebrations and Attacks: Thirty Years of Literary and Cultural Commentary*. New York: Horizon, 1979. 11–26.

Howkins, Alun. "The Rediscovery of Rural England." *Englishness: Politics and*

Culture, 1880–1920. Ed. Robert Colls and Philip Dodd. London: Croom Helm, 1986. 62–88.

Hunt, John Dixon. "The Garden as Cultural Object." *Denatured Visions: Landscape and Culture in the Twentieth Century.* Ed. Stuart Wrede and William Howard Adams. New York: Museum of Modern Art, 1991. 19–32.

Hurtig, Annette. "Site Seeing." *Jin-me Yoon: Touring Home from Away.* Vancouver: Presentation House Gallery, 2003. 7–17.

Ikuta, Shogo. "Modern Japanese Nature Writing: An Overview." *The Literature of Nature: An International Sourcebook.* Ed. Patrick D. Murphy. Chicago: Fitzroy Dearborn, 1998. 277–80.

Iyer, Pico. *The Global Soul: Jet Lag, Shopping Malls, and the Search for Home.* New York: Knopf, 2000.

Jen, Gish. *Mona in the Promised Land.* New York: Knopf, 1996.

Jonassaint, Jean. "For a Caribbean Intertext: On Some Readings of Maryse Condé's *Crossing the Mangrove.*" *French Civilization and Its Discontents: Nationalism, Colonialism, Race.* Ed. Tyler Stovall and Georges Van Den Abbeele. New York: Lexington, 2003. 147–71.

Julien, Isaac. "Black Is, Black Ain't: Notes on De-essentializing Black Identities." *Black Popular Culture.* Bay, 1992. Rpt. in *The Film Art of Isaac Julien.* Annandale-on-Hudson, NY: Center for Curatorial Studies, 2000. 73–77.

———. "Creolizing Vision." *Créolité and Creolization: Documenta 11 Platform 3.* Ostfildern-Ruit, Ger.: Hatje Cantz, 2003. 149–55.

———. "Isaac Julien in Conversation with Shaheen Merali." *Isaac Julien.* Montreal: Musée d'art contemporain de Montréal, 2004. 83–87.

———. "The Long Road: Isaac Julien in Conversation with B. Ruby Rich." *Art Journal* 61.2 (Summer 2002): 50–67.

———. "States of Desire: Isaac Julien in Conversation with bell hooks." *Transition* 53 (Fall 1991): 168–84. Rpt. in *Diary of a Young Soul Rebel.* London: British Film Institute, 1991. 125–40.

———, dir. *Paradise Omeros.* 2002.

———, dir. *True North.* 2004.

Kaplan, Caren. *Questions of Travel: Postmodern Discourses of Displacement.* Durham: Duke UP, 1996.

Kazin, Alfred. *A Walker in the City.* 1951. San Diego: Harcourt Brace, 1979.

Keeshig-Tobias, Leonore, ed. *Into the Moon: Heart, Mind, Body, Soul.* Toronto: Sister Vision, 1996.

Kermode, Frank. "In the Garden of the Oppressor." Rev. of *The Enigma of Arrival,* by V. S. Naipaul. *New York Times* 22 Mar. 1987: 11.

Kincaid, Jamaica. *Among Flowers: A Walk in the Himalaya.* Washington: National Geographic, 2005.

———. *The Autobiography of My Mother.* New York: Farrar, Straus & Giroux, 1996.

———. Interview with Katherine M. Balutansky. "On Gardening." *Callaloo* 25.3 (2002): 790–800.

———. Introduction. *My Favorite Plant.* Ed. Jamaica Kincaid. New York: Farrar, Straus & Giroux, 1998. xiii–xix.

———. *Lucy.* New York: Plume, 1990.

———. *My Garden (Book):.* New York: Farrar, Straus & Giroux, 1999.

———. "On Seeing England for the First Time." *The Best American Essays.* Ed. Susan Sontag. New York: Ticknor & Fields, 1992. 209–17.

———. Preface. *In the Land of the Blue Poppies: The Collected Plant-Hunting Writings of Frank Kindon Ward.* New York: Modern Library, 2003. xiii–xvi.

———. "Sowers and Reapers." *New Yorker* 22 Jan. 2001: 41–45.

King, Thomas. *Truth and Bright Water.* Toronto: HarperCollins Canada, 1999.

Kinoshita, Takashi, and Masataka Ota. "Nature in Modern Japanese Literature: Fiction, Nonfiction, and Poetry." *The Literature of Nature: An International Sourcebook.* Ed. Patrick D. Murphy. Chicago: Fitzroy Dearborn, 1998. 284–89.

Kinsella, John. "Doubting Derek." Rev. of *Tiepolo's Hound,* by Derek Walcott. *Observer* 10 Sept. 2000: 14.

Klein, A. M. "Indian Reservation: Caughnawaga" and "Pastoral of the City Streets." *Complete Poems: Part 2: Original Poems, 1937–1955, and Poetry Translations.* Ed. Zailig Pollock. Toronto: U of Toronto P, 1990. 641–42 and 694–96.

Klein, Marcus. "The Sadness of Goodness." *Bernard Malamud and the Critics.* Ed. Leslie and Joyce Field. New York: NYU P, 1970. 249–60.

Kogawa, Joy. Interview with Jeanne Delbaere. *Kunapipi* 16.1 (1994): 461–64.

———. *Itsuka.* Toronto: Penguin, 1992.

———. *Obasan.* 1981. New York: Anchor, 1994.

Kornhauser, Elizabeth Mankin. "Introduction: 'All Nature Here Is New to Art'—Painting the American Landscape in the Nineteenth Century." *Hudson River School: Masterworks from the Wadsworth Atheneum Museum.* By Elizabeth Mankin Kornhauser and Amy Ellis with Maureen Miesmer. New Haven: Yale UP, 2003. 3–17.

Kwon, Miwon. *One Place after Another: Site-Specific Art and Locational Identity.* Cambridge: MIT P, 2004.

Lafleur, Brenda. "'Resting' in History: Translating the Art of Jin-me Yoon." *Generations and Geographies in the Visual Arts: Feminist Readings.* Ed. Griselda Pollock. London: Routledge, 1996. 217–27.

Lamm, Norman. "Ecology in Jewish Law and Theology." *Torah of the Earth: Exploring 4,000 Years of Ecology in Jewish Thought.* Ed. Arthur Waskow. Vol. 1. Woodstock, VT: Jewish Lights Publishing, 2000. 119–20.

Lamming, George. *The Pleasures of Exile.* 1960. Ann Arbor: U of Michigan P, 1992.

Lamoureux, Johanne. "The Meeting of Two Americas." Landry 138–46.

Landry, Pierre. *"Nous venons en paix . . .": Histoires des Amériques*. Montreal: Musée d'art contemporain de Montréal, 2004.

Lefebvre, Henri. *The Production of Space*. Trans. Donald Nicholson-Smith. Oxford: Blackwell, 2001.

Lewis, R. W. B. *The American Adam: Innocence, Tragedy and Tradition in the Nineteenth Century*. Chicago: U of Chicago P, 1955.

Lim, Shirley Geok-Lin. "Japanese American Women's Life Stories: Maternality in Monica Sone's *Nisei Daughter* and Joy Kogawa's *Obasan*." *Feminist Studies* 16.2 (Summer 1990): 289–312.

Lionnet, Françoise. *Postcolonial Representations: Women, Literature, Identity*. Ithaca: Cornell UP, 1995.

Lok Chua, Cheng. "Witnessing the Japanese Canadian Experience in World War II: Processual Structure, Symbolism, and Irony in Joy Kogawa's *Obasan*." *Reading the Literature of Asian America*. Ed. Shirley Geok-lin Lim and Amy Ling. Philadelphia: Temple UP, 1992. 97–108.

Love, Glen A. *Practical Ecocriticism: Literature, Biology, and the Environment*. Charlottesville: U of Virginia P, 2003.

Lowenthal, David. "European and English Landscapes as National Symbols." *Geography and National Identity*. Ed. David Hooson. Oxford: Blackwell, 1994. 15–38.

Lyons, Bonnie K. "American-Jewish Fiction since 1945." *Handbook of American-Jewish Literature: An Analytical Guide to Topics, Themes, and Sources*. Ed. Lewis Fried. New York: Greenwood, 1988. 61–89.

MacDonald, Mary Lu. *Literature and Society in the Canadas, 1817–1850*. Lewiston, NY: Edwin Mellen, 1992.

MacLaine, Brent. Introduction. *Landmarks: An Anthology of New Atlantic Canadian Poetry of the Land*. Ed. Hugh MacDonald and Brent MacLaine. Charlottetown, PEI: Acorn, 2001. 12–20.

Makabe, Tomoko. *The Canadian Sansei*. Toronto: U of Toronto P, 1998.

Malamud, Bernard. *Dubin's Lives*. New York: Penguin, 1979.

———. *A New Life*. 1961. London: Penguin, 1968.

———. *The People and Uncollected Stories*. New York: Farrar, Straus & Giroux, 1989.

———. "A Talk with the Novelist." Interview with Ralph Tyler. *New York Times Book Review* 18 Feb. 1979: 31–34. Rpt. in *Conversations with Bernard Malamud*. Ed. Lawrence Lasher. Jackson: UP of Mississippi, 1991. 80–86.

Malkki, Liisa. "National Geographic: The Rooting of Peoples and the Territorialization of National Identity among Scholars and Refugees." *Cultural Anthropology* 7.1 (1992): 24–44.

Mandel, Eli. "Imagining Natives: White Perspectives on Native Peoples." *The Native in Literature*. Ed. Thomas King, Cheryl Calver, and Helen Hoy. Toronto: ECW, 1987. 34–49.

Marranca, Bonnie, ed. *American Garden Writing: An Anthology.* New York: Taylor Trading, 2003.

Marx, Leo. *The Machine in the Garden: Technology and the Pastoral Ideal in America.* New York: Oxford UP, 1964.

Massey, Doreen. "A Global Sense of Place." *Marxism Today* (June 1991): 24–29. Rpt. in *Exploring Human Geography.* Ed. Stephen Daniels and Roger Lee. London: Arnold, 1995. 237–46.

McCracken, Donal P. "The Jewels of Empire: British Imperial Botanic Gardens." *Gardening in the Colonies.* Spec. issue of *SPAN* 46 (April 1998): 19–30.

McGregor, Gaile. *The Wacousta Syndrome: Explorations in the Canadian Langscape.* Toronto: U of Toronto P, 1985.

McKinsey, Elizabeth. *Niagara Falls: Icon of the American Sublime.* Cambridge: Cambridge UP, 1985.

Mercer, Kobena, and Chris Darke. *Isaac Julien: With Essays by Kobena Mercer and Chris Darke.* London: Ellipsis, 2001.

Meyer, Adam. "The Persistence of the Pastoral and the Growth of the Gangster: The Urban Jewish-American Immigrant Novels of Mike Gold and David Fuchs." *Yiddish* 9.3 (1994): 162–71.

Miller, Christopher L. *Nationalists and Nomads: Essays on Francophone African Literature and Culture.* Chicago: U of Chicago P, 1998.

Miller, Perry. *Nature's Nation.* Cambridge: Harvard UP, 1967.

Mirzoeff, Nicholas. "Pissarro's Passage: The Sensation of Caribbean Jewishness in the Diaspora." *Diaspora and Visual Culture: Representing Africans and Jews.* Ed. Nicholas Mirzoeff. New York: Routledge, 2000. 57–75.

Mishra, Vijay. "The Diasporic Imaginary: Theorizing the Indian Diaspora." *Textual Practice* 10.3 (1996): 421–47.

Mootoo, Shani. *Cereus Blooms at Night.* Toronto: McClelland & Stewart, 1996.

———. *He Drown She in the Sea.* Toronto: McClelland & Stewart, 2005.

———. *Out on Main Street.* Vancouver: Press Gang Publishers, 1993.

———, dir. *Her Sweetness Lingers.* Toronto: V-Tape, 1994.

———, dir. *The Wild Woman in the Woods.* Toronto: V-Tape, 1993.

Mootoo, Shani, and Richard Fung. "Dear Shani, Hiya Richard . . . ." *Felix* 2.1 (1995): 26–35.

Mootoo, Shani, and Wendy Oberlander, dirs. *A Paddle and a Compass.* Toronto: V-Tape, 1992.

Moraes, Dom. "Changes of Scenery." *Voices of the Crossing.* Ed. Ferdinand Dennis and Naseem Khan. London: Serpent's Tail, 2000. 83–91.

Murray, Heather. "Women in the Wilderness." *A Mazing Space: Writing Canadian Women Writing.* Ed. Shirley Neuman and Smaro Kamboureli. Edmonton: Longspoon / NeWest, 1986. 74–83.

Mustafa, Fawzia. *V. S. Naipaul.* Cambridge: Cambridge UP, 1995.

Nadon, Robert Joseph. "Urban Values in Recent American Fiction: A Study of the City in the Fiction of Saul Bellow, John Updike, Philip Roth, Bernard Malamud, and Norman Mailer." Diss. U of Minnesota, 1969.

Naipaul, V. S. *The Enigma of Arrival.* New York: Knopf, 1987.

———. *A House for Mr. Biswas.* 1961. London: Penguin, 1992.

———. "Jasmine." 1964. Hamner 16–22.

———. *The Middle Passage.* London: André Deutsch, 1962.

———. *Reading and Writing: A Personal Account.* New York: *New York Review of Books,* 2000.

———. *A Way in the World.* New York: Vintage, 1995.

Nash, Charles C. "From West Egg to Short Hills: The Decline of the Pastoral Ideal from *The Great Gatsby* to Philip Roth's *Goodbye, Columbus.*" *Publications of the Missouri Philological Association* 13 (1988): 22–27.

New, W. H. *Borderlands: How We Talk about Canada.* Vancouver: UBC P, 1998.

———. *Land Sliding: Imagining Space, Presence, and Power in Canadian Writing.* Toronto: University of Toronto Press, 1997.

Nixon, Rob. *London Calling: V. S. Naipaul, Postcolonial Mandarin.* New York: Oxford UP, 1992.

Oberlander, Wendy, dir. *Nothing to be Written Here.* Toronto: V-Tape, 1996.

O'Brien, Susie. "Articulating a World of Difference: Ecocriticism, Postcolonialism and Globalization." *Canadian Literature* 170/171 (Autumn/Winter 2001): 140–58.

———. "The Garden and the World: Jamaica Kincaid and the Cultural Borders of Ecocriticism." *Mosaic* 35.2 (June 2002): 167–84.

O'Gorman, Edmundo. *The Invention of America: An Inquiry into the Historical Nature of the New World and the Meaning of Its History.* Westport, CT: Greenwood Press, 1961.

Olwig, Kenneth R. *Landscape, Nature, and the Body Politic: From Britain's Renaissance to America's New World.* Madison: U of Wisconsin P, 2002.

Orum, Anthony M., and Xiangming Chen. *The World of Cities: Places in Comparative and Historical Perspective.* Oxford: Blackwell, 2003.

Osborne, Michael A. *Nature, the Exotic, and the Science of French Colonialism.* Bloomington: Indiana UP, 1994.

Ozick, Cynthia. "The Pagan Rabbi." *The Pagan Rabbi and Other Stories.* Syracuse: Syracuse UP, 1995. 3–37.

Papastergiadis, Nikos. *The Turbulence of Migration: Globalization, Deterritorialization and Hybridity.* Cambridge: Polity, 2000.

Paravisini-Gebert, Lizabeth. "Colonial and Postcolonial Gothic: The Caribbean." *The Cambridge Companion to Gothic Literature.* Ed. Jerrold E. Hogle. New York: Cambridge UP, 2002. 229–58.

Pineau, Gisèle. *The Drifting of Spirits.* Trans. J. Michael Dash. London: Quartet, 1999.

———. *La Grande Drive des esprits.* Paris: Le Serpent à Plumes, 1993.

————. Interview with Nadège Veldwachter. *Research in African Literatures* 35.1 (Spring 2004): 180–85.

Pollan, Michael. *The Botany of Desire: A Plant's-Eye View of the World*. New York: Random House, 2001.

————. "Introduction to the Modern Library Gardening Series." *In the Land of the Blue Poppies: The Collected Plant-Hunting Writing of Frank Kingdon-Ward*. By Frank Kingdon Ward. New York: Modern Library, 2002. ix–xii.

————. *Second Nature: A Gardener's Education*. New York: Delta, 1991.

Porter, Dennis. *Haunted Journeys: Desire and Transgression in European Travel Writing*. Princeton: Princeton UP, 1991.

Pratt, Mary Louise. *Imperial Eyes: Travel Writing and Transculturation*. London: Routledge, 1992.

Pulsipher, Lydia Mihelic. "The Landscapes and Ideational Roles of Caribbean Slave Gardens." *The Archaeology of Garden and Field*. Ed. Naomi F. Miller and Kathryn L. Gleason. Philadelphia: U of Pennsylvania P, 1994. 202–21.

Punter, David, and Glennis Byron. "Postcolonial Gothic." *The Gothic*. Malden, MA: Blackwell, 2004. 54–58.

Quimby, Karin. "This is my own, my native land": Constructions of Identity and Landscape in Joy Kogawa's *Obasan*." *Cross-Addressing: Resistance Literature and Cultural Borders*. Ed. John C. Hawley. Albany: SUNY P, 1996. 257–73.

Renk, Kathleen J. *Caribbean Shadows and Victorian Ghosts*. Charlottesville: U of Virginia P, 1999.

Rennó, Roseângela. *Vera Cruz*. 200/2004. Landry 88–93.

Richler, Mordecai. *The Apprenticeship of Duddy Kravitz*. 1959. Harmondsworth, UK: Penguin, 1967.

————. *Solomon Gursky Was Here*. Markham, ON: Penguin, 1989.

Robinson, Bradley. *Dark Companion: The Life Story of Matthew Henson*. New York: National Travel Club, 1947.

Robinson, William. *The Wild Garden: Or the Naturalization and Natural Grouping of Hardy Exotic Plants with a Chapter on the Garden of British Wild Flowers*. 1895. Portland, OR: Sagapress, 1994.

Rodríguez, Illeana. *House/Garden/Nation: Space, Gender, and Ethnicity in Post-Colonial Latin American Literatures by Women*. Durham: Duke UP, 1994.

————. *Transatlantic Topographies: Islands, Highlands, Jungles*. Minneapolis: U of Minnesota P, 2004.

Rodriguez, Richard. *Brown: The Last Discovery of America*. New York: Viking, 2002.

Rose, Aubrey. "A Personal View." *Judaism and Ecology*. Ed. Aubrey Rose. London: Cassell, 1992. 4–6.

Roth, Henry. *Call It Sleep*. 1934. New York: Noonday, 1997.

————. *Mercy of a Rude Stream*. Vol. 1: *A Star Shines Over Mt. Morris Park*. New York: St. Martin's, 1994.

Roth, Philip. *American Pastoral*. New York: Vintage, 1997.

――――. *The Counterlife*. New York: Vintage, 1986.

――――. *The Ghost Writer*. New York: Vintage, 1979.

――――. *Goodbye, Columbus and Five Short Stories*. 1959. New York: Vintage, 1987.

――――. *The Human Stain*. Boston: Houghton Mifflin, 2000.

――――. *The Plot against America*. New York: Houghton Mifflin, 2004.

Roumain, Jacques. *Masters of the Dew*. 1944. Trans. Langston Hughes and Mercer Cook. Oxford: Heinemann, 1978.

Roy, Patricia E., J. L. Granatstein, Masako Iino, and Hiroko Takamura. *Mutual Hostages: Canadians and Japanese During the Second World War*. Toronto: University of Toronto Press, 1990.

Saint-Pierre, Jacques-Henri-Bernardin de. *Paul et Virginie*. 1788. Paris: Garnier-Flammarion, 1992.

Sassen, Saskia. "Spatialities and Temporalities of the Global: Elements for a Theorization." *Public Culture* 8.2 (Winter 1996): 215–32.

Schama, Simon. *Landscape and Memory*. New York: Vintage, 1995.

Schwarz-Bart, Simone. *The Bridge of Beyond*. 1972. Trans. Barbara Bray. Oxford: Heinemann, 1982.

Scott, Kitty. "Touring Home, Jin-me Yoon: An Essay." *Constructing Cultural Identity: Jin-me Yoon, Bob Boyer, Liz Magor*. Edmonton: Edmonton Art Gallery, 1991. n.p.

Scott, Sir Walter. *The Lay of the Last Minstrel*. 1805. Oxford: Woodstock, 1992.

Sheller, Mimi. *Consuming the Caribbean*. New York: Routledge, 2003.

Smith, Anthony D. *Myths and Memories of the Nation*. Oxford: Oxford UP, 1999.

Smith, Bernard. *European Vision and the South Pacific*. 2nd ed. New Haven: Yale UP, 1985.

Smith, Henry Nash. *Virgin Land: The American West as Symbol and Myth*. Cambridge: Harvard UP, 1950.

Smyth, Heather. "Sexual Citizenship and Caribbean-Canadian Fiction: Dionne Brand's 'In Another Place, Not Here' and Shani Mootoo's 'Cereus Blooms at Night.'" *Ariel* 30.2 (April 1999): 141–60.

Soja, Edward. *Postmodern Geographies: The Reassertion of Space in Critical Social Theory*. London: Verso, 1989.

Solatoroff, Theodore. "Bernard Malamud's Fiction: The Old Life and the New." *Commentary* 33.3 (Mar. 1962): 197–204. Rpt. in *Bernard Malamud and the Critics*. Ed. Leslie and Joyce Field. New York: NYU P, 1970. 235–48.

Sollors, Werner. "Literature and Ethnicity." *Harvard Encyclopedia of American Ethnic Groups*. Cambridge: Belknap-Harvard UP, 1980. 647–65.

Soto-Crespo, Ramón E. "Death and the Diaspora Writer: Hybridity and Mourning in the Work of Jamaica Kincaid." *Contemporary Literature* 43.2 (Summer 2002): 342–76.

Strong-Boag, Veronica, Sherrill Grace, Avigail Eisenberg, and Joan Anderson. "Constructing Canada: An Introduction." *Painting the Maple: Essays on Race, Gender, and the Construction of Canada.* Ed. Joan Anderson, Avigail Eisenberg, Sherrill Grace, and Veronica Strong-Boag. Vancouver: UBC, 1998. 3–15.

Suleri, Sara. *The Rhetoric of English India.* Chicago: U of Chicago P, 1992.

Suzuki, David. Interview. *The Greatest Canadian.* CBC. Ottawa: CBOT. Nov. 17, 2004.

———. *Metamorphosis: Stages in a Life.* Toronto: Stoddart, 1987.

Terada, Rei. *Derek Walcott's Poetry: American Mimicry.* Boston: Northeastern UP, 1992.

Thieme, John. "Reconstructions of National Identity in the Recent Work of V. S. Naipaul." *Nationalism vs. Internationalism.* Ed. Wolfgang Zach and Ken L. Goodwin. Tubingen: Stauffenburg Verlag, 1996. 407–15.

Thoreau, Henry David. *Walden and Civil Disobedience.* New York: Penguin, 1983.

Tiffin, Helen. "'Flowers of Evil,' Flowers of Empire: Roses and Daffodils in the Work of Jamaica Kincaid, Olive Senior and Lorna Goodison." Spec. issue of *Span* 46 (Apr. 1998): 59–71.

Tobin, Beth Fowkes. "'And There Raise Yams': Slaves' Gardens in the Writings of West Indian Plantocrats." *Eighteenth-Century Life* 23.3 (1999): 164–76.

Tölölyan, Khachig. "The American Model of Diasporic Discourse." *Diasporas and Ethnic Migrants: Germany, Israel and Post-Soviet Successor States in Comparative Perspective.* Ed. Rainer Münz and Rainer Ohliger. London: Frank Cass, 2003. 56–73.

Torgovnick, Marianna. *Gone Primitive: Savage Intellects, Modern Lives.* Chicago: U of Chicago P, 1990.

Truettner, William H., ed. *The West as America: Reinterpreting Images of the Frontier, 1820–1920.* Washington, DC: Smithsonian Institution Press, 1991.

Virgil. *The Eclogues of Virgil.* Trans. David Ferry. New York: Farrar, Straus & Giroux, 1999.

Walcott, Derek. "Another Life." *Collected Poems, 1948–1984.* New York: Farrar, Straus & Giroux, 1992. 143–294.

———. "The Garden Path." Rev. of *The Enigma of Arrival,* by V. S. Naipaul. *New Republic* 13 Apr. 1987: 28.

———. "Leaving School." 1965. Rpt. in Hamner 24–32.

———. *Omeros.* New York: Noonday, 1990.

———. "The Road Taken." *Homage to Robert Frost.* By Joseph Brodsky, Seamus Heaney, and Derek Walcott. New York: Farrar, Straus & Giroux, 1996. 93–117.

———. "Ruins of a Great House." *Collected Poems, 1948–1984.* New York: Farrar, Straus & Giroux, 1992. 19–21.

———. "Thinking Poetry: An Interview with Derek Walcott." Interview with

Robert Brown and Cheryl Johnson. *Cream City Review* 14.2 (Winter 1990): 209–33. Rpt. in *Conversations with Derek Walcott.* Ed. William Baer. Jackson: UP of Mississippi, 1996. 175–88.

———. *Tiepolo's Hound.* New York: Farrar, Straus & Giroux, 2000.

———. *Walker and The Ghost Dance.* New York: Farrar, Straus & Giroux, 2002.

Waldinger, Roger, and Jennifer Lee. "New Immigrants in Urban America." *Strangers at the Gates: New Immigrants in Urban America.* Ed. Roger Waldinger. Berkeley: U of California P, 2001. 30–79.

Walker, Kara. *Darkytown Rebellion.* 2001. Landry 120–21.

Weiss, Timothy. "V. S. Naipaul's 'Fin de Siecle': 'The Enigma of Arrival' and 'A Way in the World.'" *Ariel* 27.3 (July 1996): 107–24.

Williams, Raymond. *The Country and the City.* New York: Oxford UP, 1973.

Woodcock, George. "Possessing the Land: Notes on Canadian Fiction." *The Canadian Imagination: Dimensions of a Literary Culture.* Ed. David Staines. Cambridge: Harvard UP, 1977. 69–96.

Yaeger, Patricia. "Introduction: Narrating Space." *The Geography of Identity.* Ed. Patricia Yaeger. Ann Arbor: U of Michigan P, 1996. 1–38.

Yezierska, Anzia. *Bread Givers.* 1925. New York: Persea Books, 1975.

Yoon, Jin-me. *A Group of Sixty-Seven.* 1996. *Jin-me Yoon: Between Departure and Arrival.* By Julie Radul. Vancouver: Western Front, 1998. 58–63.

———. *Souvenirs of the Self.* 1991. *Crossings.* By Diana Nemiroff. Vol. 1. Ottawa: National Gallery of Canada, 1998. 182–83.

———. *Touring Home from Away.* 1998–99. *Jin-me Yoon: Touring Home from Away.* By Annette Hurtig. Vancouver: Presentation House Gallery, 2003.

Young, Robert. *Colonial Desire: Hybridity in Theory, Culture, and Race.* London: Routledge, 1995.

Zamora, Lois Parkinson. *The Usable Past: The Imagination of History in Recent Fiction of the Americas.* Cambridge: Cambridge UP, 1997.

Zamora, Lois Parkinson, and Wendy B. Faris, eds. *Magical Realism: Theory, History, Community.* Durham: Duke UP, 1995.

Index

Jessica Adams, Michael P. Bibler, and Cécile Accilien, editors, *Just Below South: Intercultural Performance in the Caribbean and the U.S. South*

Valérie Loichot, *Orphan Narratives: The Postplantation Literature of Faulkner, Glissant, Morrison, and Saint-John Perse*

Sarah Phillips Casteel, *Second Arrivals: Landscape and Belonging in Contemporary Writing of the Americas*